COMPARATIVE

MARKETING

Wholesaling
in
Fifteen
Countries

COMPARATIVE MARKETING

Wholesaling in
Fifteen Countries

Edited by
ROBERT BARTELS, Ph.D.
Professor of Business Organization
The Ohio State University

Sponsored by the
AMERICAN MARKETING ASSOCIATION

GREENWOOD PRESS, PUBLISHERS
WESTPORT, CONNECTICUT

Library of Congress Cataloging in Publication Data

Main entry under title:

Comparative marketing.

 Reprint. Originally published: Homewood, Ill. :
R.D. Irwin, 1963.
 Studies prepared by the Comparative Marketing Com-
mittee, American Marketing Association, under the
chairmanship of R. Bartels.
 Bibliography: p.
 1. Wholesale trade. I. Bartels, Robert, 1913-
II. American Marketing Association. Comparative
Marketing Committee.
HF5420.C65 1983   658.8'6   82-25149
ISBN 0-313-23838-3 (lib. bdg.)

Reprinted in 1983 by Greenwood Press
A division of Congressional Information Service, Inc.
88 Post Road West, Westport, Connecticut 06881

Printed in the United States of America

10 9 8 7 6 5 4 3 2 1

FOREWORD

Sensing the rapidly increasing American interest in marketing abroad, the American Marketing Association in recent years has been vigorously expanding its activities in the international marketing field. The Association's National Conference in Boston in June, 1957, centered around international marketing. Soon thereafter, a section of the national organization and several committees were created to establish international contacts and promote research. Their activities included, among other things, an exchange of marketing delegates with the Soviet Union, publication of an International Marketing Newsletter, and promotion of marketing studies throughout the world. This work led directly to the AMA initiative in forming an International Marketing Federation of all professional marketing Associations.

One of the first monographs of consequence reflecting the new interest in the international field and presenting a comparative type of analysis described marketing in Egypt. It was written by two American-educated Egyptians, Abdel Aziz el Sherbini and Ahmed Fouad Sherif, both of the faculty of Cairo University. They had been encouraged in this work by Wroe Alderson and his colleagues at Alderson and Sessions. Since then, studies in reference to marketing in other nations have appeared frequently in the *Journal of Marketing*.

In 1959 a standing committee was appointed by the Association to develop a broad program for the study of comparative marketing. Its members, who were already then associated for the production of a work on comparative marketing, planned the present book and established contacts with scholars abroad who might supply all the basic data. It was essential of course that the data collected be as uniform as possible so that a single standard of reporting and evaluation might apply to all countries. Only one who has attempted such a task can comprehend the problems and difficulties it presents. If coverage studies in the present volume are not completely comparable, it should be recalled that it is a pioneering effort and one of unusual significance.

The membership of the Comparative Marketing Committee, through whose efforts this book has come to fruition, has included the following: William Applebaum, Harvard Business School; Harper W. Boyd, Northwestern University; David Carson, Boston University; Lawrence Dowd, San Francisco State College; Marshall Goldman, Wellesley College; Leon V. Hirsch, United Research Incorporated; Stuart L. Mandell, Lowell Technological Institute; Donald F. Mulvihill, Kent State University; and Robert Bartels, The Ohio State University, Chairman.

The officers and directors of the Association are very grateful to Professor Bartels and his Committee for their dedication to this task and its completion. They have made a major contribution to our knowledge of comparative marketing. We hope other studies will follow this initial effort.

DONALD R. LONGMAN
President
American Marketing Association

PREFACE

This book is the product of two circumstances: first, a growing world-wide consciousness of marketing and, second, the perseverence of a small group in gathering accounts of marketing in different countries. The objectives of all who have participated in compiling this material have been to depict marketing practice in various cultural settings, to interpret it, and to draw such conclusions as may be warranted.

The way in which this project was conceived and executed is relevant to the type of book which has been produced. The roots of the undertaking extend back into middle 1950's. Americans at that time had little knowledge of how marketing was carried on outside their country. Interest in this subject was increasing, however, because of the expansion of United States export business, because of increasing investments in overseas production facilities, and because of the growing demand abroad for American marketing technology. Publications in English dealing with the domestic marketing practices and problems of other nations were then virtually nonexistent.

The initiative passed to academicians, to a group of American professors of marketing in a few eastern and middle western schools, who for their discussions gravitated several times to the Harvard Business School. Recently returned in 1957 from separately observing and studying marketing in Europe, James A. Hagler and I were convinced of the importance of understanding marketing in its varied national settings, and we undertook to arouse interest in research in this area. The idea of interpreting marketing in terms of its social setting was known to us as "comparative marketing," imputing to marketing the comparative analysis which has long characterized studies in religion, art, education, and other fields.

The group of professors who sought to develop this concept were convinced of its ultimate destiny to play an important role in understanding marketing. Therefore, they devoted time throughout two years to crystalizing the concept of comparative marketing and to establishing their identification with the concept. Under the leadership of James A. Hagler, they explored far-reaching projects of research and publication, but limitations of finance and personnel thwarted tangible progress while strengthening their resolve. In 1959, recognition was given the group and their efforts by the American Marketing Association in appointing them as a standing committee of the Association and in providing program time for introducing the subject of comparative marketing at the annual meeting of the Association.

During the years following the original association of this group, a number of means were considered for advancing the understanding of marketing through comparative analysis. Initially the publication of a series of book-length studies dealing with marketing in different countries was contemplated. Such books would have been unlike any contemporary book on marketing then available in the United States, for it would have been a study of *marketing viewed comparatively* and not merely a study of marketing *per se*. That is to say, it would have been not merely a description of foreign marketing experience but an interpretation of it in terms of the socioeconomic environment of foreign markets. The likelihood of producing such a series of studies seemed as small as the desirability of them was great, for no one then seemed capable of writing such a book. Americans, even if they understood marketing, were too little familiar with foreign marketing practice and too little appreciative of the differences among nations which made their marketing practices *socially explainable from their viewpoint*, although perhaps not *economically justifiable from ours*. On the other hand, foreign marketing students and practitioners were, as we had been in earlier years of the development of marketing thought, more concerned with technology than with social interpretation. Such studies, moreover, would have required resources greater than those at the disposal of the Committee but less than needed if widespread acceptance of the idea of comparative marketing were to be achieved.

As a more expeditious undertaking, the Committee selected the subject of wholesaling in a number of countries as an initial study of workable proportions. The cooperation of both Americans and other nationals was sought in the preparation of manuscripts on wholesaling around the world. While using all assistance that could be obtained, an effort was made to assemble manuscripts representing a balance of interests between eastern and western countries, large and small, developed and underdeveloped, and those of the free and of the Communist nations. The manuscripts thus collected comprise this book. Of fifteen, ten have been prepared by nationals of the countries about which they wrote. Some have been written under the supervision and with the cooperation of Americans who were in those countries or who maintained close contact with the authors during their preparation. Some manuscripts originally written in other languages were translated abroad; others were translated by collaborators in this country.

As the concept of a comparative marketing analysis grew clearer to the editors and supervisors, the instructions given to the writers were simply these: (1) descriptions or discussions of the respective national wholesaling practices should emphasize contrasts between those of that country and those of another country; and (2) the practices of their country should be interpreted in terms of the prevailing socioeconomic conditions. Mere description was insufficient; comparison and interpretation were expected. This objective was achieved in a large measure, but not fully.

Articles were arranged so that the Communist countries were grouped apart from those which provide a more democratic, capitalistic environment for the practice of marketing. Dominance of the government in relation to business was felt to be sufficiently important to give precedence to this grouping over any other. Except for this factor, countries were grouped according to areas, as in Europe and in the Middle East, and according to the order in which they would be encountered in an eastward circling of the globe, countries of the Northern Hemisphere being considered first. Within the area groups, the countries were arranged to achieve the best contrasts and comparisons.

Throughout this study, the Committee has been motivated primarily by the desire to know and to make known the facts about the ways in which human needs are being met through marketing in different parts of the world. This, it is felt, constitutes an extension of our knowledge of marketing. Such information should be useful to both the marketing practitioner and the academician. The former will find in it some insights into the ways in which domestic marketing systems are organized and operated in other countries. The success of both export trade and overseas operations is dependent upon knowledge of such facts. The teacher will find in this material content for courses in comparative and international marketing and also illustrative material for any course or seminar on marketing. It also furnishes an example of the application of behavioral science findings to marketing analysis.

At this stage in exploration of comparative aspects of marketing, one may notice its similarities to the original study of marketing dur-

ing the early decades of this century. Before any established pattern
of research was developed, scientific inquiry consisted mainly of first-
hand observation, investigation, and description. Early marketing
treaties were neither conceptual nor theoretical, but rather factual
and graphic. That stage was followed by distillation of the "elements"
and "principles" of marketing. Those generalizations have well served
in the development of management talent and citizenry.

Again today, in the study of domestic marketing systems and practices of other countries, observation and description constitute a
contribution to knowledge. However, having the benefit of an already
developed structure of marketing thought into which these foreign
instances and new observations can be fitted, the student of marketing may proceed more speedily toward the development of marketing
theory based upon comparative marketing study. Such theory will
not consist merely of the truisms and technical cause-effect relationships which have been accepted as marketing principles. They will
consist more of a body of *interpretations*—interpretations of the *whole*
marketing activity as a socially evoked, socially oriented means of
meeting social need, and of *particular* marketing activity as the interaction of individuals in roles in which they participate *in their society*
in the production, distribution, and consumption of the materials and
services needed by people. This kind of knowledge is yet at the stage
of basic research. One can expect at present only elementary findings.
Any generalizations which may be drawn from these present observations are necessarily immature in comparison to those which it is
hoped will be developed later.

ROBERT BARTELS

Columbus, Ohio
June, 1963

TABLE OF CONTENTS

INTRODUCTION

What is "comparative marketing"?

Although newly applied to marketing, use of the term "comparative" has precedence in other fields of thought. *Webster's New International Dictionary* defines comparative literature as "the study of literature by the comparative method; the comparison of the same or similar forms, movements, etc., in various literatures"; comparative religion as "the study of the origin, development, and interrelations of the religious systems of mankind"; and comparative method as "the method of concomitant variations." Thus by the term "comparative marketing" is implied the study of marketing through its attendant or associated variations; the study of the origins, organization, and interrelations of marketing practice as found in the various cultural settings of mankind.

Precedent for comparative analysis of marketing is found also in the comparative analyses which have long been made of economic systems. The applicability of a comparative approach to the study of marketing, however, requires recognition that the *differences* in marketing practice in various places are as important as the *similarities*. This fact has not been generally appreciated in the United States, during the years that the basic knowledge of marketing was being developed. Differences in marketing practice have too often been regarded as deviations or variations from a universal, from a "principle" held to be not only a mode but a model. Practices which differed from those generally accepted in the United States were often thought to be inferior, outmoded, or inefficient. Because marketing developed both as a discipline and as a practice first in this country, we have tended to judge business elsewhere from our own stand-

1

point, without appreciating that our own practices are as indigenous to our environment as those of other people are to theirs.

A comparative marketing study, however, is not simply a description of marketing in another locality. While it is interesting to know how consumers buy or how products are distributed elsewhere, there is little profit in such knowledge unless it is generalized. The critical element in comparative marketing analysis, therefore, is the manner in which experience is interpreted, related, and generalized.

Because many marketing analysts view marketing in the United States as a business mechanism of institutions performing functions in the distribution of products, there is a tendency to apply this frame of analysis to foreign systems of distribution also. Consequently, both American and other contributors to this book have explained marketing as the practices involved in the marketing of various types of products. Distinction has been made between agricultural and manufactured goods, between manufactures and handicrafts, or between products otherwise classified. Such information is useful, for it permits the making of contrasts which anyone undertaking to distribute in a foreign market may find helpful. It was expected of participants in this project that they present current marketing practices with emphasis on dissimilarities between those prevailing in their country and those in another country. Such contrasts are an essential element in comparative marketing analysis.

A second expectation of writers was that they interpret the prevalent practices in terms of the socio-economic conditions of the country. This is the second basic characteristic of a comparative marketing study, and it is in some respects more important than the first, for only in terms of social setting can the marketing practices of a nation be appraised.

It must be remembered that "marketing" itself is but a term of fairly recent origin intended to identify an activity, or a means, in the fulfillment of social ends, which in other societies have been supplied by a variety of other means throughout human history. Societies have always employed some systematic means of supplying human consumption needs, and, regardless of what form they have taken, these means have been identified as the "economy" of the society. Thus the biological, the intellectual, societal, ecological, and other aspects of social organization and orientation have influenced the specific manner in which the "economy" has operated to fulfill the social objectives. In recent times, these influences have, more specifically, determined the character of market distribution, or marketing. Hence the justification for approaching a comparative marketing analysis from the social standpoint.

The details of what is meant by the "social standpoint," however, have required some explanation, both to American and to foreign writers in this project. Consequently, for the guidance of editors and writers alike, an outline for a comparative marketing study was prepared and revised as experience with this kind of study matured. A final version of this outline is presented in the Appendix as an aid both in interpreting the studies here published and in undertaking further comparative research.

In general, comparative marketing involves three types of interpretation: (1) of the relation between social conditions in a country and the manner in which marketing is practiced there; (2) of the character and operation of the marketing mechanism itself; (3) of the patterns of personal behavior and interaction in the socio-marketing activity.

Social Conditions. Several factors must be taken into consideration as comprising the environment in which marketing takes place. Among these factors are the nation, the society, the economy, and the market.

The physical character of the nation is perhaps the principal and broadest determinant of both the society found there and the means by which that society undertakes to supply its needs. This is the combination of a number of physical and natural factors, including the following:

1. Location and size of the nation.
2. Physical features of terrain and topography.
3. Natural resources.
4. Sovereignty or political contiguity.
5. Age and history of the country.
6. Distinctive features as a community of the world.

It is obvious that physical proximity or remoteness, barrenness or fertility, and longitude and latitude have marked effect upon the market, the need for marketing, and the presence of marketable products.

The society is a second environmental aspect of the framework in which marketing takes place and in terms of which it must be interpreted. There are different useful ways in which society may be viewed and dissected for analysis, but a simple and effective approach may be made along lines of the major social institutions, as classified by sociologists:

1. The family—its typical size, composition, age cycle, coherence, formation, growth, solidarity, etc.
2. The church—basic beliefs, commitments, practices, rites, and consumption influences.
3. The school—literacy, educational levels and programs, imagination and initiative.
4. The government—the form and dominance of the government in the society; social and political philosophy expressed in government action; laws pertaining to marketing; planning.
5. The military—its claim upon economic and human resources; its dominance or subordinance; means of distributions through military channels.
6. Leisure—extra-work behavior patterns; development of art, expression, beauty, etc.

The economy—the seventh social institution—is of such magnitude and importance as to constitute a third and special aspect of the environment, one which has direct relevance to marketing. It is the immediate framework of activities, attitudes, and organization in which the specific tasks of marketing arise. Whether the economy be capitalistic or socialistic, barter or exchange, agricultural or manufacturing, underdeveloped or advanced—these are a few of the considerations which must be appraised in a comparative analysis.

The market itself is a fourth aspect of the environment which determines the nature of marketing. The market represents the sum total of the expectations that society has as consumers. It epitomizes the objectives for which marketing is the satisfying means. The character of the market—measured in terms of size, specialization, tastes, standards, etc.—determines the marketing task, and the marketing task in turn determines the manner and the extent to which marketing must be performed.

The extent to which a comparative marketing analyst feels obliged to elaborate upon the environmental determinants of the marketing activity, which it is his primary objective to analyze, depends on his own ability to relate pertinent factors to marketing and on his reader's unfamiliarity with the foreign environment in which marketing occurs. Writers of articles for this book have generally presented something of the national, social, and economic environment of marketing. The extent to which they have elaborated upon this has been dependent on the distinctiveness of their environment, as well as on other factors mentioned.

The Institutional Framework for Marketing. Within its environment, marketing has generally been interpreted mechanistically, as an institutional system comprising wholesale and retail organizations.

As few statistics for distribution are available in most places, this portion of the comparative analysis has consisted principally of comparison of types of marketing establishments in one country with those in another, usually in the United States.

One difference among the institutions of two countries relates to forms of ownership: private versus public. Another relates to variations of private ownership, as in the case of co-operatives in contrast to profit enterprises. Within the predominant types in any given country, further distinction is usually made between wholesale and retail establishments and between the various subtypes thereof, which are almost universally similar. Differences of terminology, sometimes affected by translation, give an impression of diversity that does not always actually exist.

Other than the marketing institutions, the marketing functions traditionally identified in the United States are commonly discussed as part of the comparative analysis. To the extent that they are flatly accepted as inherent and universal functions, accounts of them are little more than descriptive. In instances, however, where they are seen to be derivatives of the marketing task to be performed, discussions of functions are of a more analytical character.

Following also the organization and content of American marketing texts which have world-wide readership, even foreign writers make some comparison of entrepreneurial policies and social controls in marketing.

Social Interaction. As the making of comparative marketing analyses is a relatively new form of marketing study, the most profitable techniques are yet being developed. Indeed, this might still be said of the study of marketing in general, as new concepts and methods are steadily being adopted from the related scientific disciplines. The introduction of social-systems concepts into marketing thought has caused some shifting of emphasis from traditional *organizational* studies. Approaching marketing as a social activity rather than merely as an entrepreneurial activity, one becomes aware that marketing is what *people* do rather than what *establishments* or middlemen do. This kind of social approach is especially pertinent to comparative analysis, for the comparative study is mainly one of comparative social behavior in pursuit of a familiar objective.

Sociologists have contributed to social research the concept of roles in explanation of group behavior and personal interaction. Every individual performs in a variety of roles or characterizations in his social experience: as parent, church worker, educator, capitalist, landlord, etc. These are roles drawn from the various institutional activities, which have already been mentioned. In economic activity, and particularly in business, the related role positions are identified as manager, employee, owner, other investor, customer, resource, intermediate customer, competitor, government, and community. *Marketing is the sets of interrelationships among the role positions necessary for the achievement of the marketing objective.* The study of marketing, therefore, may be said to consist of the interpretation of behavior patterns among the sets of relationships involved in the work called "marketing." Comparative marketing, likewise, is the study of such sets of role relationships as they are found in different countries.

This type of analysis is yet new in the study of marketing; it is less common in the study of international and comparative marketing; and it is practically nonexistent in the studies comprising this book. It is, nevertheless, one which seems destined to grow in importance with further study of marketing, and it is one which has been employed, where appropriate, in the editor's introductions to each article and in the chapter on conclusions.

In the Appendix of this volume is provided an outline explaining the steps which might be followed in making a comparative study of marketing. It does not represent the outline followed by the writers of articles for this book; they were guided simply by the instructions to draw contrasts between the wholesaling practices of two countries and to interpret them in the light of prevailing social conditions. Neither does it represent the outline which the editorial committee envisioned throughout the study. Rather, it represents what at the time of publication seemed to be the most useful means of reducing marketing differences to uniform analysis so that they can be traced to social and cultural differences, rather than to arbitrary or entrepreneurial management policies alone.

EUROPE

West Germany

Finland

Italy

The Netherlands

WEST GERMANY

The author of this chapter depicts the trends of wholesaling since 1920 which resulted in the decline and renaissance of the independent wholesaler. Both political and economic factors contributed to this cycle of events. Thus is drawn a picture of wholesaling in an industrially advanced nation by one who sees whoesaling in West Germany in contrast to that in other countries.

In Germany, as described in this chapter, traditional wholesaling failed to meet the changing needs of manufacturers and retailers. Wholesalers were typically passive, lacking initiative and innovation, predatory, self-centered, and in many respects inefficient. Moreover, some political restrictions on risk venture discouraged the development of wholesaling enterprises. This deficiency was counteracted by both manufacturers' and retailers' seeking more direct means of distribution.

After World War II, following wholesaling successes in other countries, German wholesalers evidenced a renaissance. Some of them widened their assortment of merchandise and services; others increased their degree of specialization; still others undertook direct selling resembling discount-store operations. Through effective voluntary group operations, many wholesalers re-established their position in the distributive system.

The net outcome has been the emergence of a wholesaler type that is less the merchant adventurer than formerly and more a provider of essential goods and services.

Wholesaling in West Germany

*ROBERT NIESCHLAG**
(*Translation by Ferdinand F. Mauser*)

The status of wholesaling in West Germany today is one which has evolved through the past forty or fifty years. As in other countries, wholesaling itself has been criticized, as a result of an unclear distinction between wholesaling, per se, and wholesalers. The position of wholesalers was challenged, and they were eliminated from some distribution channels. Progressively, however, it has been recognized that in certain circumstances the wholesaler performs most efficiently some indispensable functions. Following a renaissance of understanding of wholesaling and with further improvement in wholesalers' technical efficiency, the wholesaler today is in an advanced stage of its maturity.

The evolution of wholesaling in West Germany since the currency reform of 1948 has been characterized by two tendencies:

1. After Germany's political debacle, the free-enterprise system, aided by the Marshall Plan, released strong entrepreneurial energies in wholesaling. Inasmuch as wholesaling by its very nature can be performed in a number of ways, the wholesaler must continually demonstrate the usefulness of his service. The fact that he exists is justification of his utility in a free market. This fact is not taken for granted, however, in a planned market economy.

2. Since World War II, wholesalers in West Germany have increasingly embraced the more advanced methods and techniques used by their counterparts in other highly industrialized nations of the Western world. Channels of communication among businessmen, it seems, lead more quickly to universal adoption of successful tactics in business than do the channels by which politicians exchange their ideas. In fact, commercial leaders seem to respond more quickly to successful innovations taking place beyond the borders of their na-

* Dr. Robert Nieschlag is Professor of Business Administration at the University of Munich. He has written extensively in the field of marketing, wholesaling being an area of special interest. He published a definitive work on German marketing in 1959, entitled, *Binnenhandel und Binnenhandelspolitik* ("Commerce and Commerce Policies").

Dr. Ferdinand F. Mauser is Professor of Marketing at Wayne State University, Detroit, Michigan.

tions than do even manufacturing or agricultural executives. This conclusion seems warranted by the fact that trends in wholesaling in West Germany have so closely paralleled those of other highly developed nations. This may also shed light on why problems confronting wholesalers in various nations are so similar, despite marked differences among wholesalers due to national characteristics, to states of the national economies, to historical factors, and to market size. It is significant that the general patterns of wholesaling in the more highly industrialized Western nations are so much alike.

WHOLESALERS CIRCUMVENTED

Following World War I, wholesaling was in a state of flux, and the outlook for the wholesaler was discouraging. Between 1920 and 1940, wholesalers strengthened their position by changing some of their ways of operation. This was accomplished not so much because of the actions of any one type of wholesalers as because of the essential character of wholesaling itself.

For some years before World War II, wholesalers waged a defensive battle. There would probably have been no questioning of the wholesalers' right to exist if they had been the initiators and pacesetters in industrialization—if they had encouraged production, increased the efficiency of the marketing process, assumed responsibility for the procurement of raw materials, or assisted with financing. Instead, manufacturers undertook much of this initiative, providing their own financing and engaging in market research. Their objective, indeed, was to become independent of wholesalers, controlling both their procurement and marketing and the channels of distribution for their products. The more mature industries had the financial strength by which they could accomplish these objectives.

Several trade developments evidenced this increasing circumvention of wholesalers:

1. Establishment by manufacturers of their own organizations for buying, selling, warehousing, and customer service;
2. Development of selling syndicates, such as those in the distribution of coal or fertilizers;
3. Licensing of brokers who serve several manufacturers, such as the specialized heavy-vehicle producers;
4. Direct exporting by producers of industrial and of branded consumer goods;
5. Direct selling to end users; and last, but not least,
6. Increased use of marketing research, which, because of its technically sophisticated approach to marketing, finds more ready acceptance with manufacturers than with middlemen.

Manufacturers switched their channels away from independent wholesalers for still other reasons. During the first half of this century, newer and larger-scale forms of retailing grew in importance, particularly the department stores, co-operatives, and chain stores. These fast-growing enterprises placed considerable emphasis on price competition, and they therefore sought to decrease their merchandise costs by purchasing large volumes directly from manufacturers, thus circumventing the wholesalers. It was not long before sales made to giant retailers exceeded sales to wholesalers.

Competition from such large retailers forced smaller retailers to band together in order to secure similar buying arrangements. Buying associations of small retailers—usually co-operatives—were frequently patterned after associations of small manufacturers who had pooled their buying power for joint purchasing of raw materials in order to compete on more equal terms with the industrial giants. Agricultural co-operatives, concerned with joint buying, selling, and financing for their members, were also solidly entrenched. Credit was a vital function of these agricultural co-operatives because of farmers' needs to borrow funds by using future harvests as security for loans.

One might have expected wholesalers to provide the above-mentioned functional services to retailers, to small manufacturers, and to farmers, but apparently the lack of prospects for doing this profitably did not encourage such action. In areas where competition between wholesalers was severely limited, as in remote agricultural districts, wholesalers did assume these functions, but they victimized the farmers to such a degree by their sharp monopolistic practices that farmers were forced into the organization of co-operatives.

Thus co-operatives pretty much replaced independent wholesalers in agriculture during the last decade of the nineteenth century, and this pattern still prevails today. In reaction to this development, many independent wholesalers undertook other operations in processing, retailing, financing, and in other facilitating marketing operations. Those wholesalers who survived did so by operating more efficiently or by switching to industries or products where there was less competition. Many wholesalers, of course, fell by the wayside, particularly in the 1920's and in the depression years of 1929 to 1932. Financial reverses caused by war and inflation took further toll.

Still another influence upon the evolution of wholesaling in West Germany has been the increasing regulation of the agricultural part of the economy, particularly many of the basic foodstuffs and cattle feeds. While such regulations did not directly limit commerce, they did result in the establishment of regulatory bodies to supervise the execution of these regulations. Thus opportunities for risk venture, which normally stimulate wholesalers' activities, were severely reduced.[1]

RENAISSANCE OF THE WHOLESALER

Wholesalers naturally shared in the general economic resurgence of West Germany after World War II, and their increased financial strength infused a new spirit of enterprise and initiative into their operations. This postwar renaissance of the wholesaler was characterized by two trends:

1. The addition of new services for customers, and
2. The large-scale return of manufacturers to the use of wholesalers as part of their distribution channels.

These trends were interrelated. Frequently manufacturers had provided their own distribution facilities because of failure of the wholesaler to render adequate services. The movement away from the wholesaler was not always successful or justified, however. While a certain independence from wholesalers on the part of manufacturers was both attractive and necessary, manufacturers came to admit that their own performance of the wholesaling functions was at best burdensome. Moreover, *competing* manufacturers were more likely to entrench themselves with competitors' *customers* when manufacturers handled their own wholesaling. The creation and control of exclusive wholesaling facilities by certain manufacturers seemed even a threat to the economy. In order to protect themselves in this situation, manufacturers in certain industries sought permission from the government to form cartels, particularly price-fixing cartels—in spite of the existence of anticartel laws in West Germany. Unsuccessful in this quest, manufacturers then turned to the newly strengthened wholesalers to provide them with strong market representation.

As wholesalers have regained status, they have also exercised new responsibility in distribution. Traditionally, large manufacturers viewed wholesalers as subordinate, denying them policy-making authority. The typical dependence of wholesalers on manufacturers

---

[1] For a more exhaustive treatment of the evolution of the wholesaler see: *Binnenhandel und Binnenhandelspolitik,* by Robert Nieschlag (Berlin, 1959), p. 496.

justified this attitude. Gradually, however, this extreme dependence by wholesalers on manufacturers has diminished, particularly in industries where patterns of distribution are being radically revised, as in foods. These changes have caused stresses and strains in the traditional relationships between the various levels of distribution.

THE PRINCIPLE OF VOLUNTARY GROUPS

The newly strengthened position of the wholesaler in West Germany is most clearly discernible in the formation of voluntary groups in the food field. This development, which originated in the United States, has spread to many lands, finding its first European foothold in The Netherlands. Such voluntary groups were virtually unknown in Germany during the Nazi era, because their basic principles were incompatible with the Nazi obsession for independence. The idea of voluntary groups found most acceptance after the war, and the growth of such groups in West Germany since then has been among the most spectacular in the Western world. There are currently about sixteen major voluntary wholesale food groups in West Germany, in which 500 to 600 wholesalers and 75,000 retailers participate. In addition, two co-operative food-wholesaling groups (EDEKA and REWE) boast a combined membership of over 50,000 retailers. Today only an inconsequential minority of food wholesalers and retailers operate outside the organizations of these wholesale groups.

A result of these developments has been heightened competition in food distribution between the voluntary and co-operative wholesale groups, the chain stores, and consumer co-operatives. Small retailers who formerly eschewed aggressive competitive tactics have embraced them with enthusiasm, since membership in the wholesale groups has furnished them new means of both price and nonprice competition. Many of these erstwhile small retailers have grown significantly, partly because, through financial assistance received from their groups, they have been able to modernize their stores and to add self-service.

Wholesalers setting up voluntary groups have usually operated on the basis of these policies: a highly selective choice of retailers and strictly defined operating areas which can be serviced profitably; restrictions in the frequency of shipments to retail accounts; and adherence to rules governing minimal order size. Increased efficiencies in purchasing and in operations have naturally followed.

Perhaps even more important, the selectivity of member customers and the limitations placed upon them by membership in the voluntary wholesale group fostered close co-operation among members. The introduction of many new services to assist the retailer was thus encouraged, including counselling on store operations, advice on merchandise assortments, financial management and credit services, central handling of bookkeeping, and sales promotion and advertising. Many independent wholesalers had long wished to be an "adviser" to his retail customers, not merely a supplier of goods, but, because of the previously informal and sporadic relations, they were unable to offer the services to their customers that co-operative wholesale groups furnished their retail members. At last the voluntary wholesaler can also do so. Voluntary wholesale groups in foods are found not only in groceries but in other areas, such as combinations of flour wholesalers and bakeries.

In West Germany, as in other nations, a lively topic of discussion in business circles is whether voluntary wholesale groups will carry over from foods to nonfoods. A textile group of this type, SELDIS, has been patterned after a French establishment, the name being a contraction of *sel*ection and *dis*tribution. Actually, without specifically forming voluntary groups, many nonfood wholesalers have added to their operating functions—e.g., carefully reviewing and selecting accounts to be serviced, systematizing delivery systems, setting up minimal order requirements, and counselling customers.

INCREASING NEEDS FOR WHOLESALERS' SERVICES

During this period of the comeback of the wholesaler, a trend toward wide assortments of merchandise has been apparent, and this expansion of breadth of assortments is still under way. Selection of merchandise by the German retailer has become considerably more complex because of the vastly increased assortments from which he must choose, thanks largely to the liberalization of foreign trade, the establishment of the European Common Market, and the growth of sources of finished goods from so-called underdeveloped countries. In addition, more highly specialized domestic manufacturers are also increasing the breadth of their assortments. As a result, the retailer is more dependent than ever on the accuracy of judgment of those selecting merchandise for him. Accurate anticipation of consumer reaction to the wider varieties of goods confronting him demands highly specialized, highly skilled buying talents.

Accurate and effective selection of merchandise is easier to manage when the middlemen—be they wholesalers or buying co-operatives—specialize in serving a homogeneous group of retailers. This factor increases the desirability of carefully selecting accounts when setting up voluntary groups. Further opportunities for wholesalers in West Germany have resulted from the renewed growth of small manufacturers and handicraft suppliers, largely as sources of more individualized, higher-priced prestige goods. As in other countries with rising incomes, the more prosperous West German also demands a more personalized touch in his merchandise.

Goaded by innovations developed by small processors, retailers have added quick-frozen foods, gourmet lines, and other products to their self-service fresh-meat sections. In similar fashion, many bakeries are gradually branching out into groceries.

Despite the traditional strength of retail specialty shops in Germany, the "give-the-customer-what-he-wants" argument has gradually changed many specialty stores into retailers carrying complementary assortments of goods. Instead of stores specializing in accordance with basic materials or skills used in production—such as leather goods, textiles, or hats—they now tend to group merchandise according to customers' needs, as in home furnishings, sporting goods, or women's ready-to-wear. This newer approach has placed considerable emphasis upon the assemblage of proper assortments. In expanding their lines, retailers have been forced into source markets about which they had little knowledge and, at least initially, in which they had little faith. Because of these circumstances, the wholesaler could provide a valuable service for the retailer by assembling goods for the retailer and by offering sound buying advice.

Such reliance by retailers on wholesalers is most marked in self-service food stores which have been expanding into nonfood lines. Since these retailers were largely unacquainted with these new lines, they have tended to rely increasingly upon wholesalers for advice. As yet, the rack jobber has not put in an appearance in West Germany, but his arrival surely cannot be far off.

The direct entry of wholesalers onto retailers' premises has some precedents in Germany, so rack jobbing will not be too great a departure from accepted practices. Tobacco wholesalers have recently assumed responsibility for servicing vending machines in retail stores, largely because of the retailer's dearth of capital and because of his lack of interest in, and appreciation for, vending machines.

SPECIALIZATION IMPROVES WHOLESALE OPERATIONS

The comeback of the wholesaler has depended not only on the extension of services rendered and the assumption of new responsibilities but also on the curtailment of services. The careful selection by certain wholesalers of their customer, noted above, meant in effect a renunciation of the small buyer whose purchases were unprofitable to those wholesalers. The specialized cash-and-carry wholesale operator has stepped in to pick up this business, either as a separate company or as a division of a full-service wholesaler, in order to take advantage of both retail markets. In spite of arguments in the trade as to whether cash-and-carry wholesaling really is efficient in view of the fact that the buyer must spend his time and facilities in picking up merchandise, until now the cash-and-carry wholesalers have been successful. They are esteemed for the service they provide for small retailers and for institutional buyers (restaurants, hotels, etc.), for the unique opportunities provided for rapid market reactions, and for the disposal of distress merchandise.

One reason for this high concentration of sales is the efficiency of large-scale operations, which abetted even further growth of those firms large enough to effect such reduced expenses per unit of business handled. Apparently a certain scale of operation is necessary to take advantage of the newer forms of wholesale operations. The process of concentration is accelerated, moreover, because of the large advantages to be gained through quantity discounts. Of course, smaller wholesalers could band together in order to earn the higher volume discounts available to their larger competitors, and, as a matter of fact, a considerable number of them do so. Whether the co-operative process will develop as extensively among smaller wholesalers as it has among manufacturers, farmers, and retailers is an open question at this time.

One result of co-operative buying groups has been a tendency among wholesalers to sell directly to end-users. This so-called direct distribution by wholesalers is, in reality, the German counterpart of "discount selling," which arose in the United States as a result of the breakdown of retail price maintenance. Direct selling in West Germany is still relatively uncommon, however.

THE WHOLESALER MATURES

The newly successful wholesaler has now reached a certain state of maturity that has gone hand-in-hand with the rebirth of manufacturers who had encouraged the broadening of wholesaler responsibilities. The economic consequences of large-scale manufacturers working in tandem with wholesalers have not been determined as precisely in West Germany as they evidently have in the United

States. Questions are being raised concerning the public desirability of concentration such as that which has occurred in certain German industries during the last decade. Such attitudes have naturally encouraged the independence of the wholesaler.

For most manufacturers the advantages of working through wholesalers outweigh the disadvantages, among which are the needs of providing funds for capital equipment and working capital and of supervising regionally dispersed personnel and activities. In addition, return to the use of wholesalers promises greater clarity as to what distribution costs actually are and perhaps wider and more thorough market distribution, since the wholesaler promotes a number of well-known lines to many types of customers and has close, long-standing associations with his accounts. The current shortage of all kinds of personnel in West Germany further militates against manufacturers handling their own wholesale activities.

Although there are exceptions among individual industries and firms, most manufacturers are seeking closer ties with wholesalers in order to take advantage of their valuable services and efficient means of distribution to selected volume customers belonging to the wholesaler group organizations. While group-oriented wholesale firms do exert considerable pressures for lower prices, their assured large volume sales make them very desirable manufacturers' channels of distribution.

In instances where manufacturers prefer not to rely entirely upon either their own distribution organizations or upon wholesalers, attempts have been made to develop still other alternatives. It is economical under certain circumstances, especially for a manufacturer, to distribute his own products with related products, so that expenses may be apportioned over a broader base. Such arrangements might suggest the establishment of a new form of wholesaling designed to meet the specific needs of individual industries. A number of German middlemen already appear to be heading in this direction, thereby contributing an aggressive element to distribution of potential value to the entire industry.

In the past, the wholesaler was a merchant adventurer with strong speculative proclivities, who frequently found attractive opportunities as a result of his intensive knowledge of markets. Today his orientation is different. He now gains his rewards primarily by providing efficient distribution and very adequate service both to suppliers and to buyers. This new role promises for him a definite place in the scheme of things and a bright future.

Because of the success in the food industry of separating whole-
ale operations into full-service and cash-and-carry units, the ques-
ion has been raised as to whether the same arrangements might not
also be successful in other branches of wholesaling—in textiles, for
instance. The policy of offering full service only to selected accounts
of larger volume is being practiced in all segments of wholesaling.
The question thus remaining unanswered concerns how to provide
for the needs of the smaller retailer. The individual full-service
wholesaler must decide whether these smaller accounts should be
left to competition or whether the wholesaler should set up his own
cash-and-carry facilities to serve them.

IMPROVED WHOLESALE MANAGEMENT

Despite the widespread influence of the newer developments
which saved wholesaling as a viable industry, merely a small fraction
of individual wholesalers either participated in these recent pioneering efforts or associated themselves with these innovations. Those
who embraced the new ideas grew rapidly, and they were in the best
position to modernize their plants and equipment and to hire the
most able management. In turn, those firms with managerial specialists had a considerable competitive advantage, and they were able to
capitalize on the renaissance of wholesaling. As a result, a large

TABLE 1

THE STRUCTURE OF WHOLESALING IN WEST GERMANY

Number of Enterprises and Sales, by Sales Volume, 1959

Sales Volume per Enterprise	Number of Enterprises		Total Sales of Volume Group	
	Number	Percentage	Total Sales (in Mil. D.M.'s)	Percentage
Up to 250,000 D.M.* (smallest enterprises)	77,057	57.2	7,031	4.8
250,000 to 2 mil. D.M. (small enterprises)	47,143	34.9	33,419	22.8
2 mil. to 25 mil. D.M. (medium-size enterprises)	10,124	7.5	51,758	35.3
Over 25 mil. D.M. (large enterprises)	500	0.4	54,557	37.1
Combined totals	134,824	100.0	146,765	100.0

* Approximately 4 West German marks (*Deutsche Mark*) equal $1 U.S. (2/1/63).

Source: *Angaben des Gesambtverbandes des Deutschen Gross- und Aussenhandels im Arbeitsbericht* (1959/60), p. 24.

and growing volume of sales is being concentrated in smaller num
bers of wholesale concerns. In 1959, only 500 wholesalers (less tha
0.4 per cent of the nation's total number of wholesalers) secured 37.
per cent of total sales (see Table 1).

FINLAND

The characteristics of Finnish wholesaling are here attributed to the cultural and economic similarity of Finland to other Nordic and Western countries. Differences are said to arise from the fact that Finland not only is agricultural but a large portion of her population supplies a significant measure of the products they consume.

By far the most unique aspect of Finnish wholesale distribution is its domination by four "blocks," or horizontally and vertically integrated groups of marketing institutions. Some are wholesaler-sponsored; others are retailer-sponsored; and still others are consumer-sponsored. Their objective has been to increase distribution efficiency, particularly through group buying, but they have shown marked political interests, lobbying on behalf of both right- and left-wing political organizations. Insofar as data are available, they are presented to show the relative activities of these blocks.

The author characterizes competition in Finland as an interaction of countervailing powers, including the cartels, the distributive blocks, and other unaffiliated wholesaling organizations. Price competition resulting from introduction of cost-saving operations, however, is little found, and restrictions are imposed on some other types of price cutting.

21

Wholesaling in Finland

*OLOF HENELL**

Finland is the only European nation founded between the two world wars that is still a democracy. The country was in a political union with Sweden until 1809, when it became a grand duchy with Russia. In 1917, it became an independent republic, which it still is. The proximity of Finland to Russia is felt commercially today, particularly in trade agreements, but in other respects their relationship is not significant to the purpose of this paper.

Size and Population. In area, Finland is about the same size as Montana. It has a population of 4.5 million, which, it is estimated, by 1970 will be nearly 5.0 million.

Urbanization is increasing in Finland. About one-third of the population lives in urban communities having more than 10,000 inhabitants. The biggest cities, the names given in both Finnish and Swedish, are as follows:

Helsinki	Helsingfors	450,000
Tampere	Tammerfors	125,000
Turku	Abo	125,000
Lahti	Lahtis	65,000
Oulu	Uleaborg	55,000
Pori	Bjorncborg	52,000
Vaasa	Vasa	44,000

Finland is a bilingual country, as is readily seen in much of the advertising and in street signs in its capital and other large cities. Finnish and Swedish are the languages spoken, the former being used daily by 92 per cent of the population and Swedish by the remainder. This, however, is not a complete picture, as it is estimated that about 20 per cent of the population speaks both Finnish and Swedish. This is important, and the active co-operation of Finland in Nordic cultural, technical, and commercial life is evidenced by the fact that, within the last few years, trade restrictions have been eased considerably.

---

* Dr. Olof Henell is Professor at the University of Lund, Lund, Sweden. He was formerly at the Swedish School of Economics, Helsingfors, Finland.

One feature of the co-operation between the four Nordic countries is that there is now free movement of labor. Finns compose the largest share of foreign work force in Sweden. At the same time, Finland is by far Sweden's largest customer for tourist services, as well as for retail goods in general.

Most Finns are oriented toward the West in their thinking. Their general outlook and living habits are much like those prevailing in other Nordic countries. Ninety-three per cent of the Finns are registered as Protestants, although it could not be said that religion plays any important part in the daily life of most Finnish citizens.

Also reflecting Western influences on Finland, Nordic schools of business are organized along lines similar to those in America, although before the war they were more influenced by the German schools of business. This is due in part to the fact that American professors are constantly at Finnish schools of business as guests.

Economy. Finland is often presented as "an economy based on wood." This is still true. Finland was industrialized later than the other Nordic countries. However, today Finland has, among others, a thriving metal industry which indeed grew strong when Finland had to pay a considerable part of the war reparations to the U.S.S.R.

TABLE 1

DISTRIBUTION OF EMPLOYMENT AND DOMESTIC PRODUCT BY BRANCHES OF
ECONOMY, 1948 AND 1959: FINLAND
(Percentages)

	Employment		Shares of Net Domestic Product	
	1948	*1959*	*1948*	*1959*
Agriculture	32.3	22.8	20.7	12.1
Forestry	10.8	7.1	11.2	8.1
Manufacturing and handicrafts	22.4	25.1	31.5	29.7
Metal industries	5.5	5.6	7.1	7.0
Wood and paper industries	4.8	4.5	9.5	6.2
Other manufactures	7.6	9.9	9.6	10.6
Construction	7.8	12.6	7.7	11.5
House construction	4.8	6.9	4.8	7.0
Other construction	2.9	5.7	2.9	4.5
Transport and communications	5.6	7.0	6.3	8.6
Commerce, banking, insurance	8.1	10.7	10.6	11.9
General government	6.1	10.7	10.6	11.9
Other services	6.9	7.1	4.0	6.4
Total	100.0	100.0	100.0	100.0

Source: *Finnish Trade Review,* V/1960.

in kind, particularly manufactured metal products. Facts shown in Table 1 indicate something of the changes in the structure that have occurred in the ten-year period.

The diversity of Finnish industry is also shown in the country's exports, by product classes:

	Percentage
Paper industry products	42
Wood products	27
Metal and engineering products	15
Timber	7
Agricultural products	5
Other	5
	100

Source: *Finnish Trade Review*, 122, (1961).

These percentages are changing, with more emphasis being given the exportation of manufactured goods. The impetus is coming from liberalization of foreign trade, which has resulted in a great increase in the flow of manufactured goods coming into the country. This is giving the Finnish producers of manufactured goods stiff competition, forcing these domestic manufacturers to compete at home as well as stimulating them to go outside Finland to get business. The stimulus to go after foreign business was not too important before, as the Finnish market up to the late 1950's was a sellers' market.

Growth of real per capita income in Finland in recent years, compared with that of other Nordic countries is shown in Table 2, from

TABLE 2

PER CAPITA INCOME, 1953–59

(1953 = 100)

	1953	1954	1955	1956	1957	1958	1959
Finland	100	108	114	115	117	116	122
Denmark	100	101	100	102	107	109	114
Norway	100	103	105	109	110	109	114
Sweden	100	106	109	112	115	115	122

Source: *Statistical Yearbook of the United Nations* (1960).

which it is apparent that Finland's economy has grown at the same rate as that of Sweden and faster than those of Denmark and Norway.

In terms of United States dollars, the per capita income of the Nordic countries, according to United Nations statistics, was as follows in 1959:

```
Finland ............$  720
Denmark  ..........   860
Norway ...........   840
Sweden ........... 1,150
U.S.A. ............ 1,980
```

Consumption patterns in Finland and in two other Nordic countries are shown in Table 3.

TABLE 3

PERSONAL CONSUMPTION EXPENDITURES

1960

(Percentages)

	Finland	Norway	Sweden
Food	39	30	27
Beverages, tobacco	9	8	10
Clothing	13	16	13
Rent, fuel and light	11	12	15
Household	8	10	9
Health	4	5	4
Transportation and communications	7	7	13
Other	9	12	9
Total	100	100	100

Source: *Statistical Yearbook of the United Nations* (1960).

Something of the orientation of Finland's commerce toward the Western countries is shown in Table 4, wherein the per cent of her exports and imports relating to different trading areas is shown.

TABLE 4

FINLAND'S FOREIGN TRADE

(Percentages)

Trading Area	Export	Import
EFTA	35.0	33.5
EEC	28.2	34.4
Eastern bloc	19.5	20.7
Others	17.3	11.4
	100.0	100.0

Source: *Finnish Trade Review*, 122 (1961).

DISTRIBUTIVE SYSTEM IN FINLAND

Finland differs from other Nordic countries in that a larger portion of its population, being agricultural, provides extensively for its own personal consumption. This has resulted in lessened need for retail stores, as is shown in the following statistics:

	Number of Stores per 10,000 Inhabitants	Year
Denmark	124	1948
Finland	81	1948
Norway	111	1953
Sweden	117	1950

Another factor contributing to this condition is the deliberate plan of two big co-operative chains to operate relatively large store units which serve a wide market area. Moreover, much retailing in Finland is carried on by "general-line" retailers, who combine a number of lines of goods. This type of retailing is most common in rural areas.

Further evidence of the distributive structure of Finland is given in Tables 5 and 6, wherein are shown for both retailing and whole-

TABLE 5

RETAILING STRUCTURE BY LINES: FINLAND

1952

Line of Business	Places of Work	Employees	Sales in Millions of Finnish Marks
Milk, dairy products, bread	1,470	3,667	14,849
Meat, fish, etc.	2,121	6,182	19,183
Groceries	3,765	10,924	39,029
Alcoholic beverages	95	1,744	22,817
Soft drinks, candy, etc. tobacco	1,463	2,419	2,683
General stores	12,356	38,515	145,389
Department stores	10	2,263	7,149
Textiles and clothing	4,729	13,244	46,567
Shoes and leather goods	690	2,299	9,242
Furniture, articles for interior decoration, etc.	459	1,549	5,285
Hardware, electric, and sports articles	1,350	5,860	23,782
Photographic equipment, jewelry, musical instruments, etc.	682	2,800	5,838
Books, stationery, etc.	1,163	3,798	7,530
Drugs	708	1,534	2,458
Apothecaries	497	4,285	5,675
Flowers, seeds	667	1,482	1,514
Fuels	438	1,858	7,708
Automobiles, accessories	365	2,394	23,778
Other goods	324	614	1,219
Total	33,352	107,431	391,696

Source: *The Official Statistics of Finland*, Vol. xxxv:1 (1953).

TABLE 6

WHOLESALING STRUCTURE BY LINES: FINLAND

1952

Line of Business	Places of Work	Employees	Sales in Millions of Finnish Marks
General line wholesalers	50	4,039	108,215
Groceries, etc.	211	3,594	51,081
Agricultural products	166	830	36,902
Other foods	274	2,418	31,662
Textiles, clothing, leather goods	340	2,671	43,616
Hardware, etc.	312	5,193	60,646
Jewelry, etc.	80	447	3,337
Paper and stationery	75	1,086	4,339
Chemicals	93	1,038	5,502
Fuel, etc.	179	2,736	28,229
Wood	368	1,630	10,028
Automobiles and accessories	41	975	19,304
Machinery and metal goods	243	3,323	39,413
Agricultural supplies	114	2,112	28,063
Other goods	499	1,387	7,912
Agencies	985	3,310	3,589
Total	3,045	33,479	478,248

Source: *The Official Statistics of Finland*, Vol. XXXV:1 (1953).

saling establishments, classified on a line basis, the number of stores, number of employees, and sales volume. Although the data are for 1952, it is thought that the relative positions of the lines remain much the same.

"Blocks" in Finland's Marketing. Not apparent in the data here presented on the structure of the distributive system is the fact that a great deal of integration, both horizontal and vertical, characterizes distribution in Finland. There are a series of more or less "voluntary" chain stores. There is also considerable integration between wholesaling and retailing. There are, too, some production plants integrated with distributive organizations. Of particular importance, however, in Finnish distribution are four large blocks or groups representing types of integration: the Wholesalers' Association of Finland, Kesko, SOK, and OTK.

The Wholesalers' Association of Finland (Finlands Grossistforbund). This is an organization consisting of a great number of wholesalers in various lines of business. The association has a dual objective: (1) to increase the efficiency of its members by educating their personnel, etc., and (2) to promote the interests of their members through lobbying and through influencing the formation of Finland's general commercial policy. Particularly important are the buying activities of the association, which are done through the part of the organization known as *Tukkukauppojen Oy* (TUKO). Through TUKO's KT department independent wholesalers have concentrated a considerable part of their purchases from domestic industry. This buying organization has been active, too, in importing groceries and in the purchasing of textiles. Similar associations are also found in other lines. The Finnish Hardware and Machinery Association was formed in 1907, the Glass and Chinaware Association in 1918, and two hardware associations—*Rautakonttori Oy* and *Rautakauppojen Oy*—in 1918 and 1929, respectively.

As is shown in Tables 7 and 8, in 1959 there were 402 members of these associations. Their sales were 196,300 million Finnish marks.

TABLE 7
SALES OF WHOLESALE ASSOCIATIONS BY LINES, 1959

	Number of Members	Sales	
		Finnish marks in millions	Per cent of total
Grocery, food and sundries, fruit, and coffee	121	85,650	43.6
Fabric and notions	65	20,590	10.5
Hardware	46	37,940	19.3
Others and Tukkukauppojen Oy	170	52,120	26.6
Total	402	196,300	100.0

TABLE 8
SALES OF WHOLESALE ASSOCIATIONS BY ASSOCIATIONS, 1959

	Number of Members	Sales	
		Finnish marks in millions	Per cent of total
Direct members of the Wholesale Association of Finland	204	125,660	64.0
Members of the Finnish Hardware and Machine Association, not being direct members of the Association	46	37,940	19.3
Other members of the member associations and Tukkukauppojen Oy (sales to outside firms, exports, etc.)	152	32,700	16.7
Total	402	196,300	100.0

The division of the membership on the basis of lines handled is shown in Table 7, the membership in the various association groups in Table 8.

Kesko. Like the associated wholesalers, private retailers, too, have organized a number of associations, in order to improve their status by pooling their buying and solving collectively their educational and organizational problems. The first association of private firms was Maakauppiaitten Osuusyhtio, formed in 1906 in Tammerfors. In 1907, Kauppiaitten Osakeyhtio was formed in Vasa. In 1915, Karjalan Tukkuliike was organized in Viborg (Viipuri), a city in the territory that was surrendered to the U.S.S.R. in World War II. In 1917, Keski-Suomen Tukkukauppa Oy was formed in Jyvaskyla. In 1941, under pressures created by the war, all these enterprises together formed Kesko Oy.

Kesko is a buying organization especially for the general-line retailers, mostly for those located in rural areas. This organization, created to take care of their economic and other interests, is known as Suomen Vahittaiskauppiaiden Liittro r.y. Retailers belonging to Kesko number about 10,500 and are active in grocery, food, hardware, textile, sundries, shoe, and agricultural-supply lines of business. Services given to members include education, business techniques, law, and building information. Kesko also provides store premises for men who want to start out on their own. Merchants who have joined and who satisfy certain requirements in regard to joint advertising campaigns are allowed to carry the K-sign. Kesko also controls a number of its own production plants, which it has inherited mainly from its four predecessors.

SOK. This is primarily a consumer's co-operative association, although it also includes, to some extent, producers' co-operatives. Their cultural and nonbusiness interests are taken care of by Allmanna Handelslagsforbundet ("General Association of Cooperatives").

OTK. This association too is an organization of consumers' co-operatives, and, like SOK, it also includes some producers' co-operatives. Their nonbusiness organization is known as Konsumtionsandelslagens Centralforbund ("Consumer Co-operatives' Central Association").

SOK and OTK are not wholly consumers' co-operatives, for they also include producers' co-operatives engaged mostly in the trade of agricultural goods. According to information obtained from SOK, they account for 55–60 per cent of the buying of grains from domestic producers. That grain is delivered both to its own mills and to others. The distribution of trade of agricultural products between associa- tions belonging to SOK and OTK is shown in Table 9. Milk for final consumption is distributed in about the same way.

TABLE 9
SALES BY SOK AND OTK, BY COMMODITIES
(Percentages)

	SOK	OTK	Totals
Grains	85	15	100
Potatoes, etc.	75	25	100
Hay	80	20	100
Meat and hides	80	20	100
Eggs	70	30	100

The co-operatives first worked in one association. In 1917, the movement whose name was SOK was divided into two movements— namely, SOK and OTK. The motives for the separation were political, but the fact that some local co-operatives represented rural interest and some urban interests also explains the tension that led to the break. SOK can be characterized as a right-wing co-operative and OTK as a left-wing one. SOK often appears under the designation "neutral"; OTK calls itself "the progressive co-operative movement."

The various blocks or groups do not exactly correspond to each other as to structure or composition, for they do not all represent the same kinds of businesses. For example, the Wholesalers' Asso- ciation of Finland has as members firms in special lines of goods, which are of little or no importance in the sales of the other groups. Thus, while the data in Table 10 show the relative size of the blocks in terms of their sales, they do not represent their competitive or comparative strength in any particular line.

Neither do the sales and relative positions shown in Table 10 present a complete picture of wholesaling in Finland, even among the associated groups, for the compilers of this information admit that they cover only 55 per cent of the country's total wholesaling. Among the other important organizations and firms for which data are missing are the following:

Hankkija (Finnish-speaking group) and Labor (Swedish-speaking group), both of which sell mainly agricultural equipment, tractors, grain, fertilizers, etc. Approximately 90 per cent of the sales from Hankkija go to the SOK local and regional co-operatives.
Valio (Dairy Co-operatives Association).
Kreaturslaget or Jarjakunta (Meat Producers' Association).

TABLE 10

SALES IN THE FOUR BIGGEST BLOCKS IN FINLAND,
1938 AND 1946–59

Year	Wholesalers' Association and Members	Kesko	Percentages SOK	OTK	Total
1938	59.4	12.7	15.8	12.1	100.0
1946	55.1	12.9	16.1	15.9	100.0
1947	56.5	12.4	15.1	16.0	100.0
1948	55.8	12.8	15.2	16.2	100.0
1949	56.0	12.7	16.0	15.3	100.0
1950	57.1	13.1	15.1	14.7	100.0
1951	57.7	13.2	15.0	14.1	100.0
1952	56.4	13.7	15.4	14.5	100.0
1953	55.0	14.7	15.6	14.7	100.0
1954	54.5	15.5	15.6	14.4	100.0
1955	54.2	16.0	15.3	14.5	100.0
1956	53.5	17.1	15.6	14.0	100.0
1957	51.2	18.0	16.3	14.5	100.0
1958	49.8	19.1	16.9	14.2	100.0
1959	49.7	20.1	16.3	13.9	100.0

Source: The Wholesalers' Association of Finland.

There are also several co-operatives for the marketing of eggs. In addition, there are special importers, wholesale firms with smaller wholesalers, and some agents.

COMPETITION AND ITS RESTRICTIONS IN FINLAND

The history of competition in Finland has been one of the organizing of the blocks mentioned and of other associations attempting to emulate their competitive power. Today, oligopoly with product differentiation is the main form of competition in Finland. This form of competition applies to most consumers' goods, as well as to producers' goods, except for raw materials.

In addition to the competition among manufacturers and others responsible for brands, there is competition among the blocks or groups: the Wholesalers' Association of Finland, the retailer-led wholesaling organization Kesko, and the co-operatives SOK and OTK. There might be some uncertainty concerning exactly how well each block is amalgamated and to what extent each block appears as a unit in its various dealings. We might, however, conclude that Finland in its distribution has more pronounced competition among countervailing powers than perhaps any other of the European countries.

Competition between the four blocks is keen. However, there has so far been very little price competition started by cost-saving operations, like discount-house operations offering little service. There has also been little development of limited-price variety stores. Price competition has become considerably more intensive in Sweden, but even there it is only a few years old. It was made more possible in Sweden when in July, 1954, resale price maintenance was forbidden by law.

Competition is sharp among manufacturers of branded products, such as Unilever and Procter and Gamble. It will increase with the liberalization of trade. Competition among domestic firms has been increased as they have learned from foreign competitors how to compete. The advertising agencies of Finland substantiate this point. The leading agencies of Finland are quite knowledgeable, having learned a good deal directly from the United States and, to some extent, from Swedish advertising agencies.

But what does this mean in terms of competition among manufacturers? For one thing, it does not mean aggressive price competition any more than it does in the United States. Obviously, other parameters of action than price are featured, such as product differentiation, advertising, etc. On the other hand, in some ways price competition is stiffer in Finland than in the United States, because of the common practice in the States to set minimum profit goals which are high according to European standards. When this practice is carried on by competing oligopolists, the consequence will be generally higher price levels.

It may be said of competition in wholesaling that when price competition is not severe at the retail level, neither is it likely to be at the wholesale level. In general, it is keener in Sweden. For example, in Sweden many wholesaling firms offer customers discounts which are graduated according to the services (in terms of small orders, deliveries, etc.) that a buyer is demanding. This practice has not yet spread to the same extent in Finland. In contrast to these conditions of competition which characterize wholesaler-retailer relations, in the relations of wholesalers and manufacturers to industrial buyers, price competition can become very active.

Conspicuous Restrictions on Competition. Cartels are one form of competition, and Finland has long had a considerable number of them. The first that appeared were export cartels. Examples of such cartels that are very important are the Finnish Cellulose Association,

Finnish Papermill Association, and Finnish Carton Association. Society has generally had a favoring attitude toward cartels in agriculture and even gives subsidies to agricultural production. That has been the case in Finland and Sweden. Denmark, on the other hand, gives no subsidies to its agriculture. Instead, it competes in the export trade. As already indicated, the agricultural activities in Finland are carried on by special organizations. There are thus two cartels in Finland dealing with the distribution of milk, cheese, butter, and, to some extent, milk powder and ice cream. The same types of cartels also apply to meat. The government sets the average price that the producers may obtain. Otherwise, the price is free to vary.

A special form of domestic cartel is the selling office, typified by the Cotton Manufacturers Sales Office, whereby restrictions are imposed on competition through the specification of product characteristics and selling conditions.

There are also a number of other types of cartels in Finland. Price cartels are common. Although their stipulations vary considerably, they often refer to "protected customers," from whom one may not attempt to solicit business without consulting the "possessor" of that customer or to whom higher prices are quoted by other than the "possessor." Another form of cartel is that organized by building firms in bidding for building projects. Sometimes the cartel selects the firm which is to obtain the job and determines the price he will get. All others are expected to quote higher prices, in order to stay out of competition.

It should be emphasized that the practices here described are monopolistic, but the cartels are not monopolies. The agricultural organizations, which are officially authorized and protected, come nearest to being monopolies. The monopolistic character of that group is blended with politics, for the Agrarian Party controls about one-fourth of the votes in Finland.

Laws against Restrictions of Competition. After many preliminaries, a law against certain restrictive practices was passed in Finland in 1957. The law was very similar to that passed in Sweden in 1953, which was broader in form.

The cartel laws now existing in Finland contain three main provisions: (1) special requests to report and to have cartels and similar agreements registered; (2) prohibition against resale price maintenance, but only after action from the official Cartel Bureau; (3) prohibition against bidding cartels of certain kinds.

It should be noted that the law, in principle, does not prohibit other forms of competitive restrictions. On the other hand, the law attempts to eliminate their negative effects by putting them more generally under official control.

The Cartel Bureau was started in March, 1958. It registers cartel agreements and follows and considers all factors that influence the restriction of competition. According to the law, bidding cartels cannot be organized without permission from the Cartel Bureau. At the same time, the Bureau cannot forbid resale price maintenance unless it is explicitly stated that the prices can be lowered. However, nobody has to report a cartel agreement to the Bureau without being specially requested to do so. The Cartel Bureau then decides whether the contents of the agreement is to be published or not. Before that, certain formalities are to be considered.

The law provides the Cartel Bureau with extensive rights to gather information. The only restriction of importance refers to information of a technical nature. When the Cartel Bureau has to investigate a special field or a certain line of business in regard to restrictions, it first sends out a questionnaire to organizations within the field and to the firms involved. The Bureau then makes up a report, which is not to be published in full until the parties concerned have had time to react to it, and even then it has to postpone the publishing a certain length of time.

In general, it can be expected that laws against restrictive business practices will become stiffer. They are likely to follow the laws in Sweden, which, so far, go further in their controls of restrictive practices of competition.

CONCLUSIONS

The economic and political environment for Finnish wholesaling and for all marketing corresponds, in general, to the environment in other Western countries. Finland is characterized by a way of living and consumption that is common in other Nordic countries and in modern countries in general.

A considerable part of the wholesaling activities in Finland are carried on by four big blocks: (1) the Wholesalers' Association of Finland; (2) Kesko, a buying organization especially for general-line retailers, mostly located in rural areas; (3) SOK, a right-wing consumers' co-operative, which is also a producers' co-operative, inasmuch as it takes care of many of the farmers' buying problems; and (4) OTK, also a consumers' co-operative, more to the left politically, which also, but to a lesser extent than SOK, is a farmers' co-operative. By far the biggest block is the Wholesalers' Association, which, however, is more loosely knit than the others.

The blocks serve as big buying organizations. They also serve as lobbying organizations, also carrying on vast educational and other efficiency-raising activities.

Competition in distribution in Finland has most of the traits of competition found in the United States and Sweden. Thus competition among manufacturers is mostly an oligopoly with differentiation. Product development and advertising and other sales-promotion activities are carried on in about the same way as in other Western countries. A few years ago, advertising outlays were reported to be somewhat smaller than in the other Nordic countries.

In wholesaling, where integration with retailers is common, and to some extent on the manufacturing level also, competition is also similar to that carried on in other countries. Retailing is characterized by chains (of more or less voluntary kind) and is going fast into self-service in the convenience-goods lines.

In retailing there are, as yet, few signs of various forms of "discounting" and flexible price competition, which is so characteristic of the United States and which is also beginning to appear in Sweden.

Finland so far has had considerable cartelization. There is fairly new legislation tending to lessen restrictions, which is likely to become more stringent. So far, resale price maintenance is, in principle, allowed, but it is likely to be forbidden in the next few years.

ITALY

Herein is given what the author refers to as an "interim report" on Italian wholesaling. By that he means that wholesaling in Italy as it might be described today is on the brink of certain change in the coming years.

Unlike Germany and the Netherlands, particularly Germany, Italy has not yet experienced the full impact of economic changes which have produced in other countries the decline and renaissance of the established wholesaler.

Preservation of the status quo in retailing has prolonged the life of the wholesaler in a system of distribution that has none too efficiently served the market. Innovation in both retailing and wholesaling has been stifled because of conformity to age-old customs in distribution, because of licensing laws, and because of the success of local interests thwarting even federal encouragement of progressive marketing.

Protection of a "superabundance of retailers" and an "excess of wholesalers," as well as slowness of manufacturers to distribute directly to retailers, have resulted in retardation of progress in wholesaling. The author feels, however, that these conditions are about to change. Increasingly, wholesalers are on the defensive as large manufacturers seek more direct channels of distribution and as new capital investments stimulate competition in distributive enterprises.

The implication is that Italian wholesalers will experience circumventive efforts until counteracting measures restore their position through new concepts of service and efficiency.

Wholesaling in Italy

PIETRO GENNARO*

Distribution in Italy can be traced back to ancient times. Unfortunately, many of the practices and regulations introduced during the Middle Ages have been continued to this day, not only in the notoriously economically backward areas of the south, but also, to some extent, in the otherwise most modern cities, which a casual observer might find difficult to distinguish from many contemporary American cities. The major inherited restraint to trade is the lack of freedom of entry—that is, the need to obtain a special permit to enter a distributive trade, whether as a wholesaler, as a retail shopkeeper, or as an itinerant peddler.

Licenses are granted only upon the recommendation of municipal boards set up for this purpose, and local merchants are well represented on these boards. According to the basic federal legislation governing these boards, licenses should be granted in accordance with such factors as the density of existing outlets of similar type in the district, the district's forecasted population growth, etc. Since the interpretation of these regulations at the local level is so broad, licenses are seldom granted. As a case in point, the president of the Merchants' Association of Milan recently stated that fewer than 10 licenses for new supermarkets had been granted in this community of over one and a half million people during the past several years, compared with over 200 applications from prospective entrepreneurs.

This effective barrier to new entries has been rationalized on the basis that chronic unemployment would drive inordinate numbers of individuals into the distributive trades, particularly into petty retailing, inasmuch as the initial investments required here are typically small. Granted that there was originally some basis for this reasoning in certain areas, there is little question that these protective measures have encouraged poor service, inadequate skills, and inefficient operations.

The licensing system is controlled by municipal inspectors who

---

* Dr. Pietro Gennaro is chief executive officer of Pietro Gennaro & Associati, Milan. He is also a professor on the faculty of the University of Pavia, teaching marketing.

continually check on whether goods sold by various outlets are covered by licenses granted for specific *items* in accordance with a very complicated set of rules. In Milan, for instance, a dairy store is permitted to sell boiled eggs and boiled rice with oil, but it is not allowed to sell boiled eggs with butter or boiled rice with tomato sauce.

Specific ordinances vary considerably from city to city, but the common end result has been the general stifling of progress in the distributive trades, the discouragement of more advanced merchandising techniques, and the granting of a premium to inefficient practices. Marketing methods at the wholesale and retail levels taken for granted in the United States are rare in Italy. The Italian National Productivity Council has tried in recent years to indoctrinate the trade in more modern methods through the dissemination of literature, the organization of lectures and conferences, and the encouragement of visits to prototypes of more efficient installations, but progress has been very slow. Reliable figures are nonexistent, but it is well known that the costs of distribution for most items in Italy are high compared with those in the United States, particularly for food. Even so, distribution costs *are lower* in certain categories, such as automobiles and industrial goods.

This exhorbitant cost of distribution, resulting both in high prices to the consumer and in low prices to the farmer, has recently spurred an interest in supermarkets including their endorsement by the federal government. But local politics have created formidable roadblocks which have prevented supermarkets from growing at more than a snail's pace. Over three years after their introduction, there are only about 200 supermarkets throughout Italy, with only four major chains in the field. At long last the federal government has also given its official blessing to variety stores, which number approximately 150 units administered by two chains. Here, too, support at the local level has been tepid or even antagonistic, since, with one and a half million people being engaged in distribution,[1] merchants (most of them small) wield considerable influence with local politicians.

This situation may change radically in the near future. During the last two years the rapid increase in industrial production has siphoned off so many of the unemployed, as well as those employed in marginal agricultural activities, that petty distributive enterprises no longer look so attractive. Moreover, the Italian system of distribu-

---

[1] Italian Bureau of the Census, July 20, 1960.

tion itself may be altered significantly during the next five years, as the European Common Market and other unifying forces of international business compel Italian industry and commerce to compete directly with more advanced, more efficient forms of distribution. As has occurred elsewhere in the West, these pressures will probably cause many retail and wholesale businesses to disappear, while at the same time encouraging the growth of large-scale distributive enterprises, particularly chains.

THE DISTRIBUTION STRUCTURE IN ITALY

The structure of the Italian system of distribution at the end of 1958 is summarized in Table 1 in terms of numbers of licenses granted. These figures overstate the actual number of operating enterprises by approximately 10 per cent, according to data published by the General Trade Confederation, since many licensed enterprises are inactive for one reason or another.

Inasmuch as the total population of Italy is now over 50 million, it is apparent from the figures in Table 1 that Italy's system of distribu-

TABLE 1
NUMBER OF DISTRIBUTIVE ENTERPRISES IN ITALY, 1958

Level of Trade	*Kinds of Merchandise*		*Number of Firms*
Wholesaling	Food		32,746
	Nonfood		34,075
	Mixed		5,828
		Total	72,649
Retailing—stores	Food		292,789
	Nonfood		347,079
	Mixed		139,845
		Total	779,713
Retailing—itinerant	Food		166,797
	Nonfood		140.944
		Total	307,741
Combined wholesaling and retailing	Food		10,584
	Nonfood		18,478
	Mixed		6,454
		Total	35,516

Source: Italian Bureau of the Census.

tion has the following characteristics:

A superabundance of retailers—about 15 families per store
An excess of wholesalers—approximately 1 of every 10 retailers
A very high number of itinerant retailers—almost 30 per cent of the total number of retail enterprises

In addition to the two variety-store chains noted above and the embryonic supermarket chains, large-scale retailing includes only one chain of seven department stores and approximately 4,500 cooperative outlets, most of which are small.

As Table 2 indicates, Italy's distributive system changes markedly

TABLE 2

NUMBER OF WHOLESALERS AND RETAILERS, BY REGION, 1958

	Regional Distribution							
	North		Center		South		Total	
Level of Trade	No.	%	No.	%	No.	%	No.	%
Wholesaling	49,297	67.8	10,953	15.1	12,399	17.1	72,649	100.0
Retailing *	399,220	49.0	157,721	19.0	258,288	32.0	815,229	100.0
No. of retailers for each wholesaling establishment	8.1		14.3		21.6		11.2	

* Includes combined wholesale and retail enterprises but excludes itinerant enterprises.
Source: Italian Bureau of the Census.

as one moves from the heavily industrialized north to the south, where more primitive forms of agriculture dominate the economy. Note that the heavy concentration of wholesalers in the north results in a ratio of only 8.1 retail enterprises for each wholesale business, compared with a ratio of 21.6 in the south.

PRIVATE EXPENDITURES AND CHANGES IN DISTRIBUTION

National expenditures for the private sector of the economy for three selective years—1938, 1948, and 1958—are shown in Table 3 in

TABLE 3

CONSUMER EXPENDITURES FOR GOODS AND SERVICES, SELECTED YEARS
(In Millions of 1960 U.S. Dollars)*

Lines of Goods	1938	1948	1958
Food	$6,109.2	$6,344.1	$13,058.2
Alcoholic beverages	781.4	835.5	....
Tobacco	460.7	495.2	....
Housing	683.5	50.9	....
Other goods and services	1,324.8	1,191.2	2,645.4
Total	$9,359.6	$8,916.9	$17,508.5

* Basic data in liras for the three selected years have all been adjusted to the 1960 value of the American dollar.
Source: Italian Bureau of the Census, Analisi Statistica Primi Studi sui Conti Economici Territoriali, Ser. 8, Vol. XII.

terms of the 1960 value of the United States dollars. Comparing expenditures for 1938 with those for 1958, it is noted that consumer spending for food and alcoholic beverages increased from 73.6 to 74.6

per cent of total expenditures, despite the fact that 1958 expenditures were more than double those of 1938 in terms of 1960 dollars. Tobacco went up from 4.9 to 6.3 per cent; housing declined from 7.3 to 4.0 per cent; and other goods and services increased from 14.2 to 15.1 per cent, reflecting greater purchases of automobiles and other discretionary items.

Unfortunately, it is almost impossible to attribute a definite share of these increased expenditures to wholesaling for the following reasons: (1) the lira was devalued to such an extent after World War II that neither total expenditures nor their channels of distribution can be measured with any acceptable degree of accuracy; and (2) many manufacturers began direct distribution to retailers only during the past decade.

Expenditure patterns vary considerably from region to region. For instance, food accounts for 48 per cent of total expenditures in northwestern Italy, as against 51.5 per cent in the northeastern and central regions, and 57 per cent in the south and the islands (Sicily and Sardinia).

SIZE OF WHOLESALERS

As shown in Table 4, at the time of the most recent census (1951)

TABLE 4

LEGAL STATUS OF WHOLESALE ENTERPRISE, 1951

	No.	*Per Cent*
Individual	50,521	78.7
Joint stock company	1,600	2.5
Co-operative	316	0.5
Publicly owned	17	....
Other	11,734	18.3
Total	64,088	100.0

Source: Italian Bureau of the Census.

approximately four fifths of the wholesale enterprises were individually owned, whereas the number of publicly owned enterprises was negligible. Roughly 88 per cent of the wholesale establishments in Italy employed fewer than six persons, compared with 59 per cent in the United States, as indicated in Table 5. At the other end of the scale, only 0.11 per cent of the Italian wholesale enterprises employed over 100 persons each, as against more than 1.0 per cent of the total number of American wholesale businesses. These facts clearly illustrate the basic nature of Italian wholesaling: a family

TABLE 5

NUMBER OF PERSONS EMPLOYED BY WHOLESALE ENTERPRISES
IN ITALY AND IN THE U.S.A.

Italy, 1951			U.S.A., 1948		
No. of Employees	No. of Firms	Per Cent of Firms	No. of Employees	No. of Firms	Per Cent of Firms
1–2	41,260	64.37	0–1	42,633	26.68
3–5	15,208	23.74	2–5	51,301	32.10
6–10	4,899	7.65	6–9	24,412	15.29
11–50	2,502	3.90	10–49	36,033	22.55
51–100	152	0.23	50–99	3,717	2.32
Over 100	67	0.11	Over 99	1,690	1.06
Total ...	64,088	100.00	Total ..	159,786	100.00

Source: *Distribution Statistics in 15 Countries* (Paris: International Chamber of Commerce, 1953).

business with low volume and relatively small net profits, which in most instances serves as a drag upon, rather than a boon to, marketing efficiency.

FUNCTIONS PERFORMED BY WHOLESALERS

Wholesalers in Italy generally perform functions similar to those handled by their counterparts in other Western nations. Naturally these functions vary in kind and in degree among different trades. Wholesalers in all trades usually extend credit to their customers, but the extension of credit to suppliers is most uncommon except in textiles. Wholesalers in most trades generally carry merchandise inventories, but they seldom provide special services to customers, such as technical assistance. Even in the industrial machinery trade, it is unusual for a wholesaler to provide adequate technical services for his customer. An increasing number of manufacturers in various fields are, therefore, bypassing wholesalers and selling directly to retailers or to industrial users of their products.

Most large manufacturers of consumer goods in foods and in toiletries have increased direct sales to retailers during the last 15 years, and, as a result, the proportion of these goods passing through wholesalers has been on the decline, with further decreases forecast for the years immediately ahead. On the other hand, wholesalers have maintained their traditionally strong position in the pharmaceutical trade despite the recent establishment by manufacturers of large networks of detail men to make direct calls on physicians and on other medical professionals. Both ethical and proprietary drugs are sold exclusively through pharmacies in Italy. Although a few small manufacturers of proprietary drugs sell directly to retail pharmacies, the total volume of sales thus bypassing the wholesaler is small indeed. In order to afford the reader a more concrete current picture of wholesaling in Italy, two specific trades—chemicals and textiles—are discussed below in some detail.

THE WHOLESALE CHEMICALS TRADE

Specialization by industries served is most important in the wholesale chemicals trade, with the principal areas of specialization being textiles, dry cleaning, photography, metal industries, leather goods, food, and soaps and detergents. Wholesalers generally carry a broad line of products representing the output of many manufacturers. It is the rare wholesaler who limits his line to the output of a single manufacturer. It is common, moreover, for a wholesaler to purchase the same types of products from different manufacturers unless an agreement between wholesaler and manufacturer should restrain the former from handling competing items and/or brands. In one segment of this trade—plastics—manufacturers almost invariably distribute their output to ultimate industrial users directly through their own sales forces.

There are somewhat more than 100 chemical wholesalers throughout Italy which have their own warehouse facilities, distributed by principal areas as follows:

Area	No.
Lombardy	24
Liguria	6
Emilia	10
Marches/Abruzzi	4
Campania	10
Apulia	8
Piedmont	10
Venetia	10
Tuscany	10
Latium	10
Sicily	6

In poorer regions such as Sicily and Apulia, the chemical wholesaler is likely to handle proprietary drugs along with chemicals. Sales territories covered by chemical wholesalers are apt to be limited to a single area, such as Lombardy (centered about Milan) or Liguria (centered about Genoa), with populations in the areas ranging from one to six million, although territories covered by certain wholesalers are even smaller. Only two chemical wholesalers could conceivably be termed national in the scope of their operations, even though neither one literally covers the entire country.

As a rule, chemical manufacturers prefer to sell accounts of over

200,000 liras (about $350) per month directly, thus leaving only the smaller accounts for wholesalers. Of course, the specific point of demarcation between direct selling and selling through wholesalers varies in accordance with the specific segment of the chemical industry, with the area, and with each individual situation. Generally, a manufacturer is likely to assume direct distribution when faced with a highly competitive situation that the wholesaler is ill-prepared to handle successfully.

Manufacturers' prices to wholesalers tend to be based on wholesale lists adjusted by quantity discounts and further adjusted by annual rebates dependent on sales volume.

Services offered by wholesalers to their customers are very limited, the most important one (and frequently the only one) being credit. Wholesalers seldom provide technical assistance to their customers even when manufacturers supplying the wholesalers are willing to do so on the wholesalers' behalf, since the wholesalers are reluctant to reveal their customers' lists. One of the major chemical manufacturers has stated that manufacturers in this industry are likely to avoid distribution through wholesalers to an increasing extent in the future, but such a policy could be affected in only a limited manner, inasmuch as distribution costs through wholesalers tend to be lower in many areas than direct distribution from manufacturer to user.

Almost every wholesaler in this trade does a certain amount of importing in order to round out his product line, with a few firms specializing in imports on a major scale. Exports are almost invariably handled directly by manufacturers.

TEXTILE WHOLESALING

Wholesalers are commonly used by manufacturers of woolens to move their fabrics to retailers, whereas manufacturers of cottons usually sell to retailers directly through their own sales organizations. Textile manufacturers, in general, tend to favor the use of wholesalers more than most other industries, especially as a means of obtaining wider distribution for their products.

Manufacturers of textiles usually grant franchises to a selected number of distributors, but such franchises are seldom exclusive. Large manufacturers using wholesalers generally employ a number of such middlemen throughout the nation, since it would be difficult to find a single wholesaler in this industry who is large enough or who has sufficient ability to offer effective distribution on a national scale. In accordance with the over-all pattern of wholesaling in Italy, textile wholesale firms tend to be small, family-owned, family-run affairs.

A possible departure from this pattern has been projected by the Textile and Apparel Wholesalers' Association of Milan as a means of increasing the group's productivity. At the heart of the plan is a "merchandise mart," in which wholesalers not only would have their offices and showrooms but would also share special services, such as deliveries to customers, data-processing facilities, advisory aids to retailers, a training center, and a marketing research department. Because of the daring nature of this proposal, its development should be of great interest to marketers in general.

There is a certain degree of specialization in the wholesale textile trade, with firms tending to concentrate on upholstery and drapery fabrics, men's-wear fabrics, women's-apparel goods, and the like. A significant recent development has been the addition of ready-to-wear apparel by a number of fabric wholesalers, some of whom have given up their piece-goods lines entirely. These changes have been motivated by the gradual shift in sales at the retail level from piece goods to ready-to-wear, similar to the transition which occurred in the United States several decades ago. Attesting to this movement is the decline in the total number of textile wholesalers in Milan from 936 in 1955 to 864 in 1960, while during this same period the number of retail stores selling ready-made men's apparel increased from 382 to 462 and the number handling women's ready-to-wear went from 365 to 458.

Few quantitative data are available concerning the sales forces used by textile wholesalers. Some employ their own salesmen, whereas others use independent sales agents who work for the wholesalers on a straight commission basis and often sell other products not directly competitive. It is the rare wholesaler who limits his source of supply to one or two manufacturers, in order to obtain more favorable quantity discounts or exclusive franchises.

In addition to stocking merchandise inventories, credit is the only other significant service that textile wholesalers usually grant their retail customers. Since much of this credit is long-term and fraught with risks, manufacturers are only too happy to have wholesalers assume these hazards. In the relatively few instances where manufacturers do offer retailers advertising and sales promotional assistance, such as window displays, the manufacturers are prone to bypass their wholesalers and work out the arrangements directly with the retailers.

PATTERNS OF CHANGE

There is a general belief among better-informed individuals in the trade that wholesaling will be increasingly on the defensive as the Italian economy continues to mature. There is a distinct trend on the part of large manufacturers toward direct distribution, and the possibility of increased competition from other member nations of the European Common Market is more than mere speculation. The considerable amount of capital—both domestic and foreign—seeking investment in the expanding Italian economy should further encourage greater competition among all distributive enterprises and will probably force long-used (and often long-outmoded) trade practices to be replaced by more efficient ones. This increased competition may result in lower gross margins for the distributive trades, hastening the demise of less efficient operators.

The wholesale trade is hardly likely to disappear *in toto* during this period of rapid economic development with its accompanying pressures and shifts, but neither is it likely to maintain the status quo. This paper is, therefore, an interim report on wholesaling in Italy. Developments during the next decade should considerably alter the situation described here.

THE NETHERLANDS

Wholesaling in the Netherlands reflects several circumstances that are peculiar to the environment: the small size of the country, its predominantly agricultural nature, and its heavy commitment to exporting. The author explains that the character of wholesaling and the role of the wholesaler reflect these factors.

His presentation of wholesaling in the Netherlands shows that the rationalization of this activity there corresponds closely to that given it in other places where classical concepts of production have prevailed. Justification for trade, including wholesaling, is based upon the "economic transformation" of goods which it effects. In explaining the value-creating processes of wholesaling as sorting, blending, storing, etc., he employs terms characteristic more of contemporary marketing thought than of classical economic analysis. Traditional social justification for wholesaling, however, is found in the fact that it increases values and decreases costs.

Although no census of distribution has been made in the Netherlands, the author has given some quantitive substantiality to his discussion by using findings of a trade survey which was made. They show a stage of early inquiry, a step beyond theoretical exposition through which wholesaling and marketing thought pass in transition toward maturity.

Principal attention has been given to analyses of the customers of industrial enterprises and wholesale establishments, showing channel patterns and the external and internal factors influencing vendors' distribution policies. Finally, inferences are drawn as to the possible strengthening that may result from rising economic prosperity in the country and from anticipated participation in the European Common Market.

47

Wholesaling in the Netherlands

J. F. HACCOÛ*

In the Netherlands, it was widely believed for a long time that certain categories of wholesalers had outlived their functions. This was thought particularly about the secondary wholesaler during the two decades following World War I. However, more recent economic developments have demonstrated that this group of distributors is still useful. The significance of this will be illustrated in this chapter.

ECONOMIC CONCEPT OF MARKETING

It may be useful to set forth at the outset something of the regard in which trade is held by economists in the Netherlands. They see trading as a particular economic activity that conforms to the general laws of economic organization. Like other forms of production, trading contributes to the economic transformation of goods.

The contribution that trading activity makes to the transformation of goods is to help bring them into the form or condition in which they are desired by the market. The successive relations of buyers and sellers throughout the economic process differ, and these differences constitute a type of tension which is relieved only by the performance of certain actions. These tensions may consist of conditions in which the quantities of goods available do not match the quantities of goods desired. The same may be said of the quality, the time, and the place of goods in the market. Trading activities adjust these conditions, relieve these tensions, and thus contribute to the completion of the economic process.

The fact that goods are not physically altered in the process of

* Professor Dr. J. F. Haccoû was nominated ordinary professor of economics in the University of Indonesia in 1948 and ordinary professor in the Economics Faculty of the University of Amsterdam, where he has held the chair of organization of business life since 1950. Principal publications: "Futures Dealing in Commodities" (1940, 1947), "Commerce and Commodity Market" (1948, 1957), "The Indonesian Export Products" (1947), "The Essentials of the Top-Manager's Function" (1951), "The Entrepreneur and His Function in Modern Economic Life" (1952)—all in Dutch; "Management of Direct Investments in Less Developed Countries" (1957) and "Some Fundamental Problems of Policy Formation and Organization in the Commercial Field" (1957)—in English.

distribution does not render less valuable the function which is being performed. The *economic* and not the *technical transformation* is the important consideration. A modification in the composition of a parcel of goods, as though the process of sorting out or blending, results economically in a goods with a different value, just as much as if it had been transformed by a technical operation. Similarly, a change in quantity through assembling a carlot in order to reduce shipping costs, or forming larger or smaller units to meet the requirements of the production processes of buyers, is economically just as much a transformation as a technical operation. Still another example illustrates the point: the storing of goods prevents their being wasted for want of a present market and preserves their value, which may even be greater at the time of a future market.

Commercial activities like these are socially as important as industrial activities, and it is from the value they add that those who perform them draw a reward.

According to this conception, trading improves the conditions under which goods move to the next stage in the economic process. While *enhancing their value,* commercial activities may at the same time *reduce the cost* of getting the goods to their final destination.

Wholesaling, which constitutes a part of this process, is performed by agencies which may be classified in four functional categories:

1. The *collecting dealer,* who buys small quantities and forms larger ones in order to reduce costs of handling and transportation. These dealers operate particularly in collecting agricultural products, as well as in collecting scrap material.

2. The *collecting wholesaler,* who combines supplies from various sources into larger quantities and in a central market. If necessary to conform to the requirements of the market, the goods collected may be subsequently sorted or mixed.

3. The *primary wholesaler,* whose service consists not only of collecting but of dispersing the goods.

4. The *secondary wholesaler,* who receives goods as the first link in the distributive trade and delivers them, generally as a part of an assortment of a variety of goods, to retailers and craftsmen.

WHOLESALING OF AGRICULTURAL PRODUCTS

The role of the collecting dealers and wholesalers is influenced to a great extent by the strong position of co-operatives of horticulturists and by the policy of the government, adhered to for many years, to maintain, mainly in the hands of those co-operatives, a system of compulsory auctioning. Such a system of auctioning is no longer upheld by law, but the co-operatives continue to maintain the system so far as their members are concerned. Both primary and secondary wholesalers buy directly at those auctions, the former for their foreign customers, the latter for the domestic market. Canning factories, insofar as they do not buy directly from growers on a contractual basis, also frequent the auctions, as do some retailers.

Auctions play a major role in the marketing of fruit, onions, winter potatoes for consumers' use, eggs, and some other vegetables. In the distribution of all of these products, each of the four types of wholesalers performs its characteristic functions. In the trade in bulbs, the primary wholesaler is usually the exporter.

Cut flowers, too, are sold mainly at auctions to primary exporting wholesalers and to secondary wholesalers who supply the domestic market. There are growers, however, who export and sell directly to retailers. Likewise, there are a number of retailers who use the auctions as their source of supply rather than the secondary wholesalers.

In agriculture and stock raising, products which have to be processed, such as dairy products, are, as a rule, sold to co-operatively or privately owned factories. Those factories in turn either export, directly or through primary wholesalers, or also supply the retail trade through secondary wholesalers and retail co-operatives. Milk processors, co-operative meat factories, chicken-slaughter co-operatives, and egg auctions usually sell directly to the retail trade.

The sale from farms to manufacturing industries is commonly made by a direct channel. This is true not only in the case of co-operative manufacturing but also in the private processing of sugar beets, potatoes for industrial uses, and straw for strawboard. In the distribution of grain and wool, the collecting dealer plays but a modest part, as co-operative organizations and collecting wholesalers are very active in these trades.

The marketing of cattle takes place in a number of weekly markets that are held on different days in various towns. These markets are supplied partly by collecting dealers, by co-operatives, and by the farmers themselves. There the buying is done by primary and secondary wholesalers and, to a lesser degree, by butchers. The latest development is the organizing of cattle-slaughter co-operatives of farmers, which not only sell the meat so produced to secondary wholesalers and butchers but also export it. The offal is sold through collecting wholesalers or—but rarely—through co-operatives. Some meat factories are co-operative organizations; others are privately owned enterprises. The latter usually purchase without using an intermediary. In Utrecht, pigs are traded on an exchange once a week.

Collecting dealers and collecting wholesalers also operate in the
trade in scrap, secondhand machinery, and similar materials.

Thus it is apparent that the role of the various wholesalers in the
Netherlands is much like that of wholesalers in other countries where
co-operatives are so widely used in distribution.

As a result of the influence of buying co-operatives in agriculture
in general, the supply of agricultural machinery, raw materials, and
accessories is, to a large extent, in the hands of the central organization of the co-operatives. In recent years, this organization has increased its share in the sale of petroleum products to farmers. However, the primary wholesaler still plays an important part in the sale
of machinery to farmers and their co-operatives. Petroleum products
are supplied to farmers also by other than co-operative channels, as
by primary wholesalers and oil companies, the latter distributing
through their own gas stations as well as directly and through privately owned garages.

Finally, it should be mentioned that the international trade of the
Netherlands, including both exports and imports, is handled principally by primary wholesalers.

WHOLESALING OF MANUFACTURED PRODUCTS

The significance of wholesaling in the domestic sale of manufactured goods is illustrated by information obtained in a hitherto unpublished study made in 1958 concerning channels used by manufacturers.[1]

It is shown in Table 1 that, so far as the home market is concerned,
sale through the wholesale trade is of great importance to Dutch
manufacturers. In general, it is the third most important channel—

---

[1] This study was sponsored by the Netherlands section of the European Productivity
Agency and took place on the initiative of the Netherlands Society of Commercial
Managers; the results have been compiled and analyzed by the Foundation for Economic
Research of the University of Amsterdam.

The companies surveyed were those Dutch industrial concerns employing at least
25 so-called "wage-earner units," insofar as they could be expected to have a marketing
organization (viz., metal, electrotechnical, chemical, textile, food, and luxury industries;
industries of other means of production; and industries of other consumer goods).

This measure of selection is also used in compiling the accident insurance statistics.
The number of units is found by summing the number of days on which each member
of the labor force was not absent because of illness, and by dividing the total by 300.

Questionnaires for the survey were sent to about one third of the 5,500 known technical units of industrial companies. In all, 1,088 answers were received from companies
having at least one technical unit, and 609 mentioned their marketing channels, stating
the degree of importance to the company of the three principal channels. Weights were
assigned to the answers to express more clearly the degree of relative importance to the
channels. Those channels cited as the most important were weighted by a factor of 4,
the next most important by a factor of 2, and the third most important by the factor of 1.

TABLE 1

SALES OF 609 INDUSTRIAL ENTERPRISES BY CLASS OF CUSTOMER:
THE NETHERLANDS, 1958

| Class of Customer | Per Cent of Sales Made | | | |
| | Total | Size of Industrial Enterprise * | | |
		Large	Medium	Smaller
Agriculture, fishery and their co-operatives	3	3	3	3
Manufacturing and industrial handicraft	28	28	30	30
Predominantly manufacturing, to lesser degree handicraft	20	22	20	
Equally manufacturing and handicraft	4	3	6	
Predominantly handicraft, to lesser degree manufacturing ...	4	3	4	
Wholesale trade	23	26	21	22
Retail trade	27	23	28	26
Big enterprises and co-operative ...	2	3	2	
Others	25	20	26	2
Government, transportation, hotel and catering business, institutional consumer	14	15	14	12
Professionals and ultimate consumer	5	5	4	7
Total	100	100	100	100

* The size of each enterprise has been determined in relation to its own branch.

second most important in the case of large enterprises. Although these results are drawn from a relatively small sample of firms, confidence in them is encouraged by the fact that the same picture is found in a number of branches of industry, varying somewhat, of course, according to the structure of the sale. The importance of the wholesale trade in several industries is as follows:

Per Cent

Construction workshops 3
Furniture 5
Textiles 33
Weaving mills (furniture textile).....39
Weaving mills (clothing material).....35
Ready-made clothing 14
Food 34
Building materials 33

A number of reasons are found for these conditions. The wholesale trade is relatively unimportant in construction workshops, for example, because such producers predominantly sell directly to industry (52%), to government, to transportation companies, etc. (37%). Likewise, furniture sales are commonly made directly to retailers (47%), as well as to governmental, hotel, catering, and institutional buyers (21%). In the distribution of textiles, the wholesale trade occupies a place equal to that of the retail trade. In the ready-made clothing industry the importance of the wholesale trade is rising, but the retail trade is the dominant channel (78%).

Additional light is thrown upon the position of the wholesaler by evidence of the degree to which that channel is used as the *only* one to whom or through whom manufacturers sell. In Table 2 are shown

TABLE 2

SALES OF INDUSTRIAL ENTERPRISES BY CLASSES OF
SOLE CUSTOMER: THE NETHERLANDS, 1958

	Per Cent of Sales Made			
Class of Customer		Size of Industrial Enterprises		
	Total	Large	Medium	Smaller
Industrial consumers	36	38	36	36
Wholesale trade	18	24	17	19
Retail trade	29	23	31	28
Government, transportation, hotel and catering businesses, institutional consumers	9	7	10	7
Total	92	92	94	90

the percentages of sales made by industrial enterprises *only* to the various classes of customers indicated. On the whole, the wholesale trade or institutions rank third as sole customer of manufacturers, although the larger enterprises make somewhat greater use of this channel.

As has already been stated, the sample refers to industrial enterprises employing at least 25 wage-earner units. The number of enterprises with a smaller labor force is several times larger—over 43,000. While no data are available about their marketing channels, it is highly probable that with them, too, the wholesale trade plays an important role. It is believed that, in general, direct sale to industry and sale to the wholesale trade are the two most important channels, with sale to the retail trade being third in importance.

The export trade of Dutch industrial enterprises is conducted largely through direct channels and to a lesser degree through co-operates. Nevertheless, the share of the primary wholesaler in the export of industrial products from the Netherlands is by no means small. The role of the wholesaler varies, of course, in different industries.

Information about the marketing channels of wholesale establishments in the domestic market was obtained in the same survey and is shown in Table 3.[2] It is apparent that the distribution patterns of

TABLE 3

SALES OF 387 WHOLESALE ESTABLISHMENTS
BY CLASS OF CUSTOMER: THE NETHERLANDS, 1958

| Class of Customer | Per Cent of Sales Made | | | |
| | | Size of Wholesale Establishment | | |
	Total	Large	Medium	Smaller
Agriculture, fishery, and their co-operatives	4	4	4	4
Manufacturing and industrial handicraft	31	31	32	26
Predominantly manufacturing, to a lesser degree industrial handicraft	15	16	15	11
Equally manufacturing and handicraft	6	8	6	3
Predominantly handicraft, to a lesser degree manufacturing	10	7	11	12
Wholesale trade	14	17	13	13
Retail trade	34	30	30	41
Big enterprise and co-operatives	4	2	3	8
Others	30	28	30	33
Government, transportation, hotels, and catering business, institutional consumers	14	16	14	12
Professional and ultimate consumers	3	2	4	4
Total	100	100	100	100

larger and smaller wholesalers differ somewhat. Customers of the larger wholesale establishments consist relatively more of manufacturing and industrial handicraft organizations, other wholesale establishments, and governmental and other institutional buyers. Contrariwise, customers of smaller wholesale establishments consist relatively more of the retail trade, presumably the smaller retail stores, and of the more predominantly handicraft enterprises. Considering the nature of the business done with these various types of customers, one might conclude from these patterns that, as the size of the wholesale

---

[2] The data relate to 346 wholesalers and 41 selling companies and independent selling organizations, each employing at least 10 wage-earner units. As no information is available about the total number of wholesalers, the data can be taken as a random sample of 387 wholesale enterprises, of which 93 have been classified as large, 243 as medium-sized, and 51 as smaller enterprises. The weighting of their importance was determined as for Table 1.

enterprise decreases, the importance of marketing in small quantities increases. This impression is confirmed if the enterprises are classified according to the character of their operation, as primary wholesalers or as secondary wholesalers supplying the retail trade and handicraft industries. Such a classification is shown in Table 4. Therein it is

TABLE 4

WHOLESALE ESTABLISHMENTS BY CHARACTER OF OPERATION :
THE NETHERLANDS, 1958

Character of Operation	Size of Wholesale Enterprise			
	Total	Large	Medium	Smaller
Entirely or predominantly as secondary wholesaler	35	20	37	53
Principally as secondary wholesaler, but also as primary wholesaler	19	22	20	10
Entirely or principally as primary wholesaler	26	30	24	27
Principally as primary wholesaler, but also as secondary wholesaler	9	8	11	4
Separate selling organizations of cooperating enterprises:	11	20	8	6
a) Selling also products other than those of the parent companies and functioning as:				
Primary wholesalers	2	3	1	2
Secondary wholesalers	2	3	1	4
b) Selling only products of parent companies and manufacturing as: *				
Primary wholesalers	5	11	4	...
Secondary wholesalers	2	3	2	...
Total	100	100	100	100

* Although the 28 enterprises listed in this category are not truly traders, inasmuch as they do not own the goods, they are included because their functions closely resemble those of wholesalers.

seen that 58 per cent of the enterprises fulfill a function as a secondary wholesaler; the percentage increases as the enterprises are smaller in size. This fact confirms the presumption that the function of the secondary wholesaler is even more important with wholesale enterprises employing less than 10 wage-earner units.

The importance of the different marketing channels of the wholesale trade varies from one industry to another. The wholesale trade occupies a far more than average importance (75 per cent) in the retail food trade, for example. The same is true in textiles. In machinery, engines, tools, and instruments, as well as for steel warehousing, direct sale to industrial consumers takes first place.

CONCLUSION

The data obtained in the survey show that both primary and secondary wholesalers are of great importance as marketing channels for the domestic market in the Netherlands.

The Netherlands is a small, densely populated country with a highly organized transportation system. Still, the wholesale trade appears to be fairly important. This is explained by the fact that it provides for lower distribution costs. On the one hand, the wholesale trade allows its suppliers to keep their selling organization and shipping administration departments on more simple base. On the other hand, by being able to deliver in quantities and, as a rule, in an assortment and at the date demanded by its customers, wholesale establishments enable buyers to keep a smaller stock and thus to reduce cost. Socially, too, the volume of stock will be smaller than otherwise would be necessary. However, this does not preclude the wholesale trade from fulfilling an availability function for its less regular or incidental customers; it will serve the latter in emergency needs. Furthermore, in a number of trades the wholesalers have the rather important function of financing, usually its customers and, on occasion, its suppliers.

Several current developments are also likely to affect the position of wholesalers. They are (1) the differentiation in consumers' wants resulting from greater prosperity and from growing variation in the products of many industries and (2) the expectation of further developments along this line which are likely to result from the Netherlands' joining the European Economic Community. It is expected that these conditions will further strengthen the position of the primary wholesaler in importing and exporting and that of the secondary wholesaler in domestic distribution.

MIDDLE EAST

Turkey

Egypt

Israel

TURKEY

This study of wholesaling in Turkey presents the findings of a research project intended specifically to ascertain facts about the scope and character of wholesaling in that country. It is exceptional in that, while it depicts quantitatively the size and types of wholesaling establishments, it is primarily a social study of wholesaling as sets of interrelationships and interactions.

The intention of the authors is to explore the behavior of wholesalers, in order to determine whether they behave as "a step, a hurdle, or as part of a channel" in the distributive process. In an interview survey of 77 wholesalers, their relations with both manufacturers and retailers were examined, from the standpoint of initiation of contact, dispersion of relationships, frequency, and type of interaction, and attitudes evolved from their experiences.

One of their findings was that wholesalers tended to initiate the contacts which they had with manufacturers but that they did not take the same initiative in relations with retailers. This fact varied in different trades studied, but it represented an emphasis of buying activity rather than selling. The circumstances which it is believed account for this role activity of the wholesaler are interpreted in the chapter, along with other findings of the study.

Wholesaling in Turkey

MEHMET OLUÇ,
NEZIH NEYZI,
EMRE GÖNENSOY, AND
ERNEST J. ENRIGHT*

Turkey covers an area only slightly larger than the state of Texas but, with a 1960 estimated population of 27.5 million, has over three times the number of people. Only a small percentage of the population is engaged in industry (about 800,000), versus an agricultural population of nearly 10 million. Per capita income is low by any standards—in 1955 it was estimated at less than $100.

THE ROLE OF COMMERCE IN THE TURKISH ECONOMY

Historical economic studies show that the Ottoman Empire developed a highly efficient economic organization in terms of that period and administered its vast resources with great skill until the latter phases of decline. The new Turkish Republic, which was founded in 1923, was almost completely shorn of the vast economic resources of the Empire. Also, the period of the 1920's was a time of major changes in the social and political environment of Turkey. This period saw

* Dr. Mehmet Oluç is Dean of the Faculty of Economics, Director of the Institute of Business Administration, and Chairman of the Department of Business Administration at Istanbul University. He is also a member of the Board of Directors of the Turkish Industrial Development Bank. He is the author of *Principles of Marketing and Their Application in Turkey, Principles of Business Management and Organizations,* and numerous articles.

Mr. Nezih Neyzi received his Master's degree from the Wharton School of Finance. He is Director of PEVA marketing research company; marketing consultant, Mobiloil Turk; Secretary-General Kelyos Conference Board; teacher in marketing at the Institute of Business Administration, Istanbul University; and a doctoral candidate in economics.

Mr. Emre Gönensoy received his Master's degree in economics from Columbia University in 1960 and is a research associate at the Bureau of Research of the Institute of Business Administration of Istanbul University.

Dr. Ernest J. Enright served as adviser on marketing to the Institute of Business Administration, Istanbul University, from 1959 to 1962. He is a lecturer in business administration at Harvard University Graduate School of Business Administration.

Assisting in the preparation of the material used in this report were Dr. Aydin Aydincioğlu and Mr. Yildirim Kilkiş. This report is based on material published by the Institute of Business Administration, Istanbul University, and all publication rights are reserved.

he government begin to organize a modern economic structure by Western standards.

In the midst of all this change the basic foundations of local industry were laid, particularly in the textile, sugar, cement, and mining industries. Agricultural output rose enough to make the country self-sufficient and to allow for a small export surplus. In general, commerce and industry were given an opportunity to develop without government interference, and in this atmosphere the relative growth of the economy was substantial.

The general economic depression of 1929–30 forced the introduction of varying degrees of government controls over imports, prices, and investments. New industries were set up and the production of existing ones increased. Service industries, such as commerce, transportation, and shipping, increased their volume as well. Some inflation resulted, but internal commerce grew during the decade of the 1930's.

The advent of World War II meant greater controls, including price ceilings and rationing during much of the 1940's. Even so, inflation became an important postwar factor in the economy. With Turkey, however, taking a neutral position for the greater part of the war, the economy was strengthened by a favorable balance of trade. Thus the first comprehensive breakdown of the factors of Turkish national income published in 1948 (Table 1) showed that commerce

TABLE 1

PERCENTAGE DISTRIBUTION OF TOTAL TURKISH NATIONAL INCOME
ACCORDING TO INDUSTRIAL ORIGIN AT CURRENT PRICES

Sector and Aggregate	'48	'52	'53	'54	'55	'56	'57	'58	'59 *
Agriculture	53.2	49.8	49.2	40.1	41.9	42.9	45.1	47.7	45.2
Industry	10.5	12.0	12.5	15.2	14.2	15.5	15.6	16.0	16.5
Construction	3.2	4.2	4.7	5.8	5.8	5.8	6.3	6.0	6.4
Wholesale and retail	10.9	10.6	11.2	12.2	13.1	10.1	8.4	7.4	7.1
Transp. and comm.	4.6	6.4	5.9	7.0	6.8	6.9	6.7	5.9	6.8
Financial instit.	1.4	2.0	2.1	2.7	2.9	3.0	3.0	2.8	2.9
Private services	3.7	4.1	3.7	4.3	4.6	4.7	4.4	4.2	4.4
Rent	2.7	2.5	2.4	3.2	2.9	3.4	3.3	3.5	4.0
Government service	10.0	8.7	8.5	9.8	8.2	8.1	7.7	6.9	7.3
Rest of world income	—0.2	—0.3	—0.2	—0.3	—0.4	—0.4	—0.5	—0.4	—0.6

* Estimated.
Source: Prime Ministry, Central Statistical Office, *Monthly Bulletin of Statistics*, No. 80 (Ankara, October, 1960), p. 135.

(wholesale and retail trade) accounted for 10.9 per cent of national income. The major expansion of the economy in the period 1923–48 was in the primary producing sectors—agriculture and industry—

which are directly correlated with commerce. Thus the retail an
wholesale trade had expanded correspondingly.

The trend since 1948, however, has been different. At the end o
1959 the relative importance of internal commerce had declined con
siderably in terms of national income, as is shown in Table 1. Th
relative share of commerce in national income in 1959 was 7.1 pe
cent, and this comparatively smaller share is less than should be ex
pected.

Internal trade since 1948 has grown steadily. Owing to governmen
economic policies since 1950, there was a greater expansion in thos
sectors that did not have direct linkage effects on commerce and di
not yield relative increases in porduction of goods. This caused th
relative share of commerce in national income to decline. A compari
son of the relative growth from 1948–59 in the various economic
sectors is shown in Table 2.

TABLE 2

INDEX OF TURKISH NATIONAL PRODUCT ACCORDING TO
INDUSTRIAL ORIGIN, 1959
(1948 = 100)

Agriculture	157.0	Private Services	220.5
Industry	188.7	Rent	256.5
Construction	331.0	Gov't Services	163.9
Commerce	166.3	Rest of World	−179.5
Trans., Comm.	263.7	Net National Income	181.6
Financial Inst.	318.0		

Source: Prime Ministry, *ibid.*, p. 145.

In the course of eleven years, commerce did grow in absolute
terms: from 100 in 1948 to 166.3 in 1959. This index of growth compares favorably with the growth of the agricultural and industrial
(157.0 and 188.7, respectively) sectors which have direct effects on
commerce and increase the volume of goods in the economy. On the
other hand, the greater increase in construction (331.0) and transportation and communication (263.7) and other sectors was mainly
inflationary and had much less effect on commerce.

The figures in Table 3 show the growth pattern of commerce during the 1948–59 period by specific years and show the effect on internal trade of the 1955 law, which restricted wholesale margins to 10
per cent and retail margins to 25 per cent of invoice prices.

The real volume of commerce in terms of constant prices increased
gradually from 1948 until the 1954 dip. This downturn (from 139.2
to 119.9) did not pertain to commerce. Rather, it is the result of a
drop in gross national product from 143.7 in 1953 to 130.6 in 1954.

TABLE 3

INDEX OF TURKISH NATIONAL PRODUCT ACCORDING TO INDUSTRIAL ORIGIN
(1948 = 100)

	Current Prices (Market Prices)		Constant Prices (Market Prices)	
		Gross National		Gross National
ar	Commerce	Product	Commerce	Product
48	100.0	100.0	100.0	100.0
50	101.3	103.2	100.2	103.3
51	114.3	121.9	118.0	119.1
52	141.3	142.3	126.5	129.4
53	172.9	167.1	139.2	143.7
54	183.2	170.0	119.9	130.6
55	241.6	209.2	129.4	140.6
56	211.2	241.7	139.5	150.1
57	246.0	303.3	145.4	159.6
58	276.4	382.5	165.6	178.5
59	364.4	461.0	166.3	181.6

Source: Prime Ministry, *ibid.*, pp. 141 and 145.

However, no such dip appeared in terms of market prices, indicating that, whatever the reason for a general decline in real terms, there were growing inflationary pressures.

The sudden shift of the Commerce Index in terms of current prices from 241.6 in 1955 downward to 211.2 in 1956 is worth noting. The figures in Table 3 show that, although commerce (in real volume) increased from 129.4 to 139.5 between 1955 and 1956, commerce was the only sector that did not show a substantial gain in 1956. One explanation might be that margins were substantially above the 10 and 25 per cent level in 1955 and that their reduction by law, together with the considerable but unknown quantity of "black-marketing," caused a decline in reported market prices in 1956. As the gap between current prices and constant prices increased, the Commerce Indices climbed to 364.4 and 166.3 in 1959. The law restricting margins was repealed in 1961. However, the restriction of commerce, together with the encouragement given other sectors, has drastically reduced the relative importance of commerce in the Turkish economy since 1955.

WHOLESALING IN TURKEY—GENERAL INFORMATION

There are no usable figures on the number of wholesalers operating in Turkey today, nor is there any reasonable basis for making an estimate, with the exception of the pharmaceutical field. Later estimates will be presented of the number of wholesalers operating in the four fields under study. The next census of business is scheduled for 1964, and thus reliable data will not be available for a number of years.

A rough estimate places the total number of wholesalers at 50–7. per cent more than the number reported in the 1950 census (se Tables 4 and 5). As can be seen from Table 4, those establishment

TABLE 4

WHOLESALE TRADE GROUPS IN TURKEY, 1950

Wholesale Trade Groups	Number of Places *	Sales and Revenue (1,000 TL)*
Food products	5,107	1,801,847
Agricultural raw materials	1,019	407,029
Minerals and fuels	233	287,148
Clothing	2,219	1,109,727
Medical goods and chemicals	190	79,402
Transport, vehicle, machine and		
electrical appliances	365	255,950
Building materials	483	135,070
Wholesalers of miscellaneous goods.........	1,400	371,804
Commission agents, brokers	1,570	639,625
Total for Turkey	12,586	5,087,629

* The official conversion rate of the TL is 9 to $1 United States, and most foreign exchange is converted at this rate.

Source: *Statistical Bulletin*, No. 21; *Prime Ministry Statistical Directory* (Ankara, Turkey, 1955). p. 90. Excludes villages with a population of less than 500.

TABLE 5

AVERAGE YEARLY SALES PER WHOLESALER BY TRADE GROUPS, 1950

Wholesale Trade Groups	Yearly Average Sale (TL)*
Food products	352,819
Agricultural raw materials	400,000
Minerals and fuels	1,232,400
Clothing	500,100
Medical goods and chemicals	417,900
Transport, vehicle, machine, and	
electrical appliances	701,233
Building materials	280,000
Wholesalers of miscellaneous goods	265,570
Commission agents, brokers	407,420
Average for Turkey	404,229

* See note to Table 4.
Source: Same as Table 3.

selling food products were most numerous (5,107), with clothing wholesalers next (2,219). Table 5 reveals that the group with the highest average yearly sales was the mineral and fuel wholesalers; and the one with the lowest average was wholesalers of building materials. As the transportability, in the economic sense, of many building materials is low and the market of a single wholesaler relatively narrow, his sales were inevitably limited.

Sales of minerals and fuel were concentrated in a few hands; thus average sales per wholesaler in this group (1,232,400 TL) were three times greater than the average for all the groups combined (404,229 TL). Transport vehicles, machines, and electrical goods had average yearly sales of 701,233 TL, which was nearly twice that of the average for all groups.

From the above, it might be assumed that wholesaling in Turkey was relatively small scale with little capital requirements. But we must remember that there were both small and big wholesalers within these groups, as witness the data contained in Table 6.

TABLE 6
WHOLESALE TRADE GROUPS VOLUME DIFFERENCES

	Those with the Lowest Sales		Those with Highest Sales	
Groups	No. of Working Places	Average Yearly Sales (TL)	No. of Working Places	Average Yearly Sales (TL)
Food products	783	7,853 *	2,162	775,444 *
Agricultural raw materials	146	5,829	421	911,875
Minerals and fuels	36	7,333	111	2,543,153
Clothing	141	6,808	1,241	756,218
Medical goods and chemicals	13	4,700	106	713,670
Transport, vehicle, machine, and electrical appliances.	26	6,700	249	981,959
Building materials	84	5,441	253	506,140
Wholesalers of miscellaneous goods	214	6,785	640	535,658
Commission agents, brokers	217	4,888	96	890,750
Total for Turkey .	1,660	6,880	5,459	786,565

* Calculated from the results of the 1950 census of working places.
Source: Prime Ministry, *op. cit.*, pp. 102-3.

In the food products group, the average yearly sale of 2,162 high-volume working places was 775,444 TL, versus average yearly sale of the 783 low-volume working places of 7,853 TL, which was almost as low as the sales of a small grocer.

The same conclusion applies to other groups as well. When those establishments with the highest sales are considered, their average yearly sales were about two times that of the average for the total number of establishments in the group. Even so, wholesaling in Turkey is not organized on a large-scale basis, despite the fact that total sales of a few individual firms are quite substantial.

One of the main determinations of this scale of operation is the lack of capital, since few wholesaling firms are organized as corporations to procure capital. Another reason is the relatively underdeveloped condition of transportation and communications. Consequently, wholesaler operations cover limited market areas. This latter limitation is an obstacle to integration and concentration in the wholesaling trade. Further, the lack of managerial knowledge and of ability to manage personnel makes many wholesalers unable to expand the volume of their business. In addition, since the credit standing of many Turkish retailers is very low, many buy from several wholesalers rather than one. Thus risk of loss is divided among several wholesalers in the event that the retailer is unable to pay his debts, but, at the same time, this practice limits the business volume of individual wholesalers.

According to the 1950 census of working places, 6,086 out of a total of 12,586 wholesalers were concentrated in Istanbul, Ankara, Izmir, Adana, and Bursa, with 4,344 in Istanbul, 1,026 in Izmir, 289 in Ankara, 212 in Adana, and 215 in Bursa. Gaziantep (225), Mersin (188), Samsun (169), Trabzon (121), and Konya (110) are other important wholesaling centers of Turkey. To summarize, wholesalers were and are concentrated either in ports, exporting or importing, in railroad centers, or in big cities.

Excluding Istanbul, Ankara, Izmir, and partially Adana and Eskisehir, the majority of wholesalers in other cities, towns, and villages are really semi-wholesalers. A few statistics may be useful to visualize the position and the role of semi-wholesalers in Turkey. Turkey covers an area of 296,185 square miles, and two thirds of the Turkish population live in 60,000 villages throughout the country, and only 6,000 of these villages have roads to nearby highways and villages.

The semi-wholesalers are the larger retailers of the towns and villages who also supply goods to the small general stores in the surrounding villages. The semi-wholesaler travels to Istanbul, Ankara, Izmir, and other cities, buys his goods in bulk quantities, and has these goods shipped to his store. By buying and shipping in bulk the semi-wholesaler gains substantial savings in costs and earns some additional profit from his wholesaling activities. In effect he is both wholesaler and retailer, and, while his personal concern may be his store, he is the important marketing link between the major marketing centers and the isolated rural population.

A CONCEPT OF THE ROLE OF WHOLESALING

The relative smallness of marketing institutions is often taken as strong evidence of an inefficient marketing system; however, because

Turkey has neither mass markets nor mass-production facilities, other approaches must be considered as a basis for studying the effectiveness of wholesaling in Turkey.

One of the classical approaches to the study of marketing systems has been concerned with the "transfer of title" as goods and services moved from the producer to the consumer or end user through the "channels" of distribution. In one sense this approach was contradictory because "transfer of title" brought forth word pictures of the manufacturer turning over the goods, together with the task of marketing, to the wholesaler. The manufacturer thereby removed himself from the marketing scene. The wholesaler in turn moved the goods and the marketing problems to another wholesaler or to a retailer. The retailer then displayed his wares to the consumer.

So the process of marketing was described as a series of distinct steps, or separate marketing hurdles, whereas the term "channel" brought to mind a smooth, continuous passageway from one point to the next. Studies have been made to determine roughly the efficiency of the Turkish marketing system by conducting research to discover the extent to which this process resembled a channel rather than a series of distinct, separate steps.

More recently, marketing experts have described marketing as the process used to deliver a standard of living. This concept of the marketing task implied the existence of goals as well as a mutual responsibility to reach these goals on the part of all those whose work involved marketing. This responsibility, in turn, required adequate communication channels, a mutual interest in the economic health of the various marketing institutions, and a mutual desire to help each marketing unit do a more efficient job.

To a considerable degree, the marketing concepts of "channel" and "mutuality" were different means of expressing the same standard by which the effectiveness of a marketing system might be judged. These concepts have been based on "relationships"—relationships of the manufacturer, to wholesaler, to retailer, to consumer, and to each other. Our study of the Turkish structure of marketing has tried to determine the extent of these relationships.

More specifically, we have attempted to study the role of the wholesaler in the Turkish marketing system by inquiring about the various relationships of the wholesaler and, from this study, to determine whether his activities classified him as a step, a hurdle, or part of a channel. Our purpose in this chapter, however, has not been to pass judgment, since there was no equitable standard on the basis of

which one could fairly judge. Our attempt, then, is to describe th
Turkish system and hope that, from a comparative study of whole
saling practices in a variety of countries and economies, a suitabl
standard may be induced.

RESEARCH METHOD USED

The research on which this description of wholesaling in Turke
was based consisted of a study of a selected sample of 77 wholesalers
of which 22 were drug; 15, margarine; 20, electric home appliance
and 20, cotton textile wholesalers. Most of these wholesalers wer
located in Istanbul. Interviewing for this survey was carried out dur
ing the months of August and September, 1961. The wholesaler
interviewed were selected as "the more responsible wholesalers'
from various listings. As a result, it was not possible to compute an
of the results with statistical accuracy. The descriptions, however
presented in the following pages should provide an adequate pictur
of the role of the wholesalers in Turkey.

CHANNELS OF DISTRIBUTION IN TURKEY

The first question asked of the wholesalers was as follows: "From
your knowledge, what channels of distribution are being used in
your field?" The answers received are shown in Table 7.

TABLE 7

CHANNELS OF DISTRIBUTION BEING USED IN TURKEY
IN MARKETING OF DRUGS, MARGARINE, ELECTRICAL APPLIANCES, AND TEXTILES *
(Percentages)

Channel	Drug	Margarine	Electric Appl.	Textile
Mfr-consumer	0	13	19	7
Mfr-retailer-consumer	32	27	56	31
Mfr-wholesaler-retailer-consumer	100	100	100	100
Importer-wholesaler-retailer	91	0	75	0
Mfr-large wholesaler-wholesaler-retailer ...	0	40	0	70
Mfr-agent-wholesaler-retailer	0	0	0	19

* Percentage of wholesalers having knowledge that channels are being used. In many cases, a
wholesaler cited knowledge of more than one channel.

In the four product fields under study, wholesalers claimed knowledge that a few manufacturers were selling direct to consumers, except in the case of drugs. Around one third to one half of the wholesalers indicated that the manufacturer sold his goods directly to the
retailer. The importer appeared to be important in the drug and electrical appliance fields, while the large wholesaler was mentioned in

the margarine and textile channels. Use of an agent was mentioned only in the textile channel. Information regarding the relative importance (in terms of volume handled) of each of these channels was not available, but all evidence indicates that the bulk of goods moves through the manufacturer-wholesaler-retailer channel.

WHOLESALER-MANUFACTURER RELATIONSHIPS

General

Two aspects of the wholesaler-manufacturer relationship are examined in this section. First, the buying-selling contact is considered so as to determine *which of the two parties customarily takes the initiative* in making this contact (in other words, to determine whether there is more buying than selling, or vice versa). Second, figures are presented to show *what proportion of wholesalers receive the variety of manufacturers' services that they expected to receive.* However, with the exception of credit, no detailed information is available about the extent to which a particular service is offered.

Also missing from this section are facts that would permit a description of the spirit of the relationship between wholesaler and manufacturer. While the following story may not be typical, one feels that similar manufacturer attitudes are all too common. At lunch one day the general manager of a large Turkish firm mentioned that he had a marketing problem he would like to discuss. One week later his comment was, "I have no marketing problem now. I sold those goods to the wholesalers."

Specific Characteristics of Wholesaler-Manufacturer Relationships

Number of Manufacturers from Whom Wholesalers Buy. In the margarine field a wholesaler buys from only 2 of the 6 margarine manufacturers. The wholesaler of cotton textiles buys, on the average, from 10 out of an estimated 122 cotton-textile manufacturers; the electrical home appliances wholesaler from 44 of 245 manufacturers, and the drug wholesaler from 88 of 118 manufacturing sources. These figures are more interesting when they are studied in the light of two additional factors. The first factor is the size of the wholesaler as indicated by the average number of employees. The cotton-textile and the margarine wholesaler employ 3 to 4 people on the average, the electrical appliance wholesaler 11 persons, and the drug wholesaler 15 persons.

The second factor to be considered is that the wholesalers say they do not buy continuously from the same manufacturers, although we have no evidence from the survey of the extent of shifting. These wholesalers claim to shop the various manufacturers and importers, seeking new products, better quality, better prices, and services.

Buying-Selling Contact between Manufacturers and Wholesalers. A survey of a selected group of manufacturers provided some information about the extent to which manufacturers circumvented the wholesaler. In general, manufacturers sold most of their products to wholesalers, although 6 per cent of the textile manufacturers (including the largest textile company in Turkey) and 14 per cent of the electrical appliance manufacturers did not sell to any wholesalers. Also, 18 per cent of the drug firms, 81 per cent of the textile, and 79 per cent of the electrical appliance producers sold part of their goods directly to retailers. These figures indicated a substantial amount of bypassing the wholesaler.

A brief description of the manufacturers' sales departments may be helpful at this point. Table 8 shows the number of sales managers

TABLE 8

MANUFACTURERS' SALES STAFFS

	Drug	Textile	Elec. Appl.	Margarine
No. of companies responding	19	16	14	3
No. of sales managers	14	12	6	2
Average no. of salesmen	18	4	2	24
No. of companies having:				
No salesmen	6	3	7	0
One salesman	0	4	4	1
2–5 salesmen	6	4	3	0
6–10 salesmen	0	3	1	0
Over 10 salesmen	7	2 *	0	2

* Number of salesmen not given and not included in the average number.

and the number of salesmen employed by the companies interviewed.

These figures are presented, in order to determine whether manufacturers had the manpower available to make the sales contact with their wholesale customers. Of those interviewed, 75 per cent of the drug and textile manufacturers, 67 per cent of the margarine companies, and 44 per cent of the electrical appliance manufacturers employed sales managers. However, 32 per cent of the drug, 19 per cent of the cotton-textile, and 50 per cent of the electrical appliance companies used no salesmen. Half of the remaining electrical appliance companies employed only one salesman. The seven drug companies employing more than 10 salesmen used these men primarily to detail their products to doctors. Only five cotton-textile firms, one electrical appliance company, and two margarine companies used salesmen to distribute their products widely throughout Turkey.

Table 9 indicates which party made the manufacturer-wholesaler

TABLE 9

BUYING-SELLING CONTACTS BETWEEN MANUFACTURERS AND WHOLESALERS

	Margarine	*Textile*	*Drug*	*Elec. Appl.*
Percentage of wholesalers who contact manufacturers	6	93	95	100
Percentage of manufacturers who contact wholesalers				
Reg.	100	27	47	36
Sometimes	0	45	5	7
Of manufacturers contacting wholesalers				
Percentage of manufacturers using:				
Phone	87	63	89	92
Mail	6	69	84	100
Salesmen	60	69	79	15

contact, and the methods used by the manufacturer in contacting his wholesalers.

Except in the margarine field, the wholesaler took the initiative of making the majority of the buying-selling contacts. When the wholesaler wanted goods, the practice was for him to shop the various manufacturers for his needs.

When manufacturers were asked whether they made any selection of the wholesalers to whom they sold, 23 per cent of the drug firms, 36 per cent of the electrical appliance, and 69 per cent of the textile companies said "yes." When asked if they signed exclusive agency agreements with any wholesalers, 17 per cent of the drug, 8 per cent of the textile, and 14 per cent of the electrical appliance firms answered that they did.

The telephone was the most widely used means of contact. A considerable number of firms, however, made use of mail and personal selling to reach wholesalers.

In general, working relationships between manufacturers and wholesalers have not been very strong. A great many manufacturers do not have assured wholesaling channels for their goods, and wholesalers have not been content with a minimum number of manufacturing sources. The presence of these conditions helps to explain the apparent lack of strong mutual feelings of interest and responsibility between manufacturers and wholesalers. However, when manufacturers were asked whether they would be interested in seeing that wholesalers made a profit, 93 per cent of the textile manufacturers, 88 per cent of the drug, and 77 per cent of the electric appliance companies replied affirmatively.

Services Received by Wholesalers from Manufacturers. Table 10 lists the various kinds of services offered by manufacturers to wholesalers and shows what percentage of the wholesalers received these services. In general, Turkish manufacturers offered the standard inducements to wholesalers to buy their goods.

A brief description of the competitive situation in the four markets may be helpful in providing some reasons for the differences in practice among manufacturers in these four product fields. The electrical appliance market is a "seller's" market for many products. A few large manufacturers produce or assemble appliances in competition with imports, which are still a major factor in this field. The manufacture of drugs is carried out by roughly 8 large firms and 100 small firms and laboratories. Most of these large firms are Turkish affiliates of well-known European and American drug companies. Competition on the basis of reputation and quality is very keen. The cotton-textile market has reached a point where supply is greater than local demand at present. This field is dominated by a state-administered holding company, although there are many new and efficient privately owned factories. The margarine field is dominated almost completely by one company.

Credit and Cash Discounts: About 90–95 per cent of the wholesalers receive credit from manufacturers with the exception of a few small companies, and almost all of the wholesalers receive discounts for cash payment, except from the margarine companies. Credit terms vary considerably from 15 days to margarine wholesalers to an average of 118 days to drug and electrical appliance wholesalers and 142 days to textile wholesalers. In most instances the wholesaler gives the manufacturer a bill of exchange similar to a promissory note dated 90–120 days in exchange for the goods. The manufacturer usually discounts this bill at the bank. When the wholesaler pays cash for the goods a discount of up to 5 per cent of the "credit" price is given.

Quantity discounts are received only by some 50–60 per cent of the various wholesalers. Additional research will be needed to supply the reasons, but several guesses can be made as to why this is so.

TABLE

SERVICES RECEIVED BY TURKISH WHOLESALERS, 1961 *

(Percentages)

Services Received	Frequency of Service Received †	Wholesalers						
		Large Elec.	Small Elec.	Large Drug	Small Drug	Large Textile	Small Textile	Margarine
Credit	NR	7	43	5	5	0	6	8
	UA	93	57	95	95	100	94	92
Cash discounts	NR	14	31	9	0	5	0	100
	UA	86	69	91	100	95	100	0
Quantity discounts	NR	44	57	32	46	40	50	100
	UA	56	43	68	54	60	50	0
Delivery	NR	21	31	23	19	55	46	7
	UA	79	69	77	81	45	54	93
Cover loss in transportation	NR	0	16	18	18	65	74	7
	UA	100	84	82	82	35	26	93
Return of defective goods	NR	0	21	23	14	25	14	14
	UA	100	79	77	86	75	86	86
Equitable rationing of short goods	NR	39	67	45	59	60	67	0
	UA	61	33	55	41	40	33	100
Merchandise information	NR	0	15	29	48	35	33	43
	UA	100	85	71	52	65	67	57
Buy on consignment	NR	85	84	86	73	90	92	92
	UA	15	16	14	27	10	8	8
Drop shipments	NR	65	61	82	73	65	54	40
	UA	35	39	18	27	35	46	60
Sales help	Yes	78		97		45		
	No	22		3		55		
Quality guarantee	NR					50	54	
	UA					50	46	
Off-season discounts	NR					25	40	
	UA					75	60	

* Per cent of wholesalers receiving.

† N = Never; R = Rarely; U = Usually; A = Always or Continuously.

First, most of the wholesalers' operations are small in volume, and these wholesalers may not buy in sufficient quantities to earn discounts of this kind. Second, the ever-present threat of shortages (except in the textile field) leads businessmen to prize inventories as a guarantee to a continuing operation, which means that they are reluctant to move stocks rapidly by cutting prices. According to the wholesalers, 25 per cent of the textile wholesalers sometimes experience a shortage of some goods; in drugs, sometimes 68 per cent, continuously 27 per cent; in electrical appliances, sometimes 70 per cent, and continuously 25 per cent. Third, the wholesaler, for additional or other reasons, does not perform the "stock or inventory-holding" function in Turkey to the same extent that wholesalers in other countries do. According to the study, wholesalers in margarine try to keep 10–15 days' stock on hand, in cotton textiles 2¼ months, in drugs 2½ months, and in electrical appliances 4 months. Fourth, the practice of bargaining over price may replace the need for granting quantity discounts.

Delivery service is given to 70–80 per cent of the wholesalers in the drug and electrical home appliances field and to almost all margarine wholesalers. Only 45–55 per cent of textile wholesalers are given delivery service by the manufacturers. There is also a considerable correlation between giving delivery service and the service of assuming the responsibility for damages and losses sustained during transportation. In three fields, 82–100 per cent of the wholesalers are freed from this liability, but in textiles, only 26–35 per cent of the wholesalers are relieved of this risk.

Most wholesalers (75–100 per cent) usually, or always, are allowed the privilege of returning defective goods. Again one quarter of the wholesale customers of the large textile companies are not allowed this service, and, surprisingly, the same is reported to be true of the large drug companies. About 50 per cent of the textile wholesalers say that they receive no product quality guarantees from their manufacturers.

As mentioned earlier, shortages are a significant factor in the electrical home appliance and drug fields. This condition is a source of some annoyance to 40–65 per cent of the wholesalers, who say that manufacturers do not ration goods in short supply equitably among them.

Most wholesalers are provided with information about the merchandise they buy; however, this help is never, or rarely, received by 48 per cent of the wholesalers when they deal with small drug companies, or by 25–33 per cent of the cotton-textile wholesalers.

Few wholesalers receive goods on consignment from manufacturers, but a greater percentage (between 30 and 45 per cent) are able to have shipments delivered direct to their customers when necessary.

Eighty per cent of pertinent wholesalers believe that the electrical home appliance manufacturers engage in helpful marketing activities through the printing of sales materials and the use of advertising and salesmen which help them sell goods to retailers. Almost all (97 per cent) of the drug wholesalers receive this type of assistance but only 45 per cent of the textile firms.

In the matter of over-all services offered the wholesaler, a majority in the drug, electrical home appliance, and margarine fields receive a full range of assistance, although the smaller manufacturers are not as able to give as much as the larger companies. By contrast, the record of the textile manufacturers is much less impressive, despite the fact that the industry is in domestic trouble saleswise.

Several explanations have been advanced for this relatively poor showing by the textile industry. One reason advanced is that of "traditional" relationships. The textile industry was one of the first established in Turkey, and present relationships are those which were formed during the sellers' market period, which ended in 1959. Another reason given is that the largest companies are state-administered, which prevents them from being solicitous about the welfare of the privately owned wholesale establishments who would be opposed to "state interference."

Other Relationships. Wholesalers were asked whether manufacturers made them buy larger quantities than they needed. The answers went as follows:

Industry	Percentage of Wholesalers Answering		
	Yes	Sometimes	No
Textile	15	10	75
Drug	9	27	64
Electric appliance	12	12	76
Margarine	0	0	100

It is not known whether the quantities "needed" by wholesalers are less than the manufacturers' minimum order requirements or whether the quantities sold in this manner are in excess of wholesaler requirements. The fact that about 25 per cent of the wholesalers are expected to buy more goods than they want, particularly in view of a very tight money situation, may be a source of irritation between the manufacturer and wholesaler.

A second question asked was whether manufacturers required wholesalers to buy goods they did not want at the time. The wholesalers replied as follows:

Industry	Percentage of Wholesalers Answering		
	Yes	Sometimes	No
Textile	15	0	85
Drug	9	18	73
Electric appliance	0	11	89

Here again the merchandise in question may belong to a line of goods that the manufacturer expects the wholesaler to handle, or it may be "tie-in" merchandise. The manufacturer may sell scarce goods to a wholesaler only on the condition that he buy other regular merchandise. The result of such a practice may be an additional strain on good relationships.

Seventy-five per cent of the cotton textile wholesalers also replied that the manufacturers with whom they deal will sell direct to their retail customers when possible, without giving the wholesalers a commission on these sales.

In the cotton-textile field the closest relationship reported concerned the qualities of the cotton textiles to be manufactured. Wholesalers reported that 90 per cent of the manufacturers either asked for, or were given, product characteristics and quality advice by the wholesalers and that 84 per cent welcomed this advice.

When wholesalers were asked about the relative number and size of manufacturing firms they would like to have in Turkey in the future, the following percentages of wholesalers gave these answers:

Relative Number and Size	Textile	Electric	Drug	Margarine
Fewer—Larger	50%	26%	32%	20%
More—Larger	20	47	27	60

Other answers to this question favored the status quo or were for smaller units. These answers reflect, in part, the competitive situation (among manufacturers) within the industries. The manufacturing facilities in the drug and textile industries are more than adequate to meet present demand, while the production of electrical appliances s only starting to develop. As noted earlier, the margarine industry has one company that accounts for a great share of the total volume.

Street Vendors. Some mention must be made of the thousands of street vendors and door-to-door peddlers that are found in the cities. These vendors are not important in marketing goods in the four fields under study. In selling other goods, such as cosmetics, houseware items, women's accessories, men's furnishings, and fruit and vegetables, these vendors account for as much as 20 per cent of total sales of some of these items, according to some estimates. The street vendor buys his daily supply of goods from the wholesaler, the manufacturer, or the importer. Thus the street vendor is a way of circumventing the traditional retailer, and in many cases the wholesaler; with his variable pricing practices he keeps retail pricing in a state of confusion.

WHOLESALER-RETAILER RELATIONSHIPS

General

The analysis of the relationships between wholesalers and retailers will be approached both from the viewpoint of the wholesaler and, wherever information is available, from that of the retailer. This section will consider what type of sales contact is made between these middlemen and then the services offered by wholesalers to retailers.

Most of the wholesalers, 80–95 per cent, reported making some part of their sales to retailers outside Istanbul, and 50 per cent of the cotton-textile and electrical appliance wholesalers reported that they operated 1 or 2 depots each, although few of these branch depots were located outside Istanbul. In general, the wholesalers did not seem willing or able to take the sales initiative, as we can see in Table 11.

The average drug wholesaler reported selling to 99 drug stores, the margarine wholesaler to 183, the cotton-textile wholesaler to 334, and

TABLE 11

CONTACTS BETWEEN TURKISH WHOLESALERS AND RETAILERS (IN PERCENTAGES)
Wholesale Study

Sales Methods	Margarine	Cotton Textile	Drug	Electrical Appliance
Per cent of times retailers contact wholesalers	77	70	8	35
Wholesalers contact retailer personally	11	16	11	16
Wholesaler's salesman	3	9	3	7
Mail	1	9	22	33
Telephone	8	6	56	9

the electrical home appliance to 420. When asked how many accounts made up 50 per cent of his total business, the drug wholesaler said 24; the margarine wholesaler, 29; the cotton-textile wholesaler, 110; and the electrical home appliance wholesaler, 49. The ratio of large customers to small customers was 1 to 3 for drugs; for margarine 1 to 5; for cotton textiles 1 to 2⅓; and for electrical home appliances 1 to 6. These ratios indicate that some retail stores had a significantly greater volume of sales than others or that some retailers concentrated their purchases to a greater degree with a single wholesaler.

When retailers were asked whether they purchased most of their goods from a single wholesaler, 52 per cent answered affirmatively. Seventy per cent of the electrical appliance and clothing retailers said they concentrated their purchases; 52–61 per cent of the grocers, drug, and butcher stores said they did likewise. Only 33–42 per cent of the greengrocers and perfumery stores bought most of their goods from one wholesale source.

However, to obtain the complete stock of goods he wished to carry, the retailer said that he bought from an average of 17 wholesalers (see Table 12). Food retailers spread their purchases among more wholesalers (21) than do other retailers (37). Clothing retailers said they purchased from an average of 19 wholesalers, while electrical appliance retailers bought from 12. Drug, perfumery, and furniture stores had the smallest number of wholesale contracts (6–9).

Whether the retailer preferred to purchase most of his goods from one wholesaler or preferred to shop around, the reasons he gave for adopting one or the other of these buying practices were the same. In order of their importance these reasons were:

  a) Good quality products
  b) Cheaper prices
  c) A variety of goods
  d) Ease of transporting goods to retail store

Buying-Selling Contacts between Wholesalers and Retailers

In the eight retail groups studied, most retailers purchased most of their goods from wholesalers, except in the case of furniture stores, where 23 per cent bought from wholesalers. Tables 11 and 12 give a summary picture of the buying-selling relationships between wholesaler and retailer.

In the margarine and cotton-textile field the retailer visited the wholesaler to buy the goods needed. Margarine wholesalers reported that 77 per cent of the time the retailer came to them, and in cotton

TABLE 12

Contacts Between Turkish Wholesalers and Retailers
Retail Study

	Grocer	El. App.	Drug	Clothing	Perfumery	Butcher	Green-Grocer	Furn.	Av.
From how many whole-salers do you buy? (No.)	21	12	6	19	9	25	37	9	17
Do you buy most goods from one whlse? (Yes)	61%	70%	57%	70%	40%	52%	33%	42%	52%
Do you go to whlse. to buy? (Yes)	93%	100%	50%	100%	90%	95%	100%	95%	92%
Does whlsr. contact you? (Yes)	53%	55%	67%	39%	74%	10%	5%	78%	44%
How is contact made?									
Mail	12%	33%	10%	22%	15%	9%	6%	26%	19%
Telephone	35%	33%	53%	41%	30%	63%	62%	42%	39%
Personal	53%	33%	37%	37%	55%	28%	31%	32%	42%

textiles 70 per cent. In contrast, the electrical home appliance wholesaler reported that only 35 per cent of the sales contacts were made
by the retailer, and the drug wholesaler, 8 per cent. However, retailers with the exception of druggists (50 per cent), said that almost
all of them (90–100 per cent) went habitually to the wholesalers to
buy their goods.

Managers of wholesale firms also reported that their personal calls
on customers plus calls by their salesmen made up the following percentages of the sales contacts: margarine, 14 per cent; cotton textile,
15 per cent; drug, 14 per cent; and electrical appliances 23 per cent.
According to wholesalers, the remaining contacts were made by
either of both parties, by mail, or by phone in the following percentages: margarine, mail 1 per cent, telephone 8 per cent; cotton textile,
mail 9 per cent, telephone 6 per cent; drug, mail 22 per cent, telephone 56 per cent; and electrical appliances, mail 33 per cent and
telephone 9 per cent.[3]

Less than half of the retailers (44 per cent) reported sales contacts
from wholesalers. This average figure was affected considerably by
the lack of sales activity on the part of the fresh-fruit and produce
(5 per cent) and meat wholesalers (10 per cent). Also, only 39 per
cent of the retailers reported that the clothing wholesalers made sales
contacts. A little more than half (53–55 per cent) of the grocers and
electrical appliance retailers reported that wholesalers approached
them. Between 67 and 78 per cent of drug, perfumery, and furniture
stores were solicited by wholesalers.

Retailers said that about 40 per cent of all wholesaler contacts were
made personally; 40 per cent were made by telephone and 20 per
cent by mail. Furniture (26 per cent) and electric appliance (33 per
cent) wholesalers made more use of mail than did others, and drug
wholesalers used the telephone a little more than half the time (53
per cent), while at least half of the grocery (53 per cent) and perfumery (55 per cent) wholesaler contacts were made personally.

In summary, most of the time the customer came to the wholesaler
to buy in the margarine and cotton-textile fields. In the cotton-textile
field particularly, the explanation for this practice might be traced
to the small size of the wholesalers and their financial inability to use
personal selling methods in a market in which sharp bargaining over
price was the practice and where, too often, the quality of goods of-

[3] Undoubtedly the telephone would be used much more frequently, but there is a
shortage of telephones in Istanbul and Turkey. Only a few of the retailers have been
able to secure a telephone.

fered varied considerably. Thus retailers were forced to shop a number of the wholesalers to obtain better prices and quality.

In the electrical appliance field the wholesalers and retailers appeared to split the tasks of buying-selling. This field has been plagued by the continuous shortage of almost all products. Consequently, wholesalers had to notify retailers when supplies of new goods arrived in stock.

Marketing practices in the drug field were much more aggressive than those practiced in other fields because of the strong competition existing between the Turkish and Turkish-foreign firms. Wholesalers and retailers are in fairly constant contact with each other through use of the telephone, with the wholesaler taking the initiative.

Services Offered to Retailers by Wholesalers

Tables 13 and 14 show the extent to which services were reported offered by wholesalers and received by retailers.

Credit. In all four fields, 80–95 per cent of the wholesalers claimed to give credit to retail customers, and retailers agreed to these figures. The average length of credit extended was estimated by the wholesaler at 35 days for margarine, while the retailer indi-

TABLE 13

TURKISH WHOLESALER-RETAILER RELATIONSHIPS
Services Offered to Retailers by Wholesaler, 1961
Wholesale Study

Type of Service Offered	Frequency of Service	Per Cent of Wholesalers Offering			
		Margarine	*Cotton Textile*	*Drug*	*Electrical Appliance*
Credit	NR *	21	15	5	10
	UA *	79	85	95	90
Cash discounts ...	NR	93	15	5	53
	UA	7	85	95	47
Quantity discounts	NR	86	65	82	68
	UA	14	35	18	32
Delivery	NR	80	35	28	55
	UA	20	65	72	45
Loss in transportation	NR	67	70	19	70
	UA	33	30	81	30
Return of defective goods	NR	7	15	4	0
	UA	93	85	96	100
Sell on consignment	NR	93	95	100	95
	UA	7	5	0	5
Equitable rationing of short goods	NR	7	—	0	6
	UA	93	—	100	94

* NR = Never, rarely; UA = Usually, always.

TABLE 14
SERVICES RECEIVED BY TURKISH RETAILERS *
Retail Study

	Grocer	El. App.	Drug	Clothing	Perfumery	Butcher	Green-Grocer	Furniture	Av.
Does whlsr. give credit? (yes)	80%	96%	100%	96%	91%	91%	72%	53%	83%
For what period of time? (days)	40	96	87	113	95	16	13	81	
Delivery service (yes)	73%	33%	96%	74%	81%	32%	7%	83%	55%
Allow returns (yes)	60%	38%	74%	65%	71%	27%	51%	28%	53%

* Percentage of retailers receiving.

cated 40 days; 113 days (retailer said 96 days) for drugs and electrical home appliances; and 145 days for cotton textiles. When asked whether they gave retailers more credit than manufacturers gave them, and how much more, the answers of the wholesalers were as follows:

Gave More Credit	Margarine	Cotton Textile	Drug	Electrical Appliance
Percentage of wholesalers saying:				
Yes	80%	50%	52%	93%
No	20%	50%	48%	7%
If "yes," how much more credit given to retailers than received from manufacturers........	87	38	37	51

Half the wholesalers in the cotton-textile and drug fields and almost all the wholesalers in the margarine and electrical appliance fields believed that one of their main functions was that of financing the retailer through the extension of credit. As noted earlier, the wholesalers did not "finance" the manufacturer to any great extent through "inventory stocking" except possibly in the electrical appliance field, where this practice might be related more to the continuing threat of shortages rather than to any desire to perform the "stocking" function.

Cash Discounts. The practice of giving cash discounts to retailers appeared to be similar to manufacturer-wholesaler practices. In the margarine field few cash discounts (7 per cent) were allowed, while in cotton textiles (85 per cent) and drugs (95 per cent) cash discounts were the rule. In the electrical appliance field, however, only 47 per cent of the wholesalers said they granted such discounts, as compared with 75 per cent of wholesalers receiving such discounts. According to retailers, 57 per cent of them received cash discounts from electrical appliance wholesalers. About 85 per cent of the druggists said they received these discounts from the wholesalers, while 80 per cent of the textile retailers claimed such discounts.

Quantity Discounts. The percentages of wholesalers granting quantity discounts, excluding the margarine field, were between 20 and 35 per cent, whereas 50–60 per cent of the wholesalers received such discounts. Some of this difference in practice was probably explained by the propensity to bargain for price in certain fields. In answer to one question, 80 per cent of the textile wholesalers said that they bargained with retail customers. Retailers claimed that, on the average, only 10 per cent of them were given quantity discounts. In the four fields under study, 15–20 per cent of the retailers said wholesalers permitted these discounts.

Delivery and Responsibility for Damage or Loss during Transportation. As a general rule, one half to two thirds of the wholesalers said that they offered delivery service. Fifty-five per cent of the retailers said that wholesalers delivered. The margarine retailers were the exception, with only 20 per cent receiving this service from wholesalers. The comparisons between delivery service *received by the wholesaler* from the manufacturer and *given by the wholesaler* to the retailer are shown below.

DELIVERY SERVICE RECEIVED USUALLY OR ALWAYS

	Margarine	Cotton Textile	Drug	Electrical Appliance
Manufacturer-wholesaler	93%	50%	75%	75%
Wholesaler-retailer (wholesaler answers)	20	65	72	45
Wholesaler-retailer (retailer answers)	Na *	Na	96	33

* Na = Not available.

RESPONSIBILITY FOR LOSS DURING TRANSPORTATION USUALLY OR ALWAYS

	Margarine	Cotton Textile	Drug	Electrical Appliance
Manufacturer-wholesaler	86%	30%	82%	90%
Wholesaler-retailer	33	30	81	30

From the above it appears that the drug and cotton-textile wholesalers pass on to their customers the service given them, while in the margarine and electrical home appliance field the wholesalers were either unable or unwilling to do so.

Return of Defective Goods. Almost all of the wholesalers, 85–100 per cent, allowed the return of defective goods. Return allowances policies of wholesalers appeared to reflect the allowances offered to them by manufacturers. Retailers did not agree with these estimates. Only 38–74 per cent of the retailers said that wholesalers allowed such returns. The difference in answers might reflect some disagreement as to which goods were defective.

Equitable Rationing of Short Goods—Consignment Sales. In contrast to the poor treatment they seemed to receive from manufacturers when short goods were to be rationed, 95 per cent of all wholesalers claimed they rationed goods fairly among their customers. Similar to manufacturers' practice, only 5 per cent of the wholesalers reported a willingness to sell goods on consignment to retailers.

Size and Number of Retail Stores in the Future

When asked about the number and size of retail stores they would prefer to see in the future, wholesalers answered as follows:

Relative Number and Size	Textile	Electric	Drug	Margarine
More—larger	53%	58%	27%	47%
Fewer—larger	5	0	32	13
Status quo	42	37	36	34
More—smaller	0	5	5	6

Thus about half of the wholesalers would like to see more and larger retail stores, and about a third of all wholesalers were fairly well satisfied with the present number. The exception was the drug field, where a relatively sizable number of drug stores have been opened recently, and it has been reported that credit accounts have been more difficult to collect as the volume per drug store has decreased.

When retailers were asked what they would like wholesalers to do better for them, the main request was for better-quality goods and reasonable prices (76 out of 217 requests). In second place was a desire for an increase in credit limits (59). Twenty-one requests were made for regular delivery service. Few retailers requested stable prices (5), but some retailers asked that wholesalers tell them the truth in describing the products they handled (18).

OTHER WHOLESALER RELATIONSHIPS AND PRACTICES

When questioned about several aspects of their relationships with other wholesalers the following answers were given (Table 15).

Sales to Other Wholesalers

The figures in Table 15 show that only one quarter of the margarine wholesalers and one half of the drug wholesalers questioned sold goods to other wholesalers in the regular course of business, while almost all of the electrical appliance and cotton-textile wholesalers had other wholesalers as customers. No information is available to indicate what proportion of the interviewees' sales were made to other wholesalers. The reasons for the different wholesaler-to-wholesaler sales pattern in these four fields are fairly well known. The leading

TABLE 15

TURKISH WHOLESALER-WHOLESALER RELATIONSHIPS
(IN PERCENTAGES)

Question		*Margarine*	*Electric*	*Drug*	*Textile*
1. Do you sell to other whole-	Yes	26	85	27	90
salers as a matter of sales	Sometimes	0	5	23	5
policy?	No	73	10	50	5
2. Do you sell to other whole-	Yes	53	89	50	84
salers in case of need?	Sometimes	13	0	18	10
	No	33	11	32	5
3. Have you been asked to	Yes	0	10	5	26
merge with another whole-					
saler?	No	100	90	95	74
4. Do you agree that most	Yes	60	47	59	0
wholesalers are inefficient					
and should be eliminated?	No	40	53	41	100
5. Are you a member of a	Yes	*	10	100	32
wholesaler's association?	No		55	0	68
6. For the future what should	Fewer—larger	27	42	50	50
be the relative size and	More—larger	40	31	9	5
number of wholesalers?	Same—larger	13	0	14	5
	More—same	7	0	0	5
	More—smaller	0	0	0	5
	Same as now	13	27	27	33

* No association available to join.

margarine manufacturer has an extensive branch, depot, and sales system, perhaps the most effective marketing department in Turkey. The leading drug firms employ relatively large detailing (sales) staffs and account for most of the drug sales made in Turkey. The wholesaler-to-wholesaler sales in drugs are, in all probability, those of the products of the numerous small companies and laboratories who have no detailing staff. On the other hand, the electric appliance and cotton-textile wholesaler sales represent transactions with the semi-wholesalers described earlier, who travel to the major marketing centers to buy goods for themselves and for the small retailers in surrounding villages. With one major exception in the textile field, the electrical appliance and cotton textile manufacturers do not make use of a country-wide sales force.

In response to the question, "Do you sell to other wholesalers in case of need," at least two thirds of all wholesalers answered affirmatively. This response indicated a fairly high degree of co-operation among Turkish wholesalers and has the effect of keeping goods moving into the markets.

Trends toward Mergers and Larger-Size Units

These questions were asked to find out whether any significant signs of a trend existed toward larger units through consolidation and merger. Unfortunately, the questions asked were inadequate for the task, and a great deal of additional research is needed. Obviously, little serious consideration has been given to the feasibility of merging; yet at least half of the drug and cotton-textile wholesalers and almost half of the electrical appliances wholesalers stated that there should be fewer and larger wholesalers in their fields in the future.

This survey did not examine a widespread report that, during the period of legal limitations on margins from 1955 to 1961, a number of wholesalers and manufacturers and wholesalers and retailers merged "on paper" to obtain a better distribution of gross margins. These merger arrangements are said to have now been dissolved since the law has been repealed (1961). Nor did this survey check the more recent reports that some manufacturers and wholesalers have artificially fragmented their businesses by means of partnership arrangements to reduce their tax liabilities under a recent law. The inference behind these reports is that legal conditions have not been favorable for wholesaler mergers. Only in the case of the cotton-textile wholesalers has there ever been very much discussion about merging.

Wholesale Associations

All the drug wholesalers belong to the drug wholesalers association, whereas only 32 per cent of the textile wholesalers and 10 per cent of the electrical appliance wholesalers claimed membership in similar organizations. In the case of the electrical appliance wholesalers, 35 per cent of those answering said they had no knowledge of such an organization.

Those answering affirmatively were asked what help they received from such an association. The drug wholesalers answered as follows: no help, 32 per cent; representation to government, 32 per cent; help with various affairs and relations, 14 per cent; contacts with manufacturers and importers, 9 per cent; help in distribution, 4 per cent. The textile wholesalers said: credit information, 83 per cent; contract with government, 17 per cent. The textile wholesalers association operates the only credit information service in Turkey. The electrical appliance wholesalers did not answer the questions on association benefits.

Inefficiency in Wholesaling

Wholesalers were asked: "In a recent survey some Turkish businessmen stated that most wholesalers were inefficient and should be eliminated. Do you agree?" With the notable exception of the textile wholesalers, 50–60 per cent of the wholesalers agreed with this statement. In view of their answers to question 6 in Table 15, at least a substantial number of the wholesalers answering "yes" agreed that some wholesalers should be eliminated. We can infer only that the remainder agree that some wholesalers are inefficient. To be more useful, this question should have been asked as two questions. The textile wholesalers, who receive fewer services from manufacturers and who are circumvented more often than the other wholesalers, completely rejected the idea that any of their group should be eliminated.

THE WHOLESALER IN TURKEY—A SUMMARY VIEW

The Turkish wholesaler operates a relatively small business and, in general, does not have strong working relationships either with the manufacturers who supply him or with the retailer to whom he sells his goods. One interesting way of visualizing the role of the wholesaler is shown in the following figures:

Industry	Av. No. of Manufacturers from Whom Wholesaler Buys	Av. No. of Retailers to Whom Wholesaler Sells	Ratio
Drug	88	99	1–1.13
Electric	44	420	1–9.5
Textile	10	334	1–33.4
Margarine	2	183	1–91.5

A principal contribution of the drug wholesaler has been to concentrate the products of the many drug manufacturers and laboratories. The electrical appliance wholesaler performs this task to a much lesser extent. Conversely, the basic task of the electric appliance, cotton-textile, and margarine wholesalers has been that of channeling their goods to the numerous small retail units. These functions of concentration and dispersion required the services of a wholesaler because most retail units and many manufacturers were so small.

Various services have been offered by manufacturers and wholesalers to facilitate both the transfer of title and the physical handling of goods through the marketing channels. The willingness and ability of the wholesaler to offer such services may depend on the extent to which he is offered similar services by the manufacturers from whom he bought. The figures in Table 16 give a rough picture of the "serv-

TABLE 16

SERVICES RECEIVED AND GIVEN BY TURKISH WHOLESALERS

Services	Electrical Appliance			Cotton Textile			Drug			Margarine		
	% of Whols. Receiving	% of Whols. Offering	Comparative Ratio	% of Whols. Receiving	% of Whols. Offering	Comparative Ratio	% of Whols. Receiving	% of Whols. Offering	Comparative Ratio	% of Whols. Receiving	% of Whols. Offering	Comparative Ratio
Make sales contact	36	55	1.55	27	30	1.10	47	67	1	100	25	0.25
Credit	60– 95	90	1.15	90–100	85	0.90	95	95	1	95	90	0.95
Cash discounts	70– 85	45	0.60	95–100	85	0.87	90–100	95	1	0	10	—
Quantity discounts	40– 60	30	0.60	60	35	0.60	55– 70	20	0.32	0	15	—
Delivery	70– 80	45	0.60	45– 55	65	1.30	75– 80	75	1.1	95	20	0.21
Assume loss in transportation	85–100	30	0.33	25– 35	30	1.00	80	70	0.87	95	35	0.37
Return of def. goods	80–100	100	1.10	75– 85	85	1.10	75– 85	95	1.2	85	95	1.1
Consignment sales	15– 25	5	0.25	10	0	0	15– 25	5	0.25	10	0	0

ices" record of the wholesalers and suggest a relationship of "services received" to "services given."

As noted in earlier discussions, a large percentage of the wholesalers did not offer the retailer many of the services that might expedite the marketing of goods and that might lead to closer relationships between wholesaler and retailer. The figures in Table 16 indicated that the cotton textile passed on 60–100 per cent of the services given him and that the drug wholesaler appears to pass on 87–120 per cent, except quantity discounts. The record of services transferred in the two remaining fields was not so impressive. To the extent that a service given to a wholesaler by a manufacturer enabled this wholesaler to pass the service to his retail customer, the grant of a service by the manufacturer might be said to have a slight "multiplier" effect.

To summarize, a substantial number of manufacturers and wholesalers have a core of steady customers for their goods. Too often, however, the Turkish marketing process cannot be described conceptually as a "channel" through which goods flow smoothly from manufacturer to consumer.

The majority of marketing transactions must be characterized as "hunting expeditions." The customers search among the retail stores; the retailers shop continuously among the wholesalers; the wholesalers go from manufacturer to manufacturer. The objectives of these hunts are good quality, cheaper prices, and more services, such as credit and delivery.

To the extent that this latter description is valid, the activities in the marketing channels work backward, and the doors to marketing offices open inward to customers far more often than they swing outward as company salesmen depart.

Concerning the transfer of title, a greater amount of time and marketing energy is spent in finding goods to sell than is used in an effort to market these goods after they are in stock.

As far as the physical handling of goods is concerned, the manufacturer does somewhat more than the wholesaler. The wholesaler does little in arranging for the physical movement of the goods to the retailer.

The basic problems in Turkish wholesaling can be said, then, to be those connected with the relatively small size of the units, the lack of sufficient capital and credit, and the need to shop for quality and price, which limits the services offered and weakens the relationships between manufacturer, wholesaler, and retailer.

EGYPT

Wholesaling in Egypt today is compared by the authors with wholesaling in the United States in the early 1800's. It is subject, however, not only to the usual attitudes of businessmen in an under-developed agricultural society but also to the circumstances of a country in which the government, through business regulation and through direct participation in distributive activities, is attempting simultaneously to achieve social and economic objectives.

Little justification for many Egyptian wholesalers can be found in their performance of the usual wholesaling functions. They have held their position rather by taking advantage of fortuitous circumstances: through their contacts with distributors through whom new products may be introduced to the market and through their capital resources, however limited, with which retailers' purchases may be financed.

Where wholesalers are unprogressive in an economy that is progressing, or where they are uninitiative in a business system where others may take the initiative, they are particularly vulnerable to actions of other parties who may undertake to bypass them. The authors make it clear that such pressures are beginning to work on Egyptian wholesalers from two directions. The government is in some instances supplanting private enterprise in the role of whole-sale agent, and manufacturers are recognizing the advantage of their performing more of their own selling function.

This chapter presents a picture of wholesaling in the midst of social, economic, political, ideological, and technical conflict.

Wholesaling in Egypt

HARPER W. BOYD, JR., AND ABDEL AZIZ EL SHERBINI *

Before the 1952 Revolution, the Egyptian economy was literally stagnating, and it is still tragically poor by Western standards. But during the past several years the United Arab Republic has launched an economic development program which it is hoped will raise per capita income substantially. Over 200 factories have been built or started recently, and the 1960–65 five-year plan calls for an investment of some 1,700 million Egyptian pounds in economic development, of which 425 million pounds will be invested in the industrial sector.[1]

Such an industrialization program will place a heavy burden on the present inefficient marketing system and create a number of problems. One of the most important of these is the failure of the marketing sector to keep pace with industrialization. Certainly, the progress of underdeveloped countries depends not only on their attainments in agriculture and manufacturing but also on the development of an efficient marketing system.

In many ways Egypt's distributive system engages only in simple trading. It has little concern with consumer wants and needs or with ways of better serving the consumer. Its primary purpose is physically to distribute the available goods. It does not even ration goods through a pricing system because the prices of most staples are controlled by the government.

---

* Dr. Harper W. Boyd, Jr., is Professor of Marketing and Chairman of the Marketing Department at Northwestern University, where he obtained both his M.B.A. and Ph.D. degrees. In 1960 and again in 1961 he spent the summer in Egypt as Visiting Project Director of the Egyptian Management Development Institute's first executive training program in business administration.

Dr. Abdel Aziz el Sherbini is Professor of Marketing on the staff of the Management Development Institute and is also a director of that organization. Formerly he served as Associate Professor in the Department of Business Administration, Faculty of Commerce, Cairo University, Egypt.

[1] The official exchange rate for the Egyptian pound is $2.87, about the same as the British pound; however, the pound sells at about a 25 per cent discount on the European market.

Egypt's distributive system has undergone a substantial change over the last several years, owing to the departure of many foreigners (French, British, Greek and Italians) who were important traders. There is, however, some question about the value of the services rendered by these trader middlemen in an underdeveloped country. Frequently such individuals were able to obtain excessive profits because they provided the sole link between the market and the producer. They often financed the manufacturer and hence were in a position to dictate prices and quantity produced.

Egypt is roughly the size of the combined states of Texas, Oklahoma, and Illinois, but only about 2.8 per cent of her land area is cultivable; the rest is desert. Egypt has one of the highest population-density ratios in the world; and the estimated population increase of 25 per cent during the next ten years will increase this ratio substantially, despite the optimistic hopes of new areas of cultivable land resulting from the High Dam at Aswan and the New Valley Project (which involves the use of underground water for irrigation). And Egypt has few natural resources of any importance.

Egypt has textile factories, petroleum refineries, cigarette factories, fertilizer plants, airlines, ships, railways, sugar refineries, pharmaceutical plants, metal-fabrication companies, iron and steel works, cement companies, ceramic plants, jute mills, and major banking and financial institutions. But, even so, Egypt is still primarily an agricultural country. Nearly a third of her total national income comes from agriculture and only about 10–12 per cent from manufacturing. Cotton is Egypt's most important crop, accounting for 75 per cent of her total exports.

The annual rate of population growth is 2.5 per cent; thus, from a current 25 million, Egypt's population is expected to grow to 28.6 million by 1967 and to 35 million by 1977. The economy will have to progress rapidly to maintain even the present low national income of approximately $120 per capita.

Over 50 per cent of the population is nineteen years of age or less. Such an age distribution requires heavy investments in health and education. The rate of literacy has increased substantially in recent years and now stands at 40 per cent for men and 17 per cent for women.

Most of the population (58.2 per cent) derives its livelihood from agriculture, and only 23 per cent of the population resides in the metropolitan areas of Cairo, Alexandria, and the Suez Canal Zone. About 13 per cent is engaged in manufacturing; this percentage has not increased significantly in recent years, reflecting the fact that modern industry does not absorb large amounts of labor because of intensive mechanization. There has been a consistent and rapid increase in the per cent employed by the government and services (13.7 per cent in 1947, as compared with 16.1 per cent in 1958).

Efficient wholesaling facilities are extremely important to Egypt because of the press to industrialize, the relatively poor internal transportation and storage facilities, the prevalence of small manufacturers, and the concentration of manufacturing in Cairo and Alexandria. A close look at wholesaling of Egyptian institutions will provide a better understanding of the role of marketing in an underdeveloped country. This chapter discusses the wholesaling of both consumer and producer goods.

Some 80–90 per cent of the total expenditures of rural families is for food, and the remaining 10–20 per cent is spent for tobacco, tea, coffee, kerosene, and basic clothing. Because of the importance of food and related items in the economy, it seems advisable to start the discussion of wholesaling at this point with an analysis of food wholesaling.

FOOD WHOLESALING

In 1957 there were 2,921 firms (38.9 per cent of all wholesalers) classified by the census as food wholesalers. This figure does not include, however, hundreds and perhaps thousands of firms which sell at both retail and wholesale and are classified by the census as retail institutions, since more than 50 per cent of their sales is at retail.

Food wholesalers employ 15,077 persons, or 35.5 per cent of all employees working in wholesale firms. On the average, the food wholesaler employs 5 employees (excluding the owner), including a bookkeeper-clerk, an assistant, and perhaps 3–4 salesmen.

Food wholesaling in Egypt is usually an owner-operated business. A typical grocery wholesaler managing five workers has an annual sales volume ranging from $150,000 to $200,000. This volume is generated from a small initial investment of from only $7,500 to $10,000. Stock turn runs about 20 in an average year, and the average net margin (which includes the owner's salary) is about 1.5 per cent of sales. The average return on investment is much higher, of course, ranging from 30 to 35 per cent.

Food wholesaling is heavily concentrated in metropolitan markets; 48.4 per cent are so located. Almost all of the large food wholesalers are headquartered in Cairo and/or Alexandria. The average number of employees per metropolitan firm is about 6.1 versus 4.5 for non-metropolitan firms.

The nature of the wholesaling functions performed varies with the lines of goods carried and according to the stage in the distributive channel where the intermediary operates.

Agent

The first rung in the distributive chain connecting the manufacturer with the retailer is the "agent." He is very important in the distribution of many locally produced food and nonfood products. He is particularly important in the distribution of such items as canned fruits and vegetables, candy, and some household cleaning articles, such as soaps and detergents.

The case of a major chocolate and candy agent illustrates the typical functions performed by an agent. He assumes responsibility for selling the entire output of a domestic manufacturer. He handles no other products. He operates several small warehouses in Cairo, Alexandria, and two other towns and owns and operates a small fleet of trucks to transport merchandise from the manufacturer's plant to his own warehouses and subsequently to his customers.

A sales force of some six men is employed, whose basic job is collection rather than selling, since most orders are received by telephone. Orders from town and rural markets are solicited by travelling salesmen. Inventory is small because orders from wholesalers (and other subagents) and institutional consumers are placed in advance. Subsequently, these orders are filled on a hand-to-mouth basis. Inventory turnover is, of course, remarkably high, but this figure is meaningless, since the agent carries no inventory and his warehouse is only a depot where merchandise is simultaneously unloaded, sorted, and reloaded to fill outstanding orders. Subagents, who are large wholesalers, may sometimes receive their orders direct from the manufacturer, but such arrangements are made through the agent, who, in such cases, still collects his regular commission.

Most agents deal with a large number of wholesalers, subagents, and institutional buyers. Terms are usually on "open account," which must be settled in 30 days from the date of purchase. In effect, the agent acts as a "collector" for the manufacturer.

Typically, the manufacturer determines the price at which the items will be sold to the retailer. The agent receives a discount in the form of a percentage often as high as 15–20 per cent. The agent then gives the wholesale intermediaries a specific per cent of the retailer's price, usually about 5 per cent. Some question can be raised concerning the economic justification for the survival of the agent. There is no doubt that his remuneration is far larger than can be justified by his costs of operation and the risks incurred. In Egypt, his strategic role appears to be the introduction of new products. The returns obtained thereafter are, in reality, long-term dividends accruing from an initial investment of marketing know-how.

In certain cases the agent assumes the role of the manufacturer's sales department. While it would be expected that small manufacturers could not afford to maintain an adequate sales force and hence would require the services of an agent, it is surprising to find that many medium and large-scale producers do not use agents in this fashion.

Import restrictions have forced certain import agents to alter their way of life. A few (International Products, Inc., and Colonial, Inc.) now contract with domestic manufacturers to produce specific articles in conformity with rigid standards. In some cases the agent has obtained, in his name, the exclusive rights to produce certain "foreign" brands on which the agent pays royalties. An example is "Lux" soap.

Since 1956, the government has also entered the market as a major "agent." The establishment of the Misr Domestic Trading Company, an affiliate of the Economic Development Organization, marks the beginning of an era in the government's "interest" in domestic trade. At the moment, this company acts as a giant import wholesaler in the importation and distribution of such basic items as tea, coffee, sugar, and the like. It operates in close contact with its sister company, Misr Foreign Trading Company, which monopolizes the importation and exportation of many consumable food and nonfood products.

The establishment of the General Pharmaceutical Organization in July, 1960, is another step toward governmental control of activities and functions previously performed by import agents. This organization will be the sole importer of all pharmaceutical products. Domestic manufacturers may also sell through this organization or may sell directly to pharmacies. With hundreds of small pharmacies and drug stores scattered all over the country, direct selling will prove to be very costly. Therefore, little attempt will be made to bypass this organization.

There is great variation between agents as to the functions they perform. Some do not carry inventory, while others operate only as brokers by merely soliciting orders, which are transmitted to the manufacturer for further action. The future appears relatively grim for the agent, owing to increasing government intervention and the emergence of large-scale manufacturing and retailing units, which will ultimately seek shorter channels.

The Service Wholesaler

Full-line service wholesalers are almost nonexistent in Egypt; the majority carry a limited line. Extreme specialization is frequently encountered; thus some firms limit their activities to olives, others sell only cheeses, and some handle only canned foods. But such specialization is typically associated with large-scale operation as well as with importation. Before 1956, the separation of wholesaling from importing was the rule rather than the exception. Government control of imports and the wholesale margins for many products, as well as the designation of specific foreign sources of supply with whom Egypt had entered into trade agreements, have practically eliminated the specialized importer.

Medium-sized and small wholesalers carry diversified lines. A medium wholesaler typically carries such basic supplies as sugar, rice, tea, and the like, the price of which is controlled by the government. These represent about 70 per cent of his total sales and contribute a net profit of about 1.5 per cent of sales. Other items, numbering about 80 to 100, comprise the remainder of his sales and contribute a net profit of between 2 and 3 per cent of sales. A typical small wholesaler carries a wider line, including such items as cigarettes, matches, candies, groceries, soaps, and detergents. Such a firm may buy the cigarettes directly from the local manufacturer, the candy from an agent, and the groceries from a larger wholesaler.

Sources of supply vary by size of the wholesale firm. Large wholesalers, who also import, but directly from domestic or foreign manufacturers. Their sources of supply are limited because of their concentration on one basic line. Small wholesalers buy from many sources of supply. They may buy directly from manufacturers whose salesmen call on them about once a week. For other items, especially those that are in short supply, telephone orders are placed by the wholesaler direct to the manufacturer. Other items are bought from an agent. Terms of purchase vary greatly. In some cases the transaction is settled in cash; in other cases an "open account" or "revolving account" with a maximum predetermined credit limit is used.

The typical small wholesaler employs a small sales force of 3 or 4 men who usually canvass a small territory or district. The men usually call daily on all the small retailers in the territory; solicit orders in a routine fashion; return to the office and warehouse to prepare the orders; and deliver them later in the day. They are usually compensated on a flat salary basis.

Market expansion through promotional activities and price cutting is not practiced by small wholesalers. An attitude of live-and-let-live prevails. Several factors seem to foster this lack of aggressiveness. The most important is a lack of capital with which to expand.

All wholesalers give credit. Installment buying is practiced in most instances. When orders are filled at the wholesaler's warehouse, an invoice is attached to the order. When delivery takes place, the retailer examines the merchandise and signs the invoice. This invoice becomes an "open invoice." Every day the wholesaler's salesmen make collections averaging 10–15 per cent of the amount of the invoice. A week is usually enough completely to settle an "open invoice."

The strategic function of the average food wholesaler is, therefore, one of financing. This extends to financing inventories. Conventionally and unlike the agent, the wholesaler stocks merchandise in anticipation of demand. Order solicitation from retailers usually follows the building-up of inventories, whereas for the agent it precedes the accumulation of inventories.

NONFOOD WHOLESALING

Small-scale operations also characterize nonfood wholesaling; the average firm employs 6.5 employees. The clothing group has the smallest scale of operation, with an average of 4.3 individuals per unit. The largest average-sized firm is found in the transportation and accessories group, which has 9.5 individuals per firm. The relatively small size prevailing in the clothing group is probably due to the multiplicity of small units that sell at both retail and wholesale—the so-called wholesale-retailers.

In discussing the structure and operation of nonfood wholesaling, a distinction must be made between agencies engaged in foreign trade and agencies involved in marketing the goods of domestic manufacturers.

Import Agencies

The machinery used to sell foreign goods has usually followed one of three forms; selling through commission agents or manufacturer's representatives, selling through exclusive agents or representatives, and selling through the manufacturer's own branches.

Commission agents usually act as representatives for foreign manufacturers. They take orders from importers, wholesalers, and large retailers, which are secured by travelling salesmen or through branch offices located in the principal cities. They usually handle a wide variety of goods and seldom specialize in one line of trade.

Between 1952 and 1956, the process of combining importing and wholesaling into one activity began to take place. The narrow import margins allowed by the government made specialization in importing an unprofitable venture. Importing and wholesaling were subject to much speculation, because of the instability of price levels and the uncertainty concerning foreign exchange and import licenses. With a continuing price rise, importers and wholesalers became more interested in speculation than in performing their regular functions. During this period several large import houses resorted to illegal maneuvers in an effort to keep substantial amounts of hard currency for their account in Europe. This was done through the use of fictitious invoices with higher margins.

Following the 1956 events of the nationalization of the Suez Canal and of the British and French financial establishments in Egypt, wholesaling changed radically. The Economic Development Organization emerged as an institution of great importance in the nation's economic life. This meant that the government had actually entered the business sector and had become virtually a genuine importer and wholesaler by the formation of the Misr Foreign Trade Company. This company was given exclusive right to import basic foodstuffs, such as tea, coffee, beans, and other agricultural products. It was also given priority over most other importers in issuing import licenses and the like. In some cases this company acted as an import-wholesaler, in others as an importer only, and in a few cases as a broker simply selling import licenses to other importers.

In the face of the severe economic siege imposed on Egypt by some Western powers, the country entered into trade agreements and many other barter agreements with the Eastern bloc. This has had some definite repercussions on the wholesaling structure. For one thing, importers were now not so "choosy" as to their foreign sources of supply, which provided another reason for combining importing with wholesaling.

It is also of interest to point out some basic characteristics regarding dealing with Eastern bloc sources of supply. For one thing, the

trade here is with the foreign government and its agencies rathe
than with business enterprises. Eastern bloc sources of supply do no
use the practice of selling through their own agencies in foreig
markets. Exclusive representation also is not granted by these source
of supply. Once a trade agreement is reached, the Egyptian govern
ment issues import licenses to whatever import-wholesale houses ar
involved in a specific line of business to procure the merchandis
from Eastern bloc sources on a predetermined quota basis. This ha
led to the rise of some genuine Egyptian wholesale firms, togethe
with public corporations dealing in these commodities. Other import
wholesale houses with relations with Western sources of supply hav
suffered greatly as a result of these circumstances. Some had to switc
and operate according to the new development.

The ambitious industrialization projects embarked upon after 195(
were, in many ways, designed to produce products that would re
place imports from foreign sources, in order to ease the drain on th
country's foreign-exchange resources. Once a product was produce(
by a domestic firm, its importation came under strict control, and, i
many instances, it was prohibited completely.

It is interesting to cite as an illustration of the above what happen:
to the wholesale structure when a product is manufactured in the
domestic market and its importation is banned; for example, bicycles
There were at least a dozen importers of bicycles, each tied up with
a distinctive foreign source of supply and a special brand. Each im
porter did his best to obtain the largest import license that would
enable him to import as many bikes as possible. Once he received the
import license, he obtained the help of a commercial bank to provide
him with a documentary credit enabling him to receive the shipment
from abroad. The shipment arrived in crates containing bike parts,
which were deposited in the Customs at Alexandria or Port Said. The
"Customs" was used as a bonded warehouse, and the merchandise
remained the property of the bank that provided the credit. The
importer-wholesaler would "feel the market," and when prices were
to his advantage, he would pay the bank a specified amount and
thereby obtain release of part of the merchandise, which would then
be assembled at his own warehouse or be shipped directly to some
of his retail customers. It is evident from this illustration that the
bank does all the import financing, that the Customs is the conven
tional warehouse, and that the role of the import-wholesaler is re
stricted to assembling, accomplishing some storage of assembled
goods, and financing the retail business.

When the bike is manufactured by the Nasr Bicycle Company, the question arises as to whether there is great need for a dozen import-wholesalers. Instead of many foreign sources of supply, there is now one—and only one—domestic source of supply. The skill required in dealing with the import business and the mysteries involved in foreign-trade transactions are no longer a handicap to small whole-salers, semi-wholesalers, and even retailers. Similarly, the role played by commercial banks is of this nature. The bank does not now have the ideal bonded warehouse that was provided by the Customs. The Nasr Company does sell on credit and discounts the bills at the bank.

In June, 1961, a law was passed making all kinds of import business the *sole* right of public corporations. Only a limited number of public corporations—seven, to be specific—are allowed to engage in the import business. Attempts have been made to co-ordinate the activities of these public corporations, and some decisions have been reached whereby they would specialize on a product-group basis. Some of the public corporations in question have never engaged in the importation of some of the product groups that were assigned to them. For example, a pharmaceutical organization was assigned all the importation of calculating equipment and adding machines.

In view of the problems involved, it was agreed that the seven public corporations would be the only ones allowed to issue import licenses. All other previous importing houses, whatever their nature and status, would operate from thereon as wholesalers. In practice, however, the public corporations have continued to act as import-license brokers, while the actual process of importing remained with ex-importers.

In July, 1961, other official decrees were passed nationalizing the great majority of industrial and commercial corporations. The question of the seven public corporations engaged in importing was reviewed, and some sort of a new plan for co-ordinating the import business is now under study. It is best to regard all import business at present in the context of the large public organizations like the Economic Development Organization, Nasr Organization, and the Misr Organization. The idea is that each public organization will have tied to it a commercial-type or trade-type firm of relatively large size, which will take care of all the public import and export corporation's business.

Manufacturing plants under the new system are given the right to import directly their raw materials, spare parts, accessories, supplies, etc. In effect, the commercial or trade firms belonging to a particular public organization will act as the purchasing agent. For instance, the Delta Trading Company (the commercial firm for the Nasr Organization), with its offices, facilities, and contacts in Europe, will be in a position to act as an efficient purchasing agent for all public corporations belonging to the Nasr Organization. The importance of this type of operation can be best visualized when it is remembered that such public organizations as EDO, Misr, and Nasr each control, on the average, some 80–100 public corporations.

At the consumer level, another major development should be kept in mind—namely, co-operatives. Another type of public organization has been formed here, the Consumer Co-operative Organization. This organization controls a large wholesale co-operative and, among other things, the largest department store in the country. It is charged with the responsibility of importing, wholesaling, and sometimes retailing basic consumer needs, such as foodstuffs, cotton goods, and basic clothing articles. Modern consumer co-operatives selling groceries and allied articles are now beginning to lead the way and are giving the independent retailers some serious competition.

Wholesaling of Products Produced Locally

The same types of agencies engaged in food wholesaling are also important in nonfood wholesaling. The agent is of greater importance in certain selling lines, such as yard goods and other fabrics, than he is in selling food. He plays an important role in financing the manufacturer. The regular wholesaler, however, is the strategic intermediary in the movement of goods from points of production to points of ultimate consumption. The performance of these intermediaries may be gauged by an analysis of their functional activities.

Selling is an important function performed by Egyptian wholesalers, since the average Egyptian manufacturer is of small size and is preoccupied with production problems. It is generally believed that he should devote his entire efforts to production and let sales follow as a result of the efforts of the wholesaler. Unfortunately, the typical wholesaler rarely performs this function satisfactorily.

Most wholesalers regard selling as simply transferring physically the goods from the seller to the ultimate buyer. In general, they provide the manufacturer with almost no marketing know-how. Many wholesalers, including those with years of experience, often go too far in attempting to sell to uneconomical retail outlets. Surprisingly enough, few wholesalers have ever run an analysis by individual accounts to determine their relative profitability.

With regard to the buying function, most wholesalers buy on a hand-to-mouth basis. The prevalence of this policy reflects the reluctance of wholesalers to assume the risk function. Similarly, manufacturers of seasonal merchandise can seldom rely on wholesalers to place their orders in advance of the selling season or even warehouse seasonal stocks. As a result, few manufacturers are able to forecast the demand for new products, thereby providing a basis for the purchase of raw materials and production scheduling. A further result of this "hand-to-mouth" buying is that economies of scale in transporting, handling, and storing merchandise cannot be effected. Few wholesalers recognize storage as a major wholesaling function. There is a serious lack of such handling equipment as lowerators, chutes, escalators, conveyors, and elevators. Cold-storage and icing facilities are practically nonexistent. In only a few instances is storage space laid out systematically. As a consequence, many wholesalers fill orders from new and not old stock. Cleanliness and sanitation are rarely practiced.

From the foregoing, it is clear that the principal function of a wholesaler in Egypt is the furnishing of credit to retailers and less frequently to producers. The multiplicity of small retailers with practically no credit rating renders the financing of their business through banking circles impossible. Accordingly, small retailers have been forced to rely solely on the wholesaler for financial help.

Following the Suez crisis in 1956, several wholesale and selling agencies were put under sequestration, since they had been owned by "enemy" subjects. For a variety of reasons, there has been great difficulty in keeping these establishments running according to their normal pattern. The repercussions of this have disturbed many domestic manufacturers. Faced with acute marketing problems for the first time and lacking an adequate sales department to cope with such problems, several manufacturers began to reconsider the merit of their present marketing policies. At present, there seems to be a growing trend to giving increasing attention to sales departments as an integral part of the manufacturer's organization.

CONCLUSIONS

Wholesale channels of distribution reflect both the quantitative and the qualitative nature of the consumer market; the role of government in manufacturing; the lack of adequate internal transportation, storage, and communication; and the fact that most domestic manufacturers tend to be almost exclusively production-oriented.

The thin market has created a very modest demand for consumer goods and services. The lack of cultural homogeneity has further complicated the problem.

Egyptian channels of distribution, with but few exceptions, are at about the same stage as those in the United States of the early 1800's. Most food products are sold unbranded and unpackaged. They are typically of low quality. Service and repair of consumer durables create a constant problem.

Small-scale units prevail at all levels of the distributive process, with the result that high margins are necessary to offset the diseconomies of size and low turnover. At the retail level the stores are typically very small, carry poor assortments of goods of uncertain quality, lack sanitary facilities, and offer few services. At the wholesale level, few functions are performed. Essentially, the sole reason for the existence of many wholesalers is that they have strong financial resources and offer liberal credit. Thus many are more interested in the gains to be made from their "lending" operations than from their marketing activities.

There is a lack of public or semipublic services and facilities, which are required to market agricultural products efficiently. Standards, transportation and storage facilities, price information, and handling facility inadequacies all contribute significantly to the gross inefficiencies in the marketing of farm products. The inevitable result is that large quantities of these items are spoiled or wasted.

The government's sequestration policy following the attack on Suez in 1956 caused many foreigners to leave. Many were outstanding merchants. Despite the fact that such persons were too often interested in speculative profits, they represented a large part of the merchandising know-how of Egypt. Government price controls and the law which literally prevents an employer from firing or laying off workers impede the development of a more efficient distributive structure.

The management group of most manufacturing enterprises are dominated by production-oriented individuals. Because of high protective tariffs, government subsidies, price controls, and the law that prohibits firing or layoff, they are inevitably concerned about production as contrasted to sales. Selling one's surplus abroad at prices that do not even cover variable costs is resorted to and is condoned on the basis of earning foreign exchange. Since most industrial firms are financed by the government, losses arising from a failure to know the market provide no incentive to the firm's becoming market-oriented.

In conclusion, the development of a more efficient distributive sector will come in the near future. Inevitably, it will lag industrialization and will follow the development of more efficient farming and manufacturing. Its progress is also dependent on the growth in size of the local market and improved public services and facilities. At present the crudeness of the distributive apparatus is retarding the economic development of Egypt. This is certainly true when one considers that Egypt ultimately hopes to sell on a regular basis certain goods in world markets.

ISRAEL

Wholesaling in Israel manifests the characteristics of a small country in rapid transition from an importing-agricultural to a domestic-industrial stage. In the course of this transition, the wholesaler has been exposed in a short period of time to some of the influences which in older countries have evolved through many years.

Thus wholesalers, already important as importers before the independence of the country, increased in importance thereafter with the growing volume of trade. As planning of the economy progressed, they enjoyed the benefits of ample margins and the prosperity resulting therefrom. This affluence provoked some antagonistic social attitudes and encouraged manufacturers in efforts to circumvent wholesalers.

Regular wholesalers, however, continue to play an important role where they serve smaller producers or retailers, particularly where they are depended on for financing the retail outlets.

As a word of caution, attention must be drawn to the terminology used by the writer of this chapter. He has written of "wholesaling" as though it were solely the business of wholesalers, as he defines them. Not conceiving wholesaling as a generic function which may be performed by manufacturers and their sales branches as well as by specialized wholesaling institutions—specifically, wholesalers—he concludes, and reiterates, that "wholesaling is declining." If it is understood that he means that the role of wholesalers has been diminishing in Israel, unwarranted conclusions concerning wholesaling in general or fallacious contrasts of wholesaling in Israel and elsewhere may be avoided.

Wholesaling in Israel

AKIVA ILAN *

Wholesaling as a separate function, undertaken by firms specializing in that activity, seems to be on the decline throughout the world. It is quite possible that this phenomenon is the result of a common set of factors operating in most advanced countries.

The purpose of this chapter is to describe, generally, the nature and the operation methods of wholesaling in Israel and to try to explain the factors for its relative decline. A wholesaler is here defined as "any merchant who buys goods for the purpose of reselling them to other merchants, generally retailers, or to business firms for use as inputs in the productive process."

We do not include in the definition those merchants who sell mainly to the general public. Nor are manufacturers who maintain their own sales force to distribute their products to retailers included. Brokers or agents who mediate between the producer and buyer and derive their income from a commission but who do not take title to the goods nor assume commercial risks are also excluded. In Israel that means the exclusion of most co-operative marketing organizations which sell their members' products on a commission basis but do not obtain title and do not assume risk. Such organizations fulfill most of the wholesaling functions.

Trade and commerce are excluded from most statistical surveys in Israel. Thus reliance had to be placed upon secondary sources for this paper. In many cases, expert opinions and estimates had to be used instead of numerical data. The general economic data were derived from publications of the Bank of Israel and the *Statistical Abstract.* The other information was received from published or unpublished reports of the Ministry of Trade and Industry, interviews with officials of that Ministry, and members of the Chambers of Commerce. Wholesalers and manufacturers were also interviewed.

---

* Akiva Ilan is a member of the faculty of the Hebrew University, Jerusalem, teaching marketing and marketing research in the Department of Business Administration, the Eliezer Kaplan School of Economics. He has served as consultant to the Ministry of Trade and Industry, the Treasury, the Israel Government Tourist Office, and private corporations. Most of the data for this paper were collected by the author's student, Mr. Menachem Naveh.

Following a short summary and generalization is a section dealing with the economic background of Israel. A general description of wholesaling is then followed by some illustrations.

A BRIEF SUMMARY

As in many other countries, in Israel there are various kinds of marketing channels between producers and final consumers. Some manufacturers sell direct to the consumer through their own retail outlets; others maintain a sales force which distributes the goods to the retailers; some use brokers and agents, while many still sell to wholesalers.

In 1961, about IL 800 million worth of goods[1] were sold through wholesalers. This amounted to about 13 per cent of the total volume of trade, which was IL 6,250[2] million in that year. These sales were made by 1,500 wholesalers, of which 1,100 operated stores or warehouses, while 400 were truck-jobbers. Of the 1,100 resident wholesalers, 650 traded in groceries, 100 in small house and kitchenware, while the rest handled building supplies, paper, textiles, etc.

As will be seen in the illustrations at the end of this chapter, wholesalers play an important role in those industries where the number of manufacturers is large, yet, on the average, small in sales. Big producers and large-scale retailers tend to bypass the wholesaler. Similarly, wholesaling is important in selling small retailers. Where the retailer or the manufacturer needs financial help, the wholesaler has survived longer than otherwise would be the case.

In general, however, wholesaling is on the decline. In the grocery field (which has always contained the largest group of wholesale merchants), their number declined from 1,150 in 1954 to 650 in 1961 (see Table 1).

TABLE 1

NUMBER OF GROCERY WHOLESALERS IN ISRAEL
1954–61

Year	No. at End of Year
1954	1,153
1955	1,078
1956	1,012
1957	942
1958	894
1959	861
1960	767
1961	647

Source: Food Division, Ministry of Trade and Industry.

---

[1] Derived from reports of the Ministry of Trade and Industry.
[2] Derived from Bank of Israel, *Annual Report* (1961).

In the timber trade the number of wholesalers has dropped by 50 per cent since 1954. Tires are now sold by one wholesaler instead of about 30 in the early 1950's.

GENERAL ECONOMIC BACKGROUND

Several economic factors have operated together to diminish the importance of wholesalers in Israel. The small physical size of the country and the high concentration of population in the few big urban centers are certainly the most prominent factors. A similar effect may, however, be attributed to the concentration of production in a very few firms in many industries, the decline in the relative share of imports in the supply of consumer goods, and the general increase in the standard of living, with its effects on consumption and purchasing habits.

The size of Israel is about 8,000 square miles, approximately equal to New Jersey, U.S.A., and the 1962 population was 2,232,000. A third of this number lived in and around Tel-Aviv, while 75 per cent of the population lived in the central districts and the three big cities— Tel-Aviv, Haifa, and Jerusalem. There are no published data regarding the distribution of the national income by districts, but it appears that the urban population received more than a proportionate share. Thus more than 80 per cent of the national income, which amounted to IL 5,300 million in 1961, and the purchasing power is concentrated in 14 per cent of the country's areas.

A small market like this naturally favors the development of monopolies. In industries where production is conducted under conditions of increasing returns to scale, firms must maintain large plants if average costs are to be within reasonable limits. In a small market like Israel, this means that in many industries one or a few plants can supply all the local needs and even have a surplus for export. Paper, rayon, and corrugated cardboard are illustrations of one-plant industries, while tires, cement, electrical refrigerators, and beer are examples of two-firm industries. In many cases the existence of more producers has led to surplus production capacity, which, in turn, has brought about the formation of cartels for the avowed purpose of exporting but which also regulate local marketing.

Since an important function of the wholesaler is to facilitate the transfer of goods between the manufacturer and retailers, the two above-mentioned factors caused a decline in the importance of wholesaling in Israel. Short distances encouraged direct selling. In addition, the usual difficulty of maintaining such direct dealings between many suppliers and retailers is eliminated by virtue of the small number of producers present in most industries. Thus, in most cases, it is not uneconomical for manufacturers to sell directly to retailers.

Until the establishment of Israel as an independent state in 1948 and even during the first years of its existence, most consumer goods were imported. When goods were imported, the economies of scale were less significant, and similar goods were imported from various sources and by many traders. Consequently, there existed many opportunities for wholesalers to serve both importers and retailers.

The scarcity and rationing of goods which marked the early years of independence strengthened wholesaling even more. Imports were regulated because of a shortage of foreign exchange, and there existed a "sellers' market." The allocation of import quotas was done according to the principles of "past trade." Trading margins were fixed administratively and, as is usual under such circumstances, at a higher level than would otherwise have existed. The elimination of competition by the government's controls and the shortage of goods increased the profitability of trade, particularly wholesale trade, since risk was eliminated and the need for such services as credit or warehousing declined substantially.

As a result, a widespread impression was created that wholesaling was unnecessary and too profitable relative to the services performed by it. The tendency to establish wholesale businesses increased, while many industrialists and retailers were encouraged to improve their lot by bypassing the wholesaler and absorbing his "excessive" margin.

However, because of the fast industrial development, the share of imports in the supply of consumer goods has declined steadily. Many products previously imported from various sources are now locally produced by but a few manufacturers. Imports now consist, to a large degree, of producers' and investment goods, which tend to bypass wholesalers. Table 2 illustrates this development.

TABLE 2

ISRAELI IMPORTS, BY ECONOMIC DESTINATION

	1952		1960	
	IL Millions	%	IL Millions	%
Consumer goods	132.3	23	91.7	10
Producer goods	328.3	56	586.6	65
Investment goods	121.4	21	226.6	25
	582.0	100	905.0	100

Source: *Statistical Abstract* (1961).

Thus, while imports have increased by more than half from 1952 to 1960, imports of consumer goods (which are more likely to be handled by wholesalers) declined absolutely as well as relatively.

Local producers, protected by a high tariff wall and administrative prohibitions of imports can now dictate their will on the market. One result has been to transfer the marketing functions typically performed by wholesalers to sales departments of manufacturing firms.

The marketing of imported goods has undergone changes too. Once the economic situation improved and foreign-exchange reserves accumulated, the "paradise" of shortages and control disappeared. Liberalization of imports was started in 1957, and import licenses are granted to everyone who can fulfill some basic, reasonable requirements. Imported raw materials, timber, iron, imported food, and spare parts no longer sell in a "sellers'" market. Competition and commercial risk returned to the Israel market.

During this period, living standards rose steadily. Personal consumption increased between 1952 and 1959 at an average annual rate of 5 per cent. The industrial development and the steady "boom" in the building industry eliminated the unemployment that marked the early 1950's and replaced it with full employment. The increased income was used both to raise consumption and to diversify it. Many thousands of Israeli citizens spent summer vacations in Europe and brought home new needs and habits. Retailers accepted the challenge by improving their services, increasing the product lines, and introducing self-service in food retailing. Industry had to adjust itself to the conditions of a "buyers' market" in many products and, consequently, improved their products, their packaging, and their merchandising practices. Many manufacturers began to rely heavily on advertising. The number of pre-packaged goods sold under producers' brands increased steadily. The use of advertised brands and the growth in the size of the firms brought about (or perhaps were caused by) the widening of product lines. Such firms could, therefore, maintain an independent sales department and sales branches to sell direct to retailers, while the small firm which sold only a single or a few items and could not afford to presell its products by advertising had to continue its dependence on the wholesalers. But the share of the larger firms increased very fast in the growing economy.

To summarize, wholesaling is declining in Israel. The major economic factors accounting for this trend are:

1. The decline of imports and the increase in local production as a source of consumer goods.

2. The concentration of the production of many products in a few firms, and the tendency of such firms to do "their own wholesaling."
3. The strengthening of retailers through increased size and the increase in the number of chain stores which buy direct from the manufacturers.
4. The elimination of controls and the liberal trade policy which reduced trade margins.

WHOLESALING IN ISRAEL

Owing to the complete absence of any statistics about trade in general and wholesaling in particular, reliance had to be placed on indirect evidence and estimates and opinions from authoritative sources. Any information provided here must be regarded as approximations. According to informed sources, there were about 1,500 wholesalers in Israel in 1961—about half of them in the grocery field. Of the total sales of goods to customers, which amounted to about IL 6,250 million [3] in 1961, only IL 800 million,[4] or 13 per cent, passed through wholesalers.

While the sales of the average wholesaler thus amounted to more than half a million pounds, the large dispersion renders that average meaningless. It is important to distinguish between three classes of wholesalers according to their volume and trade practices. The first group includes a small number of large enterprises which have sales volume of tens of millions of pounds. Such firms are generally also importers. Some of them own or control industrial firms. Some also have their own retail outlets.

The largest of these wholesalers is Hamashbir Hamerkazi, the major supplier of the co-operative movement in Israel. This company does not specialize in any particular line but supplies everything that its customers might need. It sells groceries, textiles, building materials, fertilizers, chemicals, tractors, machinery, stationery, and varieties. Its volume of sales was IL 148 million in 1961. Hamashbir Hamerkazi has full or partial ownership of some 12 industrial firms in the food, metal, textile, printing, chemical, and cement industries, which had total sales of about IL 150 million in 1961.

While the other wholesalers in this group are "poor seconds" to this giant, their volume is still far above the average. They deal mainly

---

[3] Derived from Bank of Israel *Annual Report* (1961).
[4] Derived from reports of Ministry of Trade and Industry.

in food, building supplies, timber, and raw materials. Frequently they are exclusive agents for their major suppliers.

The second group is comprised of what are called medium and small-sized wholesale merchants. These are the "commercial center" traders. They maintain, generally, one store or warehouse and have no branches. They tend to specialize in one line of merchandise, adapting themselves to the needs of the type of retailers they serve. Such wholesalers operate in groceries, small nonelectrical home appliances, nonexpensive textiles, children's clothes, and spare parts.

Such traders are not usually exclusive agents for their suppliers, although they may have exclusive rights for a certain district or a certain type of customer. It is by providing financial aid to a small producer in the form of large cash purchases that a wholesaler gains such an exclusive dealership in his area.

The third group includes about 400 truck-jobbers. These are merchants who do not have a store or a business address. About half of these are fresh-fruit and vegetable wholesalers. They serve the small or remote retailers whose small volume does not justify direct purchase at produce auctions. These truck-jobbers have relatively steady trade relations. The other truck-jobbers do not stick to one line of trade. They buy textiles if an opportunity arises and move to canned goods or appliances when it seems advantageous to do so. They buy and sell for cash and are considered a good outlet for second-rate merchandise. Their relative advantage, according to some sources, is their "ability" to evade taxes.

The most important functions performed by wholesalers in Israel for their customers are twofold: (1) the providing of credit and (2) the maintenance of a diversified inventory according to their customers' needs. Sales promotion, whether in the form of advertising or by salesmen, is not performed by them. In those industries where keen competition exists between the various manufacturers, there has been a tendency to bypass the wholesalers, since they do not "push" the goods. The sales manager of a leading detergent manufacturer (a very competitive industry) said that he would have no business with wholesalers, since they are too "passive." Only very small and unknown manufacturers base their sales effort on the support provided by wholesalers. They have little choice to do otherwise. With the development of chains, wholesalers are even losing some of the business of their small suppliers. Only truck-jobbers, who do not have a warehouse, push sales of their goods by visiting potential customers.

The logical result is that only those firms or industries that need the two basic services of wholesaling in Israel are selling or buying through a wholesaler. Since there are many food stores and a relatively large number of manufacturers in that industry, a significant share of groceries is handled by wholesalers. A similar condition exists in the nonelectrical appliance industry. Paper, timber, and plywood are also wholesaled, because large amounts have to be bought and paid for in advance and a diversified stock must be maintained. On the other hand, most fresh produce, shoes, watches and jewels, electrical appliances, adult clothes, and raw materials now bypass the wholesaler.

Because of the chronic inflationary pressure, which is an almost inevitable by-product of a fast-growing economy, the Bank of Israel imposes severe credit restrictions. This renders the credit provided by wholesalers both to customers and suppliers even more important. In many cases the wholesaler would have been dispensed with but for his financial role.

In some cases the wholesaler has to buy large quantities in advance and pay cash. Such is the situation in the paper trade, where supply is controlled by a single producer. A textile wholesaler purchases large amounts for cash only to secure an exclusive dealership.

The common case is that the wholesaler provides credit to his customers and receives such from his suppliers; however, the credit period granted to the retailer is longer than the period given by the manufacturers.

A survey [5] conducted by the Research Department of the Bank of Israel reveals more detailed information about the importance of credit in wholesaling. In 1957 "receivables" were equal to 20 per cent of the total sales of wholesalers covered by the survey. This means that, on the average, the credit was extended to a period of 2.4 months.

Behavior was not similar among wholesalers, and, as is illustrated by Table 3, the smaller firms extended more credit.

Table 4 describes the composition of current assets, points up the same thing; that is, credit is the major function provided by wholesalers, particularly the small ones.

One explanation for the larger proportion of receivables held by small wholesalers is that it is harder for them to discount their customers' notes.

---

[5] The survey covered only incorporated firms and therefore does not include small firms.

TABLE 3

RECEIVABLES AS PERCENTAGE OF SALES BY ISRAELI WHOLESALERS,
1956 AND 1957

	1956	1957
Small wholesalers	82	116
Medium wholesalers	14	14
Large wholesalers	16	18
Total	17	20

Source: Bank of Israel, "Corporations' Survey" (unpublished).

TABLE 4

COMPOSITION OF CURRENT ASSETS HELD BY ISRAELI WHOLESALE CORPORATIONS, 1957
(IN PERCENTAGES)

	Small	Medium	Large	Total
Cash	3	6	4	4
Receivables	77	44	63	62
Inventory	20	50	33	34
Total	100	100	100	100

Source: Bank of Israel, "Corporations' Survey" (unpublished).

Food is sold on very short credit, while in the textile trade it is not uncommon to extend credit up to 5 months. For payment within 30 days, in textiles the retailer receives a cash discount ranging between 5 and 6 per cent. The credit extended to the wholesaler ranges between 30 and 60 days.

The other important function is the maintenance of wide stock as a service to retailers. Most food or hardware retailers cannot maintain a large stock. They are limited by the small size of their facilities as well as by a scarcity of capital. This is particularly true in the small towns. Such retailers rely upon the inventory held by a nearby wholesaler to whom they can "send a boy" to fetch a requested item which is out of stock.

The "Corporations' Survey" contains some data on turnover of inventory by wholesalers (Table 5).

TABLE 5

INVENTORY AS PERCENTAGE OF SALES
OF ISRAELI WHOLESALERS, 1957

	Per Cent
Small wholesalers	29
Medium wholesalers	16
Large wholesalers	10
Total average	11

Source: Bank of Israel, "Corporations' Survey" (unpublished).

The large wholesaler tends more to trade in raw materials or building supplies, which are fast-moving items. But they are probably better organized and have more efficient methods of inventory control. Similarly, small wholesalers are farther from the resources of supply and are used more by small customers, who depend on their inventories.

The wholesale margin varies according to the product. Shortening or cigarettes sell at a margin of 2 per cent, which is very low considering the fact that such items are even sometimes sold on credit. Paper, small appliances, and canned goods provide margins of 10–15 per cent. The more important the role of the wholesaler in getting the sale, the larger the margin. The margin on the better-known brands of canned foods is about 3 per cent, while less well-known products often provide a margin up to three times as large.

SOME ILLUSTRATIONS

Up to this point the discussion has been very general. Perhaps a few illustrations of wholesaling in some industries will render it more meaningful. The wholesaling of foods, appliances and kitchenware, and paper have been chosen for such a detailed description. The choice was affected by the number of wholesalers in these fields as well as by the available information.

Wholesale Marketing of Food

In food marketing a distinction is made between two main classes of goods. The first group contains fresh agricultural produce, milk and milk products, eggs, poultry, fruit, and vegetables. These products bypass almost completely the wholesaler as he has been defined in this paper.

Two major factors account for the almost total absence of wholesaling in the marketing channels of local agricultural products. In the first place, fresh products tend generally to pass through the shortest possible channel.

The second reason stems from the social nature of Israeli agriculture. Most settlements are organized on a co-operative basis. These settlements maintain a central marketing co-operative, "Tnuva," through which they sell all their products. Tnuva does not buy the produce from the farmers but handles it on a commission basis. By its organizational nature, Tnuva does not assume commercial risks, nor is it allowed to make any profits. Costs are calculated for every department and the commission rates fixed accordingly. If the commission is found to be too high, relative to actual costs in marketing a certain product, the difference has to be refunded to the member-farmers.

Tnuva markets about 80 per cent of the total agricultural produce. There are other firms marketing agricultural products on a similar basis.

Tnuva has dairies to process milk and cold storage for fruit and vegetables, as well as factories where surplus fruit and vegetables are canned. Milk products, eggs, and canned food are distributed to retailers by Tnuva's salesmen, who use trucks.

Fruit, vegetables, and poultry are auctioned each morning in the produce exchanges maintained by Tnuva and the other marketing firms in the major centers. The produce is brought to the stores during the night, and the auction starts in the very early morning. Many purchasers are large retailers and institutional buyers. A significant part is bought from the exchange by truck-jobbers, who purchase for small retailers and vendors whose small volume does not justify independent buying on the exchange. The flow of these commodities can be diagramed as follows (Chart I):

CHART I

DISTRIBUTION CHANNELS OF FRESH FRUIT AND VEGETABLES

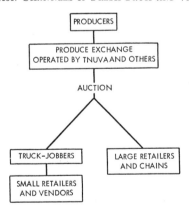

It is estimated that about half of the fruit and vegetables is bought by truck-jobbers. Each jobber has a steady circle of retailer-customers whom he serves. He provides his ability to buy on the exchange—and it requires considerable experience to buy successfully, since the prices fluctuate frequently, with the range amounting to

20 per cent. He also delivers the goods to the retailers' stores. His margin of profit depends on his success in buying at a reasonable price and is typically about 10–15 per cent of the price paid by the retailer. It is estimated that about 200 truck-jobbers are engaged in this line of trade.

The second food class consists of nonperishable foods—either those processed locally or those imported. Such foods tend, more than most other goods, to pass through wholesalers. As a mater of fact, 650 of the 1,100 resident wholesalers handle these products.

But even this line has been affected by the general factors that have caused the decline of wholesaling in general. The number of these grocery wholesalers has declined by about 50 per cent since 1954.

By examining more closely the methods of distribution of three products—edible oil, canned fruit and vegetables, and imported beans—it appears that imported foods still tend to be sold mainly by wholesalers. But the manufactured foods, oil, and canned food tend to bypass the wholesaler as the manufacturing firm becomes larger. The big manufacturers prefer to establish their own sales branches or to use agents.

The typical food wholesaler maintains a store or a warehouse in the commercial center; his sales volume ranges from IL 0.5 to IL 1.0 million per annum, and his stock consists of about 500 items. He pays cash within 15 days for his purchases and grants credit of up to three months to his customers. The selling is done on his own premises. Small retailers select and pick up their orders, while the larger customers order by telephone and the wholesaler delivers the goods. There is little competition among wholesalers, as customers tend to patronize the same supplier steadily.

Sometimes the relations are built on common cultural backgrounds when the wholesaler, retailers, and consumers are immigrants from the same foreign country. In such cases the wholesaler maintains a stock planned for the special needs of his customers, and thus the relations grow even stronger.

The wholesaler's margin fluctuates from 2 to 7 per cent, depending on the product and the reputation of the manufacturer. The more reputable brands provide a smaller margin.

Truck-jobbers operate along this line also, but on a less permanent basis. They buy from the small producers, particularly those that are in financial trouble, and drive hard bargains by being able to pay cash.

Marketing Edible Oil

Six manufacturers sold about 21,000 tons of edible oil in 1961. As illustrated in Chart II, the two largest firms did not sell completely

CHART II
DISTRIBUTION CHANNELS OF EDIBLE OIL

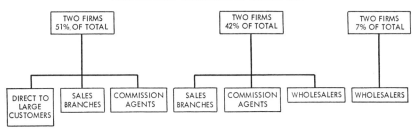

through wholesalers, and the smallest two firms, whose volume was only 7 per cent of the total sales, used wholesalers exclusively.

Officials of the Ministry of Trade estimate that about 15 per cent of the edible oil is sold through wholesalers—a large part of it to small and remote communities.

While wholesalers keep "some" oil in stock, their main function is to get orders, which are "drop-shipped" by the factory, with the wholesaler providing credit and collecting the bills.

The margin is fixed by the producers at about 2 per cent and cannot be altered by the traders, as prices to retailers are fixed. In spite of the low margin, the manufacturers have tended to sell direct to the retailer, the reason being the keen competition among the various brands and the inability of wholesalers to provide the aggressive sales effort demanded by the producers. Where direct discounts to retailers are used as a competitive tool, wholesalers are not flexible enough to discriminate between their customers. Therefore, many oil wholesalers have been relegated to agents, although they are allowed sometimes to wholesale other food items to raise their income.

Wholesaling Canned Fruit and Vegetables

In 1961 some 32 factories of varying sizes sold about IL 30 million worth of canned fruit and vegetables. Some factories are big plants employing hundreds of workers and producing a wide line of products, while others operate only during some seasons and produce few items.

The diversification in size and product line is reflected in the channels of distribution used. The large full-line manufacturers have their own sales organization and call directly on retailers and institutional buyers. Others use commission agents, while some use wholesalers. Similar to the oil industry, there is an inverse relationship between the size of the firm and its use of wholesalers' services. The large firms sell to wholesalers if asked to, but the functional discount allowed them on the well-known brands is too small. A wholesaler has a gross margin of only about 3 per cent on leading brands, while he makes about 7 per cent by selling less well-known products.

The continuous rise in the size of manufacturing firms and the growth of retailing chains have reduced the number of wholesalers in this line. While wholesalers sold 60 per cent of canned food in 1955, their share had dropped to only 25 per cent by 1961. The main reason for this was that, as production increased, the industry became more competitive and the wholesaler could not provide the required sales efforts.

Imported staples like beans or herring are still sold almost exclusively through wholesalers, but the relative importance of such products is declining.

Wholesale Marketing of Appliances

Large electrical appliances are manufactured by only a few manufacturers and sold through a selected list of retailers. Small appliances and utensils made of china, ceramics, glass, metal, and wood are manufactured by several hundred small and medium-sized firms and distributed through about a hundred small wholesalers to many retailers and vendors.

Until 1957 there was only one producer of electrical refrigerators. The demand was keen, and buyers had to wait several months for delivery of their fully prepaid order. Under such conditions the manufacturer did not need even the services of retailers, let alone wholesalers. Since 1957 a second firm has joined the industry and is now selling about 15 per cent of all refrigerators. Consequently, the waiting period has been shortened and both firms are now using retailers in towns where they do not have sales offices; however, the demand is still strong enough that customers must pay in advance of delivery.

By contrast, the local production of small appliances and utensils, replacing imports, increased the number of wholesalers in that field. Until the early 1950's, import provided most of the chinaware, kitchen utensils, and other small appliances. The high import duties and small quotas encouraged the development of a local industry. But in this case the industry consists of hundreds of small-sized plants. Retailing in this field is also on a small scale and thus there exists a basis for extensive wholesaling activity.

The large number of producers and their small size precluded the establishment of well-known brands in the field or the use of advertisement to promote sales. As a result, the main selling efforts are provided by the wholesalers who are putting more sales effort into this line and margins are larger, between 10 and 12 per cent.

Wholesaling of Paper

The paper industry is dominated by a single firm, which produced 95 per cent of the locally manufactured paper and is an illustration of a case where wholesaling survived only because of its financial function.

Eighty per cent of the paper used during 1961 was locally produced, and a third of that amount was sold through 12 paper wholesalers (Chart III).

CHART III

DISTRIBUTION CHANNELS OF PAPER

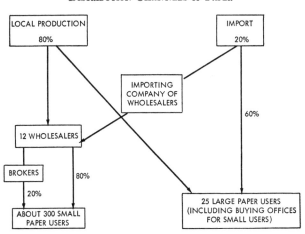

Large paper users, such as the daily newspapers and the large publishers, purchase directly from the producer or import on their own. Small printers, paper converters, and paper-bag manufacturers cannot buy directly from the producer because of his minimum order requirements. The paper mill will not sell to a client unless he pays cash, orders at least 3 tons at a time, and purchases at least 300 tons annually.

The suggested reason for these restrictions is that, since the paper mill has a monopoly, its managers prefer not to raise the price but to save on interest, storage, and selling expenses by selling big lots only. In this case the wholesaler purchases in large lots, pays cash, and sells to small customers on credit. The wholesaler's margin is about 11 per cent and, during periods of shortages, even more.

ASIA AND OCEANIA

India

Japan

Australia

INDIA

India, one of the world's large underdeveloped countries, is described by the author as a combination of Eastern and Western marketing practices, a study of transitions from a primitive to a more culturally and conceptually advanced system of distribution.

Being characterized by lack of market information and personal financial resources, agriculturists in India are much dependent on co-operatives to protect their interests in the face of monoponistic industrial buyers and strongly entrenched selling agents. Manufacturers generally approach distribution from the premise that their responsibility is to produce and not to market goods. Negligence and indifference at this point affect both subsequent market practices and marketing institutions.

Many of the unique aspects of pricing under such circumstances are discussed by the author: charging what the traffic will bear, cost-plus practices, price differentiation based on "range of buyers" rather than on functions performed, and forms of price emulation.

Among the other aspects of Indian distribution that are mentioned are the following: influences of caste upon entry into marketing activity; the role of the extended family relationships in employment, occupational opportunity, and line diversification; intrainstitutional business practices; and the lack of both vertical and horizontal differentiation in marketing.

Wholesaling in India

LEON V. HIRSCH *

INTRODUCTION [1]

India is an underdeveloped country with a population of approximately 400 million people and a per capita income of about $60 per annum. The government is committed to economic development and considers contribution to the social good as the prime measurement of the adequacy of its marketing system.

Since the wholesaling sector, considered in its broadest sense, is the heart of marketing, an understanding of its operation is necessary to evaluate the system as a whole. In this article *wholesaling* is used to refer to that aspect of marketing dealing with the distribution of goods from the primary producer through all intermediaries, but not to the ultimate consumer. For some purposes, this definition of wholesaling may be too broad; however, in an underdeveloped economy, the risk is great that important aspects of the process unfamiliar to observers from developed economies might be ignored with a limited, preconceived orientation.

This article will first examine agricultural distribution, still the most important aspect of Indian wholesaling. Next, it will discuss wholesaling of manufactured goods, developed from techniques used in agricultural marketing. Finally, observations will be made on the wholesaling system over-all.

AGRICULTURAL WHOLESALING IN INDIA

In India, a number of specialized intermediaries have developed to assemble and distribute agricultural products. Chart I illustrates, in simplified form, the agricultural wholesale chain.

Preharvest Contractors, Moneylenders, and Petty Merchants

A grower either may own his crop outright at harvest time or may have pledged it during the growing season. Pledging a crop is com-

---

* Dr. Leon V. Hirsch is Senior Associate, United Research Incorporated, Cambridge, Mass.

[1] For a fuller discussion of many of the points in this article, see the author's book, *Marketing in an Underdeveloped Economy: The North Indian Sugar Industry* (Englewood Cliffs, N.J.: Prentice-Hall, Inc., 1961).

CHART I

SIMPLIFIED STATEMENT OF INDIA'S AGRICULTURAL WHOLESALING

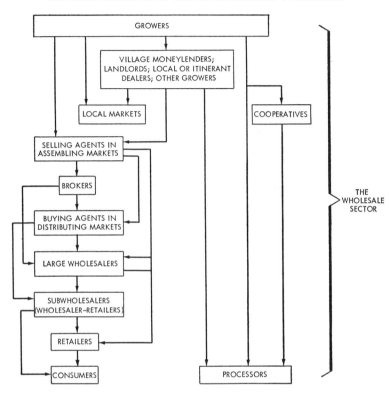

mon in underdeveloped countries, where many growers live on a hand-to-mouth basis.

Sometimes growers sell their standing crop to preharvest contractors, who then assume the responsibility of watching, picking, packing, and transporting the crop at the suitable time. It is more common, however, for growers in need of money to borrow on the maturing crop from village moneylenders, landlords, or local or itinerant merchants. At times, a well-to-do cultivator may also lend money to less well-to-do cultivators.

Some loans to growers are made on a straight interest-charge basis. The range of interest charges is very wide, but usually falls between 12 and 75 per cent per annum. When a loan is made in kind, the lender typically obtains an additional one fourth to one half of the quantity loaned at harvest time. More frequently, however, the lender obtains interest *and* the opportunity of marketing the crop, thereby making a distribution profit. For example, the terms of one type of loan are such that the grower must sell his crop at 5–10 per cent less than the going market rate to the lender-merchant, who has the exclusive right to market it.

At times, a grower may sell his crop to village merchants, itinerant dealers, or other growers, even though he may not have pledged it.

Agricultural Processors and Grower Co-operatives

In the case of agricultural products for which some processing is usual (such as rice, peanuts, coffee, and hides), growers, or those to whom they have sold their crops, may sell directly to local processors.

Producer co-operative societies also play a role in the agricultural distribution process, particularly in sales to processors. The government has stated that its aim is to promote the development of the co-operative movement in all areas of the economy; thus the role of co-operatives is expected to become increasingly important in agricultural marketing.

The grower co-operative is most important for sugar cane. Because it may set the pattern for other grower co-operatives, it will be discussed in some detail. At present, in North India (the major cane-growing section of the country), almost all cane is sold to sugar factories through co-operative societies sponsored and administered by the state governments. Where a co-operative society exists, all growers must sell their cane through it. Each sugar mill is allocated a reserved and an assigned area from which to purchase its cane. In theory, if so directed by the Cane Commissioner (a state official), the mill purchases all the cane offered for sale in the reserved area, and such quantity of the cane offered for sale from the assigned area as is decided upon by the Commissioner. In practice, however, the amount of cane a factory will actually buy is determined through consultation between the co-operative and the mill manager. In a number of instances, growers in the reserved area produce more cane than the factory concerned can absorb. In such a case, the factory purchases only a portion of the cane offered.

The cane co-operatives are really quasi-governmental organizations, although representatives of the growers, elected by villages in proportion to population, have an advisory function. The co-operatives are financed partly by the government and partly by charges to the mill based on the amount of cane handled.

The day-to-day work of co-operatives is performed by *kamdars*, village-level officials reporting to each co-operative. The kamdars are responsible for surveying the cane supply, in order to plan and schedule deliveries to the mill; they also act as general liaison with the growers.

About a month before the mills are scheduled to start their seasonal crushing, the kamdars estimate the amount of cane that will be available for factory use. Since cane sold to factories generally yields a higher return than cane used for any other purpose (such as making *gur*, a village raw sweetening product), growers generally prefer to sell all their cane to mills. If there is an excess of cane offered for sale, the growers are each allocated a pro rata share to supply. The total amount each cultivator is to supply over the crushing season is divided as evenly as possible into fortnightly periods, since (because of its heavier weight) the cultivator realizes a greater return from his crop when it is fully mature.

A corollary to the monopsonistic position which the mills enjoy is that each season the central government fixes the minimum price for cane. (In practice, this is also the maximum.) Theoretically, the price is set in relation to cost of production, the return to the grower of alternative uses of cane and of other crops, and the cost of sugar to the consumer. It has frequently been alleged that the government sets the price of cane at an economically unjustifiably high level for political advantage. Another factor that influences the government in price setting is whether or not there is a shortage or glut of sugar on the market and hence whether it wants to encourage or discourage the growing of cane.

The reasons for the importance of growers' co-operatives in cane compared with other Indian crops are grounded in the economic and technical necessities of the cultivator-mill relationship. During the crushing season, the mills work around the clock and must have a continuous supply of cane on hand to operate economically. The cane crushed should be as close to maturity as possible, since immature or overripe cane yields less sucrose. Furthermore, the cane crushed should be fresh; soon after it is cut, the sucrose content of cane begins to drop markedly. This means that it is most economical to obtain cane from the immediate vicinity of the factory.

In the absence of some mechanism such as the co-operative, the grower is in a vulnerable position in relation to the factory, unless there is a shortage of cane. Because of cane's bulk and its tendency to deteriorate, the cultivator finds it economical to sell only to the local mill. The grower is committed not only for the year he has planted his cane but, because cane is a perennial, often for one or two seasons thereafter. While it is true that there are alternative uses for cane, such as in the production of the village sweetener (*gur*), cane used for these other purposes provides a lower return than that sold to mills.

For these reasons, therefore, some system of cane procurement is needed that schedules deliveries in an equitable way, guaranteeing as far as possible sufficient cane to mills and a fair return to growers, and which discourages economic losses due to mid-season bargaining or cross-hauling. In other sugar-cane-growing countries, institutions performing functions similar to India's co-operatives have grown up, with the plantation system as a prime example.

While the Indian cane-procurement system has at times been criticized by cultivators and mill-owners, it is difficult to see how any other form of procurement could work as effectively without some radical economic change.

Agricultural Markets

Except for those products (such as cane) that move directly to processors, agricultural exchange is effected through a system of markets. Indian agricultural markets can be roughly divided into three categories: village, assembling, and distributing. These markets are also called primary, secondary, and terminal, respectively.

Village markets are small, periodic local markets near growing areas which generally serve the needs of the immediate population, although representatives of outside merchants may also buy there. Both growers and those to whom they have sold their product may sell at local markets. (As little as a headload of such products as rice may be sold at one time.)

In theory, assembling markets gather together the produce of a region, while distributing markets dispose of it in consuming areas. In general, assembling markets are located in main centers of the producing region, and distributing markets in main consuming or export centers. Frequently, however, there may be an overlap between these two market types.

Both these types of markets may be municipally or privately owned. Charges are frequently levied on merchants who wish to deal in the market or who occupy space in it. The markets may be regulated or nonregulated. If regulated, certain functionaries, such as weightmen, are licensed. The markets may consist of a piece of land surrounded by merchants' shops and warehouses or may simply be a public thoroughfare, with a number of merchants' houses lining the sides of the street. In general, the markets are characterized by poor physical conditions for display or storage and a great deal of confusion of movement.

Selling Agents

The key merchants in the assembling markets are selling agents, who, at least in theory, act on their clients' account to sell their merchandise for a commission. The cultivators or small merchants who deal with these agents frequently have continuing relations with them. To attempt to attract those sellers who have not built up such contacts, touts representing particular agents often line the main roads leading into the market. It is the practice for sellers to come to the market early in the day or the night before. If their clients arrive the night before, selling agents often provide them with some minimal food and a place to sleep. In winter, the clients of one merchant sleep in his office, on the mattresses on which business is conducted during the day. In the summer, string beds called *charpoys* are set out on the sidewalk. Buzzing and biting insects may make sleep for the uninitiated fitful and restless.

The cultivators or petty merchants turn over their crops to the selling agent, who may sell the crop immediately and pay the seller at once, collecting later from the buyer. More frequently, the agent does not conclude an immediate sale; in this case he advances sellers an amount approximating 80 per cent of the estimated value of the crop. Because the majority of Indian cultivators live on a hand-to-mouth basis, they find it important to obtain cash immediately. This is true in a number of other underdeveloped countries, where an important prerequisite to being a successful merchant in crop procurement is having the financial wherewithal to make advances.

After taking delivery, the agent usually negotiates sale of the crop on the account of the grower or petty merchant, who continues to retain title to the commodity until it is disposed of. The price the crop brings, *less* transportation charges, the advance, the interest on the advance, and a commission for selling the crop, is remitted to the cultivator. Both the commission and the interest on the advance are important sources of revenue for the agent. Interest averages between 6 and 12 per cent on an annual basis and is sometimes as high as 24 per cent. Commissions for selling the merchandise usually range from a fraction of 1 per cent to 7 per cent. Selling agents may also finance the village merchants or itinerant dealers who trade with them before taking physical possession of the crop. For this service they usually charge an interest rate of 7–9 per cent annually. In some areas, if the agent has made an advance to the seller earlier in the season, he may charge double the ordinary commission, in addition to interest. Agent advances to growers (as opposed to small merchants) before receipt of the crop are less common.

There are a number of different methods by which the selling agent offers the products he deals with for sale. Perhaps the most picturesque method is one negotiated under a piece of cloth. The buyer or his representative presses one or more fingers of the agent under cover. Every finger, except the thumb, has a value which often varies from product to product and from locale to locale. In some cases, potential buyers are allowed to rebid after the highest offer is announced.

If the seller for whom the agent is acting is present, the agent asks his approval of the final price offered. Most frequently, the successful buyer and the rate at which he has purchased are announced, although in some markets the successful bid is not disclosed.

The second major method of sale by agents is through open auctions, which are similar to commodity auctions in the United States. Although most auctions proceed on the basis of verbal bids, some operate by sealed bids.

The third method of selling is by private negotiation between agent and buyer, by inspection either of samples or of the entire lot offered.

All these methods of selling are subject to some abuse. This is particularly true for the under-the-cloth technique if the price accepted is not announced to all other would-be purchasers. The integrity of the selling agent is the prime protection for the seller.

There is also another way in which the selling agent may take unfair advantage of his position. In theory, the selling agent is supposed to be just that—an intermediary operating on the seller's account. It is not uncommon, however, for the agent to buy the seller's crop outright, often without the seller's knowledge. Opportunities for conflict of interest here are great.

In addition to the commission and interest fees previously mentioned, the seller must frequently pay many charges which vary widely from market to market. In general, charges to sellers are particularly high in markets where there is comparatively little competition among merchants, where they are levied on the basis of weight as opposed to value, and where they are collectible in kind rather than in money.

While not all of the following are collected universally, they illustrate the range of fees the sellers may have to bear. Tolls and taxes are usually levied for entering municipal limits or the market proper. Frequently, the seller is expected to tip the tax collectors. Beside the commission to his agent, the seller must pay certain handling and haulage costs; in some areas, these charges have become standardized and are levied whether or not actually incurred. Agents commonly deduct for a contribution to charity; usually, this charge is relatively minor, but in at least one market it is reported to amount to over 3¾ per cent. One of the favorite charitable contributions is for the maintenance of a *gaushala*, a home for superannuated cows, India's prime sacred animal. In certain cases, government reports have alleged that merchants, believing charity begins at home, have usurped the charitable contributions for themselves.

For poor quality or to allow for the weight of binding materials used, the selling agent may deduct up to 5 per cent from the amount due the seller. These deductions are sometimes taken, whether justified or not, and act to enhance the price the selling agent receives. Finally, sellers are also liable for a host of miscellaneous charges, such as for tips to members of the selling agent's staff.

Although market charges fall most frequently on the seller, in some cases, certain of them are levied by the agent on the purchaser.

Brokers

Brokers mediate between selling agents and further links in the chain of distribution. They take neither ownership nor possession of the products they deal with and do not perform a financial function. In effect, they sell information. They help uninformed buyers secure the goods they desire at better than average terms, and they perform the related service of providing information about possible future trends in the market. As might be expected, the importance of brokers for different agricultural commodities depends on the general availability of market information and on the physical distance separating selling agent and potential purchaser. The rate of commission paid to brokers varies but is usually small. The buyer or seller or both may pay brokers' fees.

Buying Agents

Selling agents may sell to small merchants or wholesalers (who will be described in the following section) and in some cases may help to finance them until they sell the product. In most cases, however, especially for commodities for which there are large terminal or distributing markets, selling agents deal with buying agents. Like selling agents, they are also commission agents, but they frequently conduct a much larger business. Many buying agents maintain offices in a number of trading centers. Buying agents act on behalf of a number of wholesale buyers, purchasing on their account after receiving firm orders to buy. In many cases, the buying agent is obligated to pay the selling agent before he receives full payment from his clients. A typical transaction is one in which the buying agent requires a deposit of from 5 to 30 per cent of the cost of the commodity from his client, advancing the remainder of the amount due the selling agent at a 6–9 per cent annual interest rate. Buying agents also collect a commission for their services. This can vary widely, from less than 1 per cent to several per cent.

As with selling agents, buying agents may also purchase stocks for their own account, selling from their inventory to their clients. In this situation, the buying agent is not, in fact, acting as a true agent and there is a good chance of a conflict of interest arising between him and his customer.

Especially during the harvest season, it is not uncommon for selling agents and other sellers to send commodities on consignment to buying agents.

Leading buying agents who maintain large stocks are frequently able to obtain bank financing for their stocks. They receive from 65 to 75 per cent of the value of the stocks and are usually charged interest rates of from 4½ to 12 per cent annually.

Wholesalers

Wholesalers buy on their own account and take possession. They generally service local retailers, to whom they frequently give credit. Just as many buying agents may sell as principals and in this way act as wholesalers, larger wholesalers may, to a small extent, operate as buying agents. Other smaller merchants who conduct the main part of their business as wholesalers may also, to a limited extent, sell as retailers. They may buy through buying agents or from larger wholesalers. These smaller wholesalers might be considered more explicitly as subwholesalers or wholesaler-retailers.

One of the chief differences in the mode of operations between large and small wholesalers is in their techniques of pricing. The larger, more powerful wholesalers typically vary their prices, depending on their view of market supply and demand. However, although they may initiate small variations in price to adjust to market conditions, these wholesalers do not have the economic power to make large changes *against* the market trends, since buyers shop around and are strongly price-conscious.

In contrast to large wholesalers who vary their prices according to their estimation of market conditions *virtually regardless of their cost*, smaller wholesalers generally price on a "cost-plus" basis, adding a fixed money amount to the price at which they purchased the merchandise. This method of pricing is not followed because of some conception of a "just price." Rather, the small wholesaler feels that the market dictates to him the size of the markup he can add to his cost as payment for the activities he performs. He is forced to march in step with established practice.

There are some exceptions to the strict "cost-plus" method of pricing described as usual for small wholesalers. In two related instances these merchants may try to price at a higher rate than that which their implicit formula dictates. Whenever small wholesalers have a flurry of purchasers or when they hear from their suppliers that there is a rush on them, they take this to mean that there is exceptional demand and that there will probably soon be a general price increase upward. Small wholesalers may then make a tentative small increase in the price they charge. If their buyers do not resist the increase, they will continue selling at the same level. Similarly, if wholesale prices rise, small wholesalers mark up the selling price of their inventoried goods; however, they often meet buyer resistance before they can match the full price change. If, in contrast, the price at which small wholesalers buy goes *down*, they attempt to sell their inventory at the old price, trying, as long as possible, to keep the news of the price decrease from their purchasers.

In somewhat simplified summary, the differences in pricing techniques between large and small wholesalers is that the former "buy cheap and sell dear" and the latter generally sell at purchase price plus fixed markup.

Both large and small wholesalers offer credit and inventory; however, only the larger wholesalers with capital have the means to buy on their own account for the purposes of speculation.

Other Aspects of Agricultural Marketing

Forward Markets. For many agricultural staples, there exist more or less formalized markets in futures, which operate similarly to such markets in developed countries. The usual contract is one which is to be honored in three months. Agreements on the floor of the trading hall are generally verbal and are written up at night. For products for which standardization is a problem, merchants deal mainly in differences rather than in actual deliveries, which might involve disagreements as to quality. There is little reneging on contracts; if this should happen, the guilty party would be blackballed from the market.

Government Control Periods. During wartime and periods of shortage, the government has taken over control of the distribution of a number of basic crops by making allocations to nominees it has selected in the market or by distributing directly, by establishing maximum prices, and by rationing the crop. Government control of distribution in India is a complex area of consideration; since it is an atypical distribution pattern, it will not be discussed in this chapter.

MARKETING OF MANUFACTURED GOODS

Some manufactured goods (such as a number of industrial products, automobiles and trucks, and petroleum derivatives) are distributed in ways similar to those in the West. However, distribution for most consumer goods, excluding major durables, has much in common with Indian agricultural marketing. Chart II illustrates in simplified form the wholesale chain for manufactured goods.

CHART II

SIMPLIFIED STATEMENT OF INDIA'S WHOLESALING
OF MANUFACTURED GOODS

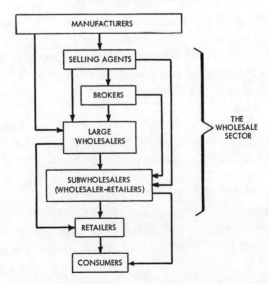

Manufacturers

Most Indian manufacturers consider their function as simply one of production and have little interest in marketing. The typical manufacturer believes that the factory as such should play no more than a rudimentary role in the selling process. This attitude is prevalent, even though particular factory owners may have other business interests primarily concerned with marketing. One manufacturer's comment summed up the prevalent attitude: "Our business is to make a product, not to hawk it."

One reason for this attitude is that the trading groups have traditionally been looked upon with suspicion by other members of society as unproductive and as profiting unfairly at the expense of both producer and consumer. This attitude is common in a number of underdeveloped and developing economies. To a large extent, the very nature of distribution contributes to this attitude. Unlike production, the economic contribution of which is concrete and easily appreciated, distribution enhances the value of a product and contributes to society in an intangible way.

Often, distributive profit margins are believed to be arbitrary, and the very fact that particular traders are well-to-do is adduced as evidence that they have extracted their wealth by impoverishing other members of society. Often implicit in this conviction is the belief that wealth is a limited quantity to be apportioned to the different members of society; it is not understood that the distributive process can be a productive activity leading to the generation of increasing wealth. Compounding this problem is that the benefits which traders themselves reap from their activities are much more readily apparent than is the dispersed and not immediately identifiable contribution they make to society.

A further factor leading to the unfavorable evaluation of distribution is that this activity cannot progress very far without the use of money, unlike production, which can develop to a considerably greater extent. In many underdeveloped countries the use of money in certain sectors of the economy is a recent innovation, and there is an aura of mystery connected with the strange thing. The lack of ease with money and a suspicion of activities that depend on it is enhanced by the fact that traders, the principal handlers of money, frequently are members of strange and exotic ethnic groups and communities. In India, particular castes have been traditionally identified with trading and moneylending. Uncomfortable feelings about money and the people who deal with it can easily spread to the distribution process as a whole.

In economies now highly developed it is quite likely that similar conditions prevailed in earlier times, producers being much less interested in marketing than they are today.

To go back into the past of New England woolen mills, I recall the son of a mill owner harking back to the "good old days" when his father ran the mill. Then they produced blue serge which they shipped to a New York suit manufacturer. The factory absorbed a certain number of thousands of yards of blue serge every year, and if it wasn't converted into suits this year it would be the following year. Neither mill nor converter had to worry about selling; the serge cloth was as good as money in the bank, so it was a simple production problem which had to be solved, not a series of marketing, planning, design, and style problems as it is now.[2]

Manufacturer lack of emphasis on marketing has a number of corollaries. Prepackaging, particularly of consumer staples, is not common. For many items, price or retailer advice is considered more important than brand, and many products are sold without the consumer's knowing who has manufactured it. As can be expected in a country with a high illiteracy rate and with a lack of emphasis on packaging and brand, advertising is rudimentary. (However, a few companies, such as Hindustan Lever, a division of Unilever, advertise extensively.) There is generally little active personal selling or sales promotion, and market research is in its infancy. This means that production may not be closely integrated with consumer needs. Much production is looked upon as an end in itself rather than as a means of helping consumers satisfy their implicit or explicit wants.

Selling Agents

Lack of emphasis on the marketing function has created a potential vacuum in the distribution chain. Commission agents have filled this gap. Many manufacturers deal through selling agents, who, for all practical purposes, can be considered as the selling arms of the factories; by promoting sales and executing orders for the mills, they relieve the producers of the necessity of carrying on most marketing activities. In many cases, the intermediaries may also carry stocks, take credit risks, and even set prices.

[2] Kenneth H. Myers, Jr., and Orange A. Smalley, "Marketing History and Economic Development," *Business History Review* (Autumn, 1959), p. 392, quoting Burleigh Gardner at a meeting, "Marketing Evolution and Implication—an Interdisciplinary Panel Session Held under the Auspices of the American Marketing Association" in Chicago in December, 1958.

The development of the Indian cotton-textile industry in the mid-nineteenth century gave a strong impetus to the agency system in manufacturing. Because many of the textile pioneers were foreigners, limited in their knowledge of Indian languages and market conditions, they took the opportunity of having a responsible Indian agent conduct their selling activities.

Factory-agent relationships vary. The most usual procedure is for manufacturers to have business relations with a number of agents, many of whom deal in several competing brands. Frequently, manufacturers will permit any merchant to act as agent for them as long as a specified minimum quantity is ordered at one time and payment made on receipt. The commission rates which manufacturers dealing with a number of agents pay are frequently on the low side of the range prevailing in the market for the particular product. Often the commission amounts to less than 1 per cent.

Other manufacturers prefer to deal with a limited number of agents, with whom they have built up continuing relationships. A few may deal with only a single selling agent. However, unless there is a family relationship between manufacturer and agent, sole agencies are relatively unusual because most manufacturers are afraid of becoming dependent on a single outlet for their product. Such dependency might hamper them in bargaining on rates of commission. Manufacturers are also concerned lest the agent's interests and those of the factory come into conflict. Although, in theory, an agent is not supposed to buy on his own account, many do. Because of this, manufacturers feel that a sole agent lacking integrity may advise them to sell so that he can buy and speculate on his own account. As a check, therefore, most manufacturers deal with a number of agents.

As implied in the foregoing discussion, the operations of Indian selling agents may deviate from what are usually regarded as traditional commission-agent functions. The term "selling agent" is used here less because it defines the role of this intermediary as for historical reasons and because this term is the common one in the market place.

Traditional Indian manufacturer selling-agent activities are closely akin to brokerage. The agent, in theory, first locates buyers for a product and then contacts the manufacturers to fill these orders. Usually, the factory has informed the agent of the minimum price it is prepared to accept. If it has not, the agent is required to clear large orders with the factory. The manufacturer expects payment for the goods upon receipt—the agent usually assuming the credit risk of the buyer. Although many of the small, capital-poor agents operate in this manner, many larger agents frequently act as principals and, to the extent that they function in this way, might more properly be called wholesalers.

Furthermore, many of the larger selling agents are important sources of capital for manufacturers. This is an extension into manufacturing of the combination financial-distribution function that commission agents perform in the agricultural sector. Manufacturers, however, unlike growers, typically do not borrow because they are short of funds as such. Rather they prefer to use the funds they generate internally for such purposes as plant expansion, instead of building up their working capital. They feel that this use of funds will yield returns that will more than repay the cost of the loan.

Typically, an agent receives a combination of both interest and marketing concessions from a manufacturer to whom he has loaned money. The commissions generally take the form of the opportunity to handle a greater than ordinary proportion of the manufacturer's output at a higher than usual commission rate. This procedure does not necessarily mean that the manufacturer is forced to pay unreasonable compensation for his loan. The interest rates that agents charge are usually quite low by Indian standards and those of other underdeveloped economies. A rate of 6 per cent annually is usual for prime operations. In many cases, it is a point of honor for the borrower to be able to obtain funds at this rate.

The possession of capital is a very important factor in allowing Indian selling agents to perform more than the traditional agent function. Agents with capital can accept their clients' goods on consignment, lending them money on the goods received until a sale is made; they can also buy on their own account and so help manufacturers dispose of their product when the market is temporarily weak. Furthermore, agents having capital are able to obtain important marketing concessions because they have the wherewithal to lend money to producers on a long-term, unsecured basis. Finally, agents possessing capital can speculate on their own account—an important way of enhancing profits in the Indian market.

Brokers

Agents generally sell to wholesalers, who in turn sell primarily to retailers, who purchase on their own account and who stock. Helping to mediate sales between selling agents and wholesalers are brokers who, in effect, sell information. They act in behalf of the uninformed buyer, helping him to secure the goods he wants at favorable prices. They also perform the related service of providing information about possible future trends in the market. Brokers do not buy on their own account, nor do they lend money.

Typically, a broker's client will meet him in the bazaar and go with him to four or five agents to compare prices. For their regular customers, brokers send out postcards periodically, quoting current rates. Many purchasers are clients of more than one broker as a check on the efficiency of these intermediaries and because they want to have more than one source of market information.

Many smaller buyers, especially those from outside the main population centers, almost always use brokers. Some larger buyers almost never do. The use of a number of typical clients makes brokers depend to a great extent on market conditions—whether there is a buyers' or a sellers' market, whether the market is steady or volatile, and so forth.

The seller, the buyer, or both may pay the broker for his services, depending on their relative bargaining power. Market terminology may be misleading on this point. For example, according to market terminology, the seller may be said to pay the broker. However, even though the actual transfer of money may be from the seller to the broker, the buyer may actually be paying for these services. This is generally a result of an established market practice, whereby buyers who do not use brokers have demanded the brokerage fee as a deduction from the price they have to pay because they claim that they are acting as their own brokers. Therefore, although there is no direct transfer of money from the buyer to the broker, it may actually be the buyer who, in effect, pays the brokerage fee, since he forgoes the opportunity of obtaining a reduction in the price charged to him.

The role of brokers in mediating sales of manufactured goods has tended to become less important for those products about which increased market information has become available from other sources, such as the government. In this situation there also usually tends to be downward pressure on brokers' fees.

Wholesalers

The term "wholesaler" is applied to those merchants who generally buy on their own account through agents, who stock, and who sell to retailers. In fact, however, there are few merchants who are pure wholesalers. Many of the larger ones may buy directly from manufacturers some of the goods with which they deal. In this case they are acting as selling agents. Smaller wholesalers may sell a small amount of their goods at retail and therefore are actually subwholesalers or wholesaler-retailers. (These smaller wholesalers may buy either from selling agents or from larger wholesalers.) Typically, all wholesalers offer credit, generally either charging a low rate of interest or a slightly higher price to their customers.

There are several other differences between the modes of operations of large and small wholesalers. The former frequently have sufficient capital to speculate in inventory on their own account. As in the case of wholesalers operating in the agricultural sector, large wholesalers dealing in manufactured goods usually price on a "buy cheap and sell dear" basis; small wholesalers on a "cost-plus" basis.

OBSERVATIONS ON INDIAN WHOLESALING

The Merchant Community

Caste. The majority of Indian merchants operating in the wholesale sector belong to castes for whom trade has been the traditional occupation. An occupational stratification as defined as that in India does not seem to be typical of other underdeveloped countries. Although there may be a strong disposition to enter one economic field rather than another, in casteless societies there is not so definite a predetermined economic role that must be played.

Furthermore, in a number of underdeveloped countries, individuals (or members of their families) who nominally engage in one type of occupation, such as agriculture, may also trade as a sideline. Eventually, they may even come to trade as a full-time occupation. None of this appears representative of the Indian economic scene, where a member of a nontrading caste, if he has the temerity to enter the field of wholesaling, may be shunned by the established merchants.

Caste restrictions are a good example of social factors that have a restraining influence on economic forces, thereby leading to unfavorable effects on the economy. The most efficient deployment of resources is hampered because there is probably less effective use of labor and more difficulty in tapping the capital of nontrading castes. In rural areas these restraints seem to encourage local trading monopolies or oligopolies. Markets are inclined to be narrower than they otherwise would be. This can lead to such unfavorable results as higher prices, aggravation of possible scarcities, price fluctuation, and a general dampening effect on economic growth.

Caste, of course, may operate in an individual's favor. Membership in a particular merchant community may often help a man establish himself in trade by giving him an ascribed status and by leading to important contacts.

Role of the Family.—The role of the family is also an important one in Indian wholesaling. The Indian joint or extended family contains many more members than the nuclear family common in the West. In most areas of India the joint family is headed by a patriarch. The patriarch's unmarried descendants and married male descendants with their wives often live in a single household, which may also include some of the patriarch's siblings and more distant relatives. Members of a joint family have an interrelated configuration of obligations to each other. Typically, all members share in the income of earning members. The existence of relatives who have a traditional claim on the resources of the earning members of the family, whether or not they themselves contribute, acts as a strong impetus to the use of these people in some manner in the family business. In a number of cases, merchants in the wholesaling sector who have the necessary capital resources expand into new areas of business or geographical locations, principally to make use of family members who might otherwise be unemployed. It is not uncommon in India to find the various members of joint families each managing a somewhat different type of business from the others but having some familiarity with them all.

The converse of the intrafamily relationship is that it is very unusual for nonfamily members to become associated with a family business in any responsible capacity. Generally, there is an abundance of relatives, compared with the available jobs. Even if this is not the case, however, outsiders are seldom hired in any important capacity because of the lack of trust between people who are not related, common in India.

Description of a Bazaar and a Typical Merchant's Office

Whole sections of cities, which often tend to be subdivided by the general type of goods sold, are devoted to wholesale selling of merchandise of every conceivable nature. The sidewalks are crowded with people on commercial errands and the streets choked with animals, usually bullocks but sometimes donkeys or even camels, hauling loads or wandering free. Driving a car is a difficult process, very slow and hardly ever accomplished in anything but first gear.

The office of a large sugar and cloth merchant is typical. Near the office is a red-pepper dealer, and the air surrounding the building is suffused with the pungent aroma of this condiment, which causes burning throats and tear-filled eyes to those not used to the penetrating odor. The first floor of the building in which the merchant is located is occupied by a rice seller. In the back is the office of an astrologer, who is one of the more popular in Delhi for picking auspicious occasion for weddings and other important events. Up a steep, rickety flight of stairs is the merchant's headquarters. The office is in the traditional Eastern style; over the door are mango leaves, now withered, a symbol of good luck and prosperity. Every day a holy man visits the office and performs ceremonies designed to bring good fortune, for which he is paid the equivalent of a few cents. Shoes are removed at the entrance to the office proper. The floor is covered with a while cloth, and the walls are lined with pillows. The various partners and clerks sit cross-legged against the walls, leaning on the pillows. They write on small desks about a foot or 15 inches high. A telephone and its extension complete the furnishings. The doors to the outside verandah are left open, and there are usually about half-a-dozen pigeons flying around the office.

The merchant partners have no objection to Westernization as such. Their homes are lushly furnished in eclectic European style. But they find several advantages in an Indian office. It is comfortable, informal, easy to maintain, and inexpensive. Most Indians feel it would be a foolish waste of money to decorate an office. Far from having a favorable effect on the business people dealt with, these men would resent this tampering with the usual and would feel uncomfortable and out of place in strange foreign surroundings. Another reason for not "modernizing" is that it is part of the tradition of Indian traders not to show too great opulence, for this may just be asking for trouble with the government tax examiners.

Lack of Differentiation between Middlemen

One of the most important characteristics of the Indian wholesaling sector is that there is often no clear-cut specialization of distributive activities, either vertically, by successive levels of distribution, or horizontally, by types of goods handled.

Lack of Vertical Differentiation. Earlier, several examples of the lack of vertical specialization by distribution levels were given. Large commission agents frequently act as principals; wholesalers may do some business as agents or, if small, as retailers.

This blurring of distributive functions appears to be a common phenomenon in other underdeveloped countries. In Puerto Rico many firms act as both wholesalers and brokers. In West Africa there is "no clear-cut division between successive stages of the distributive process. The same European or African trader may import direct, and also sell by wholesale, semi-wholesale and retail methods (and African traders sell by petty retail as well)." [3] Observers have cited similar examples in such countries as Iran and Venezuela.

This situation may simply be a reflection of the relative lack of specialization prevalent in a low-income economy. More specifically, because of such factors as the prevailing market structure, the low cost of labor, and the lack of fixed prices, it may often make economic sense for a merchant to widen the nominal distributive level at which he operates. This hypothesis is supported by the statement of several wholesalers interviewed that they would have no hesitation in varying their usual methods of sale in individual instances if they thought that they could thereby get some return over cost.[4] The Indian wholesaler here is acting like the American manufacturer of a consumer good who sells to wholesalers under his own brand name and who also sells to large retail outlets under the outlet's name at a lower price. The American decision is based on the implications of mass production, whereas that of the trader in an underdeveloped country has its rationale in his ability to differentiate his activities at low cost.

Because of the lack of vertical differentiation, it is inappropriate to talk of the price current at any particular level in the wholesale section, unless what is referred to is carefully defined. Every merchant in the market has a circumscribed group from which he ordinarily purchases and another to which he ordinarily sells. For example, small wholesalers buy from agents and large wholesalers; retailers buy from large and small wholesalers; and large wholesalers sell to small wholesalers and large retailers. The merchant, then, does not have the concept of dealing with a specified distribution link but with *a range* of sellers and buyers.

Typically, prices to comparable buyers, adjusted for the services

---

[3] P. T. Bauer, *West African Trade* (Cambridge: Cambridge University Press, 1954), p. 53.

[4] A personal incident graphically illustrated this orientation to me. I wanted to mail some books from India and tried to buy heavy wrapping paper in a number of different stationery stores but with no success. The stores advised me to look in the wholesale paper bazaar, which supplies wrapping paper to the souvenir shops that pack for export. It seemed doubtful that a wholesaler would break a full roll of paper to make a relatively minor sale. However, the first paper merchant I talked with, after making some rapid calculations, agreed to sell me a few yards. He explained that he had never sold at retail before but that he was quite willing to do this. Although he would have to sell the open roll at a discount, he figured that he would more than make up the difference from the proceeds of his sale to me.

provided, are similar, even though, according to market labels, the potential sellers may be on different levels of distribution. This is largely a corollary to the prospective purchaser's comparing the prices and services offered him within his appropriate "pricing box," in order to decide which seller offers the terms best fitting his needs.

For many purposes it would be more meaningful to distinguish among the different Indian middlemen by size rather than by market label. There are some rough similarities among many types of large, as opposed to small, middlemen. For example, the former vary their prices depending on their estimation of market trends rather than pricing on a "cost-plus" basis, and they speculate in inventory to a significant extent.

Lack of Horizontal Differentiation. With the general exception of retailers, Indian middlemen or their close relatives frequently handle a wide range of apparently unrelated products, ranging from sugar to precious metals and from textiles to chemicals. This phenomenon is generally called "scrambled merchandising." In the United States horizontal integration is not uncommon, but among businessmen of the same relative size there is probably not as much scrambled merchandising as in India. The lack of horizontal differentiation appears to be common in other underdeveloped countries too.

This situation is a result of merchant reactions to various economic factors. Middlemen who want to expand may find the scope for enlargement of their present business limited. Narrow markets often restrict the type of commodity specialization possible for a merchant, and expansion beyond a certain proportion of the market becomes progressively more difficult. Therefore, merchants in the wholesale sector who want to grow must often choose a new field rather than enlarge current operations. Such diversification has the advantage of spreading their risk.

At times, a merchant may consider diversification as a defensive move. He may begin to deal in a new product in order to compete aggressively with another relatively undifferentiated merchant who seems likely to enter the first man's home ground. For example, a firm dealing in grain may start selling cloth if it believes that a strong cloth merchant may be considering entering the grain trade.

To take full advantage of the profitable and defensive possibilities of horizontal diversification, rapid mobility is important. Because of the narrowness of markets and relative lack of information in underdeveloped countries, favorable opportunities may arise suddenly and unexpectedly. Those merchants who can quickly recognize and take advantage of such economic opportunities are most likely to benefit.

Indian merchants judge that horizontal diversification is economically practical because they believe that the various types of wholesaling operations are basically quite similar to one another. They feel that marketing ability, or, perhaps more accurately, trading ability, is much the same, no matter what the good handled. Furthermore, capital and skill in financial activities are important factors in the successful operation of a merchant business over a certain size, and these factors vary little from product to product. Because of this lack of differentiation among the factors of production, the more sophisticated middlemen can expand with little difficulty or sacrifice among a wide range of products to take advantage of emerging opportunities. (Small traders also have some of this flexibility in shifting product line. However, if they start to deal in a new good, they are generally forced to give up the previous product handled because of the thinness of their capital or managerial resources.) The important role of the joint family in India also works to encourage diversification.

There appears to be a gradual trend toward increased horizontal specialization in the Indian market. Specialization is becoming more profitable with the growing size of the market and with differentiation in techniques of distribution. These and other factors have also acted to increase the amount of capital required to carry on trading and have thereby begun to limit economic mobility.

The Competitive Environment of Indian Distribution

Background. India, like many other underdeveloped countries, is characterized by an overabundance of labor. That is, labor is excessive in relation to the other factors of production with which it must combine for productive purposes: capital, land, and entrepreneurship (including all those skills necessary for effective business management). This relative oversupply of labor leads to its underuse, that is, to chronic unemployment and underemployment, and to a generally low return for labor.

Because of the economic situation, a man who is out of a job is usually willing to engage in any type of work for a meager return, as long as the work is suitable for his caste. (Nevertheless, an individual, though presently idle, may refuse a job which would force him to give up his claim to a share of the family income, as might happen, for example, if he moved from the family homestead into the city, unless his new returns would make up for the loss.)

For members of those communities for whom it is considered appropriate, trade is a field easily entered that can provide them with some return, small as it may be. Although it is difficult to obtain a job working for someone who is not a relative, it is easy to set oneself up in business. The prospective merchant has probably been familiar with generalized trading techniques from early youth. The scale of operations in trade can be quite small. The merchant's capital needs are minimal, since his overhead costs may be low or virtually non-existent, and he can often obtain credit from suppliers. Many people start trading ventures in geographic locations or in products with which they are unfamiliar. They begin with a bare minimum of capital, frequently obtained either as loans from relatives or from saving a remarkable proportion of very low incomes. For example, one refugee wholesaler re-entered trade after fleeing from Pakistan by obtaining a bag of sugar on credit in the morning and lugging it on his back to a spot in the bazaar where he sold it in small quantities. The proceeds from the used bag were his only profit.

The considerable unemployment and underdevelopment in India and the ease of entry into the wholesale sector lead to a great overcrowding in the field. This overcrowding makes for strong competition; and it also makes for heavy downward pressure on margins and returns.

The Drive for Differentiation. Because of the intense competitive struggle, there is a great incentive for merchants in the wholesale sector to introduce an element of uniqueness into their operations. Even relatively minor differentiation, if valued enough by the consumer for him to pay a slightly higher price, means a substantial increase in profits. (Because margins are so low, a small increase in price leads to a large jump in returns.)

Trading skill alone is rarely enough to assure an Indian merchant of more than a minimum return for his efforts. (This also applies to brokers, whose skill is that of supplying market information.) As was discussed earlier, there is, however, one strikingly effective means by which continuing high returns can be achieved: the competent utilization of the power of financial resources. Access to a meaningful amount of capital is restricted to a limited number of merchants. Therefore, the merchant who can command significant funds and who has the sophistication to utilize them is directly competitive only with the small fraction of merchants who also have capital available to them.

Earlier, the union of financial and marketing activity, whereby a loan not only returns interest but also secures important marketing concessions for the lender, was discussed. Such transactions appear to be common in a number of underdeveloped areas, including West Africa and Iran.

Financial resources are also important to middlemen in enabling them to finance forward, to extend credit to purchasers. As in many other underdeveloped countries, this service is considered one of the most important that Indian middlemen supply. Middlemen in the wholesale sector who cannot extend significant credit are usually at a decided competitive disadvantage compared with their colleagues.

The command of capital can help improve a merchant's competitive position in other ways. It gives him staying power during temporary difficult periods in the market, whereas capital-poor merchants are very susceptible to market vagaries. By purchasing on their own account, capital-rich agents can help the manufacturers they deal with dispose of their stocks during temporary periods of market weakness, and, by maintaining inventories, they can often service their customers better.

Furthermore, capital allows merchants to speculate in inventory, an activity considered important and profitable for middlemen in the wholesale sector. The consensus in the Indian market is that a merchant can realize a good return only if he is able to buy and sell on his own account.

The crucial importance of capital in freeing a merchant from some of the rigors of strong price competition is reflected in the attitudes of Indian middlemen. Financial resources are looked upon primarily as a business tool rather than as a means of increasing personal consumption. The point of view that capital should be passed on enhanced to the next generation as a trust helps to account for the relatively simple life of some extremely wealthy merchants. Religious attitudes may also emphasize simple living for members of trading castes. This predilection is fortified by the economic fact that it is difficult for an Indian middleman starting with little or no capital to build a position of financial strength. As pointed out earlier, a trader cannot hire out his services for any significant sum because there is an oversupply of men with skill alone. Working for himself without sufficient capital, the merchant realizes a low return. (Of course, there have been cases of men starting from humble beginnings who amassed large amounts of capital, but these are the exception.) It might be mentioned here that, among middlemen without significant financial resources, there seems to be a more philosophical resignation and acceptance of their role than is the case in comparable situations in developed countries.

Evaluation of the Relationship between Finance and Distribution in Indian Wholesaling

In the wholesaling of both agricultural and manufactured goods in India, it was shown that financial and distributive activities are frequently interrelated. In some instances, strong middlemen who can provide a package of financial and marketing services are able to obtain monopsonistic power. But whenever the potential client can choose among a number of trader-leaders who are actively competing with each other, economic forces should insure his not having to pay an excessive price for the combination of services that he buys. The obligation of a producer to sell to a particular middleman at lower than prevailing market prices may well be balanced by his paying lower than market rates on his loan.

For most analytical purposes it is preferable not to attempt to segregate the return from distribution and that from finance. In other words, the transaction should be looked upon as yielding a return consisting of so much in interest and so much in commission as payment both for a loan of a certain amount and for marketing services. Examining one part of the transaction out of context might lead to faulty conclusions (for example, that interest rates are lower than usual or that the producer is receiving less than fair market value for his product.) It is said that certain government marketing schemes to aid cultivators failed because they were concerned only with distribution per se and did not take into account the necessity of providing credit to growers.

Many manufacturers who have sufficient resources to choose whether or not to borrow from agents decide in favor of borrowing; they prefer to use their capital resources elsewhere. This is good indication that they consider borrowing from their distributors to be in their best economic interests and that they are not being "victimized."

It may well be, however, that some sellers or purchasers would benefit if they had the opportunity to transact their financial and marketing activities separately from each other. They may not feel that the particular combinations offered by the market are best suited to them. (Some information as to the true cost of credit may be needed to help them judge the most favorable alternative.) It would not be an answer to this problem for the government to prohibit the wholesale sector from extending financial help, a policy which might well worsen the position of the producer or the consumer who is either left without funds or with limited alternative sources of funds. Rather, the government should investigate ways of encouraging new sources of marketing and financial services independent of each other which would be competitive with those presently provided by trader-lenders. Individuals would then have a wider range of business possibilities from which to make their decisions. As the economy develops, these will probably evolve naturally.

Costs and Returns in the Indian Wholesale Sector

It is difficult to determine precisely either the cost spread in the Indian wholesale sector or the average margins of individual links in the chain. The situation is similar to that in West Africa. Bauer's evaluation there is that "an attempt at detailed statistical discussion of selling margins in West African trade would be unrewarding." [5] The basic problem in India is that adequate accurate statistical information is virtually impossible to obtain. As a very rough estimate, however, charges in the Indian wholesaling sector appeared to range between 5 and 30 per cent of wholesale selling price.

Because of the lack of data and the reticence of Indian merchants to discuss financial matters, it is not possible to estimate returns in the Indian wholesale sector.

Functions in the Indian Wholesaling System

The Indian wholesale sector performs services similar to those usually rendered in developed countries but with some shifts of emphasis. The Indian wholesale system assembles, sorts, transports, stores, and breaks bulk. It assumes many of the risks associated with carrying inventory. Through storage, pricing, and other techniques, the system helps adjust supply and demand over time between different geographical areas but not without short-run fluctuations, however. Through the market information it supplies, the distributive chain gives some assistance to manufacturers in guiding their output. The system finances both backward and forward by lending money to cultivators and factories and by extending credit to retailers.

There are certain functions sometimes associated with wholesaling which the Indian sector does not perform. It does not usually grade. Market demand is taken as fixed; the wholesale sector engages in almost no promotional activity to shift demand or to increase over-all demand.

---

[5] Bauer, *op. cit.*, p. 58.

Within the wholesale distribution chain, relatively little selling effort is evident. It is the buyer who ordinarily approaches the seller, rather than vice versa. For example, the Indian retailer typically contacts the wholesaler to place an order. In the United States and other developed countries, it is more usual for representatives of wholesalers to visit retailers. This is generally considered a more efficient way to operate. Because of the smaller number of wholesalers relative to retailers, such a procedure cuts down on the total amount of traveling required and allows greater functional specialization. The Indian procedure probably arises from the desire of buyers to compare the prices of a number of different sellers before making a purchase. It would not be practical for the buyer to wait for a sufficient number of sellers to approach him; he must therefore approach them. This orientation also accounts for the tendency of suppliers of particular goods to congregate in a given area.

The Middlemen's View of Their Activities

Most businessmen engaged in marketing in economically developed countries consider the return they realize as payment for their activities in distributing goods. In other words, they feel that their markup is compensation for their function as market intermediaries. Indian middlemen in the wholesale sector, however, typically see themselves as traders—merchants who are able to buy at one price and sell at a higher price as a result of their activities in the market. These activities consist of such tasks as breaking lot size and, assuming they have the resources, in varying the amount of inventory carried to take advantage of expected price changes. The Indian middleman looks upon these operations as two sides of a merchant's activities; he does not differentiate one as "speculative." For this reason, the middleman cannot understand and resents accusations that he is a market manipulator or speculator simply because he follows what he considers normal practice in adjusting his inventory in response to expected price fluctuations. The merchants feel no responsibility for price rises or for shortages, although some admit that activities taken in expectation of these conditions can be self-fulfilling.

The pricing techniques of the large middlemen illustrate the view they have of themselves as traders. As described earlier, their technique is continually to initiate small variations in selling price (and in their offers to purchase) based on their appraisal of market conditions. They thereby realize a constantly varying margin. Smaller middlemen price on a "cost-plus" basis, not because they feel their role as traders differ from that of the larger merchants but because, to a large extent, they are price followers whose markup is circumscribed by competition.

Productivity and Efficiency in Indian Wholesaling

Unfortunately, adequate information on such particulars of Indian wholesaling as capital turnover and sales per man is not available. Therefore, labor and capital productivity cannot be measured quantitatively. It is my belief, however, that the productivity of capital can be characterized as reasonably high but that much labor is redundant.

In the wholesaling sector, little capital is invested in fixed assets. Its major use is for carrying inventory and, to a lesser extent, for extending credit backward to producers and forward to retailers. (Loans to producers are more a financial, than a distributive, use of capital, however.) Although inventory is carried not only to service clients but also for speculative reasons, turnover of capital invested in inventory appears to be rapid. That is, a relatively small inventory generally supports a large volume of sales. Over-all capital turnover is somewhat slowed because the wholesaling system as a whole is a net creditor. However, all things considered, the productivity of capital in the Indian wholesale sector seems reasonably high.

Much labor in distribution is redundant, and therefore output per man is low. In other words, fewer middlemen could carry on substantially all present distributive activities. This, however, is not a fault of the wholesaling system as such. The problem must be examined in context of the larger environment of the society as a whole. It is a malaise of the Indian economy that much of the labor force is unemployed or underemployed. It is no more the "fault" of distribution that it is overcrowded than it is the "fault" of agriculture that there are too many people on the land. Eliminating redundant traders would not mean more productivity in another sector of the economy but rather unemployment of these traders. Hopefully, economic development will generate job opportunities that will help to eliminate unemployment and underemployment throughout the economy and will thereby work to decrease redundancy in distribution.

Whatever current productivity in wholesale distribution may be, is it possible to propose an alternative that will make more efficient use of the various factors of production? Because of the lack of data, it is not possible to contrast the present system of Indian sugar wholesale distribution with a radically different alternative, such as, for example, complete government control. However, a particular change of a less basic nature that is frequently suggested as a way of improving the current method of wholesale distribution can be evaluated.

It has been held that too many stages of wholesale distribution intervene between the producer and the retailer and that some should be eliminated. The present system supposedly leads to unnecessary waste and to higher costs for both producer and consumer.

This opinion arises in part from the view that the wholesale sector does not add anything to a product's value and that each successive middleman makes a charge for his activities without concomitant benefit to producer or consumer; therefore, the more middlemen, the more of these "unnecessary" charges. The attitude is also a result of the desire for "neatness" in distribution.

In most cases, however, the clients of a particular link in the wholesale sector have the opportunity to bypass it. In such cases, it is reasonable to conclude that the clients of the link judge that it is to their economic advantage to use it and that the value of the middleman's service is greater than the charge made for it.

JAPAN

Wholesaling in Japan has been shaped by some unique historical factors. Foremost has been the feudal character of Japanese society, wherein the role of economic overseeing fell largely to the merchant class, particularly to wholesale organizations, commonly called "trading companies." Extended vertically and horizontally into other functional levels and into assorted industries, these Zaibatsu-type organizations wielded power unsurpassed by even some of the cartels of the Western world.

In this chapter, the author shows some of the wholesaling practices to be rationally based on economic circumstances and others to be peculiar to habits in that country. Unavailability of capital for financing both small-scale production and distribution except through wholesale merchants, the predominance of a sellers' market, and the prevailing practice of even large retailers to shift to wholesalers even functions normal to retailers have vested wholesalers with extraordinary authority and power.

Very gradually, however, the position of the wholesaler is being eroded as market conditions change and as concepts of marketing gain acceptance by the business community.

Wholesaling in Japan

GEORGE A. ELGASS AND
LAURENCE P. DOWD *

With an area of approximately 147,000 square miles, Japan is a little smaller than California; yet within that space she has a population of 94 million—six times that of California. The population, now growing at a rate of only 0.8 per cent per year, is expected to reach 102 million by 1970.

The literacy rate is among the highest in the world. Approximately 99.7 per cent of the adult population can both read and write. The law provides for six years of compulsory free education. Education is highly valued and important to the type of employment that one may obtain. Consequently, students typically go to high school, and hundreds of thousands attend Japan's colleges and universities.

The Japanese language is spoken with relatively slight variations throughout the land. Except for the roads, transportation and communication facilities are extensive and very good, and the Japanese have a high propensity to travel. Consequently, cultural patterns do not vary greatly. Ideas spread quickly. These basic factors patently contribute to the development of the economy.

Japan is basically a free-enterprise economy. In their own way, Japanese enterprisers generally are competitive. The nation is now in the midst of a ten-year plan of economic development by which it is hoped that the level of the Gross National Product can be doubled by 1970. Japanese economists sometimes describe the economy as neither advanced nor underdeveloped, but rather in the "in-between" stage. There is perhaps more to this than customary Japanese modesty. Substantial parts of this very large economic system have not yet had access to modern production and marketing technology. Nor has high mass consumption yet become the general condition.

Income per capita for 1961 was approximately $358; per capita

* Dr. George A. Elgass is Professor of Marketing at the Dearborn Campus, University of Michigan, Dearborn, Michigan.

Dr. Laurence P. Dowd is Professor and Director of the School of World Business, San Francisco State College, San Francisco, California.

GNP, $447. Real per capita income has doubled since 1951. Dollar income figures, however, tend to cause the true standard of living to be underestimated. The prices of staple foods, transportation, and services are very low in dollar terms.

The distribution of income is far from ideal by the standards of the Japanese people themselves. However, approximately 85 per cent of national income is distributed in the form of labor income to employees and as proprietors' income. The persons with relatively low incomes tend to be those employees and proprietors associated with organizations which, for any reason, have been unable to keep pace with the progress of the economy. This income-distribution pattern appears to be made more pronounced by the underemployment of the labor force, a problem which has not yet been overcome in Japan.

Because of the rugged mountainous territory, no more than 19 per cent of the land area is estimated to be arable. Farms are very small—about 2 acres. Employing the best technology *consistent with small units and an objective of high yield per acre* enables the agricultural sector to provide 80 per cent of the nation's food requirements. The proportion of the labor forces in the primary sector declined from 42.3 per cent in 1955 to 32.7 per cent in 1961.

Manufacturing contributes almost 30 per cent of total national income and is still growing. The product mix has become more diversified and has been changing markedly. Capital-intensive industries have been growing fast. Electrical equipment, motor vehicles, machine tools, organic chemicals, and steel have expanded greatly since 1955. High standards of quality and quality control are more widely appreciated.

Capital formation is very high in Japan. Gross domestic investment has averaged 31 per cent of GNP per year in recent years. Japan does not lack in spirit of enterprise, and thrift is still a virtue. This virtue is backstopped, moreover, by excise taxes and import duties. Furthermore, stringent measures are at times employed to combat inflation.

For some nations, a substantial amount of international trade is important, but for Japan international trade is vital. The country depends on it for acquiring sufficient food products for the survival of the people and the raw materials needed to provide the opportunity for productive full employmnet. Large-scale efficiency and the benefits of a fully employed economy also are goals that Japan could not achieve without access to international markets. Exports and imports average 22 per cent of Japan's GNP, compared with 7 per cent in the United States.

Wholesale and retail trade contributes 15 per cent of total national income, and this ratio has been quite stable. Most of the firms are very small and suffer all the well-known maladies of very small business units. At the other extreme are modern department stores with branch units and the large trading companies which act as sales (and sometimes financial) organizations for many large and small manufacturers.

MERCHANTS ASSISTED JAPAN'S EARLY GROWTH

At the time the North American continent was being colonized, Japan already had an established distribution system with large, well-organized wholesale firms which assembled and distributed products on a national scale. Apparently the earliest of these organizations was founded long before Columbus discovered America. Economic historians award substantial credit to Japan's strong merchant class for the success of the nation's transition to an industrial economy. It was the leading merchants who possessed the knowledge, the skills, and the wealth required to develop industry. As feudalism reached its end, members of the merchant elite also contributed their talents for organization to strengthen the national government and to assist in its effort to stimulate and facilitate economic development.

An interesting sidelight is that the low social position assigned to the merchant class during the period of Japanese feudal society is considered to have contributed to their economic effectiveness. Despite their theoretically low status, merchants were actually often well regarded and achieved considerable power. Nevertheless, a merchant could never enter the nobility. Consequently, successful merchants accumulated capital, which was used to finance the nation's early industrial growth. To this day there exists a cultural lag in regard to the social position of members of the merchant group. In part, this is due to a lack of appreciation of the social value of the functions performed by merchants—a condition not peculiar to the Japanese public.

DOMINANT POSITION OF WHOLESALE ORGANIZATIONS

In the second half of the nineteenth century, the reopening of Japan to trade with the Western world led to a new era of great economic growth. Commerce in general thrived, and the strongest general wholesale organization—commonly called "trading companies"—expanded into the vertically, horizontally, and circularly integrated Zaibatsu organizations, which dominated both production and distribution in the decades preceding World War II. The Zaibatsu type of organization was regarded by the Japanese as an effective means of achieving economic development for the purpose of protecting the nation's sovereign independence and gaining the fruits of industrialization. The Zaibatsu did make important contributions toward these ends. At the same time, however, the Zaibatsu came to possess great political and economic power. Moreover, both types of power were sometimes used unwisely.

It is noteworthy that the Zaibatsu were not the equivalent of most European cartels. The structure of the Zaibatsu somewhat resembled what today are called "conglomerate enterprises." A Zaibatsu enterprise included within its organization one or more banking units, manufacturing plants in diverse industries, and domestic as well as international trading companies. In addition, the complex network included co-operative arrangements with a multitude of small manufacturing and trading firms.

Following World War II, the Zaibatsu organizations were partially disintegrated. Nevertheless, individual units, such as the trading companies, continued to function on a reduced scale. These trading companies have since regained a strong position in the economy.

START OF TREND TOWARD MANUFACTURER CONTROL

A definite trend away from wholesaler control of the channels of distribution originated in the late 1950's. It was at this time that large and medium-sized manufacturers became seriously interested in modern marketing concepts and methods. Many such firms now perform a substantial part of the necessary marketing functions and exercise control over the process of distribution for their output. This trend is significant, and over a period of time the stage will be reached in which wholesalers will generally play a much smaller role. For the present, however, the general situation in Japan remains one in which large wholesalers continue to occupy a dominant position in the channels of distribution.

REASONS FOR DOMINANT POSITION OF WHOLESALERS

Large Wholesalers Function as Financial Institutions

Japanese wholesalers finance forward in the distribution of products; that is, they finance the next stage in the channel of distribution, as do American wholesalers, although not as extensively or on an equally high basis of risk. More important is the extent to which Japanese wholesalers engage in backward financing; they finance production processes even to the extent of "lending" raw or semi-finished materials for processing. Actually, this is analogous to the medieval "putting-out" system widely used in Europe.

It has been estimated that 98 per cent of Japanese firms have fewer than 100 employees. Most small firms are very limited in their sources of working capital. Since the banks typically have been unwilling to extend credit to such small firms, they have relied largely on wholesalers for necessary funds. The reluctance of most banks to finance small retailers and manufacturers is attributable to the general shortage of capital, the relatively high risk involved, the conservatism of the banking system, the force of tradition, and other similar factors.

The use of open-account financing has not been customary in Japan. Financing is carried out by the use of commercial bills or trade acceptances. Moreover, banks are reluctant to extend loans directly to either producers or retailers, preferring the additional security of the wholesaler's endorsement on a discounted draft. Consequently, if the drawee fails to make payment when the bill is due, the bank can look to the wholesaler for payment. So important is this method of financing production and distribution in the Japanese economic system that regular reports of "dishonored bills" in number and amount are published and used by economic statisticians as an indicator of the current state of the economy. However, a dishonored bill in Japan does not mean one on which the drawee is permanently unable to make payment; it is merely a bill which is not paid when due, even though it may be paid a few days later.

In respect to the impact of traditional and customary methods of finance upon present practice, it should be remembered that for hundreds of years the distribution of products has been by means of this channel of distribution dominated by wholesalers. A certain amount of rigidity, therefore, should be expected. Furthermore, there are signs of change. A number of relatively large producers have recently been able to adopt more modern methods; yet, still following traditional patterns and to satisfy bank requirements, they sometimes establish wholly owned subsidiary wholesale organizations. These are most commonly found in the large, integrated enterprises which were formerly part of the Zaibatsu empires. Such wholly owned subsidiaries, however, do not limit their activities to the parent company. They undertake the sale of products of otherwise competing producers. In a few instances these subsidiaries control the wholesale distribution of an entire industry.

Secular Sellers' Market

As far as the domestic economy is concerned, Japan has enjoyed a secular excess of demand relative to supply—a long-term sellers' market. This is undoubtedly an important reason why even relatively large producers have been rather uninterested in the marketing aspects of business. Prior to World War II, large manufacturers were primarily engaged in the production of goods for the government. The consumer market was relatively small, and sales at that time to industry involved mainly negotiation. It was not until the late 1950's that domestic demand sometimes lagged in a significant number of industries for reasons other than a decline in Japan's export sales. It was at this point that many manufacturers became seriously interested in learning about modern marketing with a view to preparing to meet the buyers' market which could be anticipated to prevail in the future.

International Balance-of-Payments Problems

The Japanese economy must rely to a large extent on foreign sources for many types of industrial raw materials. Consequently, an increase in domestic demand necessarily leads to an increase in the demand for imports. Unfortunately for Japan, her international balance-of-payments position is perennially in a precarious state. Merchandise exports are the cause of a serious bottleneck to steady economic growth, and the government is frequently under pressure to pursue policies designed to restrain domestic demands. The conflict of such policies with marketing activities designed to increase demand is apparent. On the other hand, a substantial increase in Japan's exports would tend to reduce the need for such restraint. With increased opportunities to cater to the domestic market, manufacturers would, in due course, become more generally interested in the marketing functions of business.

LONG CHANNELS OF DISTRIBUTION

Not only is wholesaling a dominant activity, but also there is an amazing multiplicity of wholesalers in individual channels of distribution. Commencing with the production of a basic commodity, such as steel sheets and billets or textile fibers, the product may pass through the hands of as many as five separate wholesalers before it finally reaches the shelves of the retailer. A somewhat typical channel for a product is shown in Figure 1, which indicates some of the in-

FIGURE 1
TYPICAL WHOLESALE CHANNEL OF DISTRIBUTION
FOR A CONSUMER PRODUCT

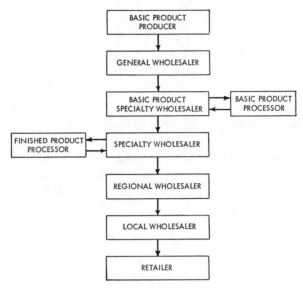

teresting characteristics of wholesale organization and activities in a channel of distribution.

As in all forms of Japanese business, wholesale organizations tend to extremes in size. At one limit there are the enormously large, highly integrated general wholesale organizations ("trading companies") which deal in products ranging from abaca or abacuses to zippers and zink. These enterprises, of which there are about twenty controlling basic distribution, are direct descendents of the prewar Zaibatsu firms; and they are some of the largest business organizations in Japan. Of particular significance to foreign marketing is the fact that the large trading companies may have almost a monopoly of the export and import trade of significant sectors of the economy. At the other extreme are small, one- or two-man organizations which may engage in no more than local distributions of abacuses.

The general wholesalers, or trading companies, typically acquire all the output of a number of manufacturers in an industry. In fact, in some industries the entire industry is controlled by one wholesaler, and that one wholesaler may control several industries. Those firms, nevertheless, do not limit themselves to basic commodities. They also control the distribution of many consumer goods. Although the general wholesalers may engage in "putting out" basic commodities for processing, more frequently they sell to specialty wholesalers who limit themselves to one line of product or even part of a line. Basic product-specialty wholesalers, in turn, may sell to specialty wholesalers who "put out" the product to finished-product processors before distribution to regional wholesalers. Regional wholesalers, who are usually located in large trading centers such as Tokyo or Osaka or Fukuoka, in turn sell to local wholesalers, located in secondary trading centers who limit their activities to the immediately surrounding territory.[1] Wholesalers in Japan are also specialized on a functional basis. There are brokers, agents, commission merchants, and a variety of limited-function distributors.

The use of a short channel is still unusual even in the case of large retail buyers. A large department store purchasing an item such as men's socks typically would not purchase its requirements for any period of time directly from the knitter or even a national wholesaler. Rather it would purchase from a local wholesaler located in the immediate vicinity of the store. Sometimes it might buy as little as three or four pairs—perhaps merely enough to fill an order for a single customer, on occasion while he waits for the order to be filled.

Actual channels of distribution are very diverse and often complex. Nevertheless, the use of long channels is the common practice for both industrial and consumer goods. The use of three or more wholesale links is not extraordinary and not limited to very small firms. Some of the key factors behind such long channels are the following:

1. The national market covers a great distance because of the long, narrow shape of Japan.

2. The 94 million consumers, with a 1961 income per capita of approximately $360, constitute a broad but thin market.

3. The buying habits of consumers make very intensive retail distribution necessary for some types of products. Housewives shop daily for food. In a large city there are strips of small convenience-goods shops within a short walking distance from almost every residence.

4. The atomistic size of the large proportion of manufacturers, wholesalers, and retailers, plus their limited capital, encourages, if not requires, that the firms which perform the functions in the channel system make use of an additional link or two.

5. Secular unemployment, coupled with cultural patterns which

---

[1] See Yukichi Arakawa, "Small Wholesalers is the Cotton Textile Marketing in Japan," *Annals of the School of Business Administration,* (Kobe University, 1957), pp. 59 ff.

favor individual proprietorship, tend to retard the growth of large-scale business units except when technology *requires* large-scale operations.

6. Manufacturers often perform little or no part of the marketing task, thus leaving a big job for the middlemen.

MULTIPLE CHANNELS

Medium and large manufacturers frequently use several different channels of distribution for a single product line. There are four reasons for this practice that are particularly worth special mention:

1. For a given product or product line the specific market tends to have a wide range of diversity—for example, from Tokyo to a tiny rural village; from cottage industry to a giant corporation. Similarly, the middlemen vary from the very large and financially strong to mamma and pappa shops.
2. With the economy's rapid growth rate and new diversification of industry, there are no traditional channels for some new products. If distribution through *several types of retail stores* is needed, this may well require the use of *several types of wholesalers.*
3. Recently, some supermarkets and discount houses have been born, to add to the diversity of retail types that the producer must reach.
4. Scrambled merchandising by established channels of distribution is not lacking in Japan.

MARKETING ACTIVITY BY PRODUCERS

At all levels, Japanese business may be characterized as an economy of extremes. There are immensely large and minutely small producers, wholesalers, and retailers. There are organizations which undertake marketing activities intensively and those which engage in almost no marketing activity. Throughout the economy there is very little "in the middle," in either size or extent of activity.

This becomes immediately apparent in the case of producing organizations. The large factories of the highly integrated enterprises are readily observed in the Tokyo-Yokohama, Osaka-Kobe, and Nagoya areas; but, in Japan's over-all production, small factories that employ less than ten workers are of equal importance. In fact, these small factories are sometimes referred to as the backbone of the Japanese economy.

In the United States one may observe some elementary marketing activity by even the smallest producer. Yet with few exceptions—notably in the production of direct consumer goods, such as processed foods for immediate consumption, tailored clothing, and similar products—small producers in Japan engage in virtually no marketing. They rely completely upon wholesalers. Until very recently it could be said that even large manufacturers seldom undertook intensive marketing activities of their products. Most firms have had no marketing or sales department as such; and even those firms with such a department would usually relegate it to a completely subordinate position. In fact, even allowing for the trend toward marketing by manufacturers described earlier, it is unlikely that the change has been sufficiently widespread for the intensive undertaking of marketing. Similarly, despite a "breaking-out" of the marketing functions in some organizations to a departmental status, this has not yet become so widespread as to outmode the typical generalized organizational chart which appears as Figure 2.

FIGURE 2
Typical Organizational Structure of a Large Manufacturer

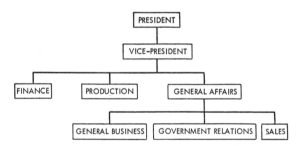

"Department of General Affairs" is the translation for the Japanese term *Somubu.*[2] This department includes such jobs as secretarial and legal, and almost all the duties undertaken on too small a scale to break out as a separate department and that are not regarded by top management as a highly important function.

Of course, there are significant exceptions, and they are increasing in number. For a considerable number of years the camera industry in Japan has been one in which the largest producers, recognizing the importance of sales promotion, have maintained well-organized and managed sales departments. The dominant firms in the beer industry, which also market a variety of soft drinks, likewise have

---

[2] See Business Administration Practices Specialists Study Team, International Cooperation Administration, Japan Productivity Center, *Business Administration Practices in Japan* (1959).

placed considerable emphasis on sales. Some years ago a large electrical appliance manufacturer elevated the position of the sales department in its organization and greatly expanded its functional responsibilities. This soon became the general pattern among larger electrical appliance manufacturers in the industry. Certain large producers of confectionery products and foodstuffs have also played a leading role in elevating the sales function.

No single reason can be cited for the lack of attention paid to marketing activities by producing organizations. Surely of high importance is the dominance in the Japanese economy of independent wholesale organizations. Furthermore, Japanese producers have typically been more interested in technological problems than in marketing. Perhaps the need for a well-developed internal marketing organization had simply not been recognized earlier.[3] The feeling seems to be quite common that if a product is produced with a high degree of technological efficiency, it will sell itself. Consequently, the executives of an enterprise with a modern factory often engage in intensive research to discover further improvements, but they give little thought to improvement in distribution of the product. On the other hand, with the shift of many markets in 1956–57 to buyers' markets, many manufacturers quickly became interested in learning about modern marketing. Japanese business leaders are very pragmatic.

Financial problems also take up a substantial part of the time of the executives. With existing over-all capital limitations and restrictions on investments, it is extremely difficult to secure approval or adequate financing for either plant and equipment or working capital.

In the Japanese educational system there are some good schools of commerce, but these institutions are too new and too few to have had any significant effect on the present leaders of Japanese business.

Although it is impossible to evaluate accurately the continuing influence of the traditional feudalistic social system on attitudes toward engaging in marketing activities, a negative influence can be observed even in a modern Japanese business society. For many hundreds of years before Japan reopened her doors to the Western world, a rigid social-class system existed, with the merchant placed in the lowest class. As in the medieval Western world, the merchant or

---

[3] For a general discussion of this problem see Peter F. Drucker, "Marketing and Economic Development," *Journal of Marketing*, Vol. XXII, No. 3 (January, 1958), pp. 252–59.

trader was considered to be unproductive and existing at the expense of other members of the community. Following the adoption of constitutional government, the social classes as such were abolished. Yet tradition remains strong, and business executives both young and old still hope to avoid the stigma of being classed as a "merchant." This condition may have helped Japan's early industrialization. However, it does not help to develop marketing.

Despite such obstacles, definite progress is being made in specific areas of marketing, such as product design and quality. We have observed this advancement in connection with recent imports from Japan. Also, media expenditures on advertising in 1959 were reported to be at three times the level of 1953. An increasing amount of marketing research is being done. Channels of distribution are being improved. Furthermore, the government, through the Japan Productivity Center, is active in advancing the state of marketing knowledge and its application. Businessmen, professors, and government experts who have studied marketing in the United States and Europe are very active in this work. Executives and owners from outstanding small enterprises have also been included in this educational effort. Through the example that they set in their respective enterprises and the educational work that they participate in as members of various business organizations, these leaders exert considerable influence within the important small-business sector.

There are recent reports that some wholesalers are engaging in marketing research with particular emphasis on market analysis and the forecasting of demand.[4] Over the years, wholesalers will lose their present dominant position. However, they may be expected to adjust to changing market conditions, adopt modern marketing methods, and continue to perform essential marketing functions in an economical manner.

CONCLUSION

The present distribution system, dominated by wholesalers, provides mass distribution and makes possible centralized mass production. However, the economic potential of Japan could not be developed to its fullest through this system. Only a few years ago there was a real basis for pessimism about Japan's future economic growth and stability. It looked as though conditions were being created that, in

---

[4] Small Business Market Analysis Team, International Cooperation Administration, Japan Productivity Center, *Japanese Small Enterprises and Their Market Analysis* (1961).

future years, would result in serious economic difficulties unless drastic changes in the distribution system took place. In the last five years, however, substantial changes in the direction of more modern marketing effort, with participation by manufacturers as well as wholesalers and retailers, have been initiated and pursued with some vigor. It is hoped that this movement will proceed with sufficient speed to avert all potential difficulties in the area of domestic marketing.

There remains, nevertheless, a serious deficiency in international marketing. Internationally, lack of responsibility by producers for the marketing of products, together with a failure by wholesalers to promote sound market development, has tended to produce unstable market penetration. Furthermore, exports have not been distributed over a sufficiently wide range of goods, nor has geographic market coverage been wide enough, to meet Japan's total export needs.

Large-scale export marketing is inherently difficult. It is costly. A large investment of capital is required to establish channels of distribution and to develop demand. There are substantial risks involved. Nevertheless, it may well be that in the future the exporters of all countries with a large export business will gradually have to make the necessary effort to contribute to the development of markets abroad. It no longer appears sufficient to ship goods on a price basis into markets developed by another nation's producers. The economic strains and the poor relations which result are well known.

Of course, progress in foreign marketing will be made in modest steps. For Japan, however, there is an urgency for more leaders in business and government to initiate and to support such steps. On the optimistic side, if Japan's exports could be expanded to levels sufficient to obtain the imports necessary for full employment and growth, the resulting opportunities for domestic industry and the social benefits would be enormous.

AUSTRALIA

For many years wholesalers have held a dominant place in the Australian distribution system, but today they are experiencing some of the identical trends that have altered the concept of wholesaling in other countries.

Noting similarities between Australian and American wholesaling, the author emphasizes their differences, which he attributes to the socio-economic circumstances of the continent: wide dispersion of large coastal cities easily accessible by water routes, lagging industrialization of smaller towns, and radial, rather than interconnecting, rail facilities.

These circumstances have nourished the development of wholesalers who combine merchandising and shipping service, provide national market coverage, and integrate, for agricultural products, assembly and dispersive activities.

Recent developments affecting traditional patterns of wholesaling include movement of population into larger centers, decentralization of industry into smaller centers, and improvement of both transportation and communication. At the same time, there have been changes in scale of manufacturing and of retailing. Together, these changes have led to producer-initiated and retailer-initiated circumvention of established wholesaling institutions, to which the latter have reacted by improvement and adaptation of their services.

Wholesaling in Australia

JOHN S. EWING *

The Australian market strikingly resembles that of the United States in many respects. Language, legal and political structure, standard of living, way of life, and particularly willingness to consume are comparable or rapidly becoming so. Research, advertising agencies, channels of distribution, and other elements of the marketing function impress American observers as generally familiar.

ENVIRONMENTAL INFLUENCES ON THE DEVELOPMENT OF AUSTRALIAN WHOLESALING

The Development of National Wholesalers

Despite the impression of similarity between the Australian and American marketing scenes, there are marked and significant dissimilarities. Particularly there exists a fundamental difference in wholesaling: the preponderance of Australian wholesaling organizations operating well beyond local markets into coverage of the entire continent—contrasting with the American tendency to function in smaller areas such as the West Coast, New England, or groups of states in the Midwest or South.

Paradoxically, the geographical structure and extent of wholesaling operations in Australia result, in part at least, from the extreme isolation of one area of population concentration from another, a circumstance that could have been expected to lead to the development of local wholesalers rather than regional or national. However, cities grew slowly in the early days of the country, and industrialization followed agricultural activities at an equally slow pace. Australians were forced by the nature of the continent to live along the coastal fringes for the most part, their settlements were small and scattered, mobility was much less common than in the United States, and communication for many years was by ship.

* Dr. John S. Ewing is visiting Associate Professor of International Trade and Marketing, Graduate School of Business, Stanford University, Stanford, California. Much of the basic research was done by Donald Fraser, M.B.A. (Stanford), Brisbane, Queensland.

Shipping companies recognized that they were particularly able to enter wholesaling, since their control of transportation gave them access to sufficient, if separated, markets. They expanded into the national wholesalers of today and, although railway and road construction in time diminished the importance of coastal transport, the wholesaling activities which began as offshoots of this continued. Some of the old companies proved unable to adapt to the new competition from local wholesalers, made possible by the growth of cities and better transportation, but others were markedly successful. Burns Philp is one example of a nation-wide Australian wholesaler with its origins in shipping. Organization and contacts developed in the early days of Australian settlement and expansion helped Burns Philp to operate successfully despite the rise of local competition. Diversification into other activities contributed further to stability and growth.

The Development of Integrated Wholesalers

Diversification was, to some extent, a characteristic of the Australian shipper/wholesalers from fairly early times and also reflected the environment in which they flourished. The major factors and their effects seem to have been these:

a) The Agricultural Economy and Isolation. Unlike farmers in much of the United States and other countries during early development, the Australian agriculturist operated (and still does) beyond easy reach of markets. The shipping companies which sprang up to provide communication and transportation found themselves buying local products to transport back to large centers for sale, doing this on their own account, as well as on an agent or brokerage basis. This was particularly true in the Pacific Islands along the north coast of the country, where coconuts were an important crop and where copra buying was one of the functions into which the shippers soon ventured.

The buying of agricultural items and the selling of the manufactured and other goods needed by the settlers led to the establishment of trading posts. Some of these were purely retail operations; others developed into combined wholesale/retail outlets, as market areas expanded and other retailers entered the scene. For some of the national wholesalers, retailing through controlled outlets became an important activity, presumably as important as the shipping and wholesale functions, although information on relative profitability is not available.

b) *The Pattern of Industrialization.* Unlike the United States, Australian small cities, towns, and villages seldom industrialized significantly. With a few exceptions, nothing like the textile and paper-mill towns of New England or the factory towns of the Middle West developed. This was partly the result of a lack of water for power, partly of the Australian's desire to live in ever-enlarging cities (Sydney, Melbourne, and Brisbane account for about 43 per cent of the total population of Australia), and later of a system of rail tariffs that had the effect of discouraging industrial decentralization.

The small centers relied and still rely for their existence on their role as marketplaces and, in these centers, the trading posts and later stores of the shipper/wholesaler were important. Because of the scarcity of local industry from which to draw, because of the over-all market areas served by the wholesalers, and because of the problems of securing goods for sale, some of them integrated backward into manufacture. Such manufacture included clothing, footwear, foodstuffs, beverages, and in time the companies offered more complete product ranges under their own names but not always of their own manufacture.

The Development of Local Wholesalers

Local wholesalers were the product of improved communications, larger cities, and industrialization in those cities. There the contributing environmental factors were more nearly identical with those of the United States, and such wholesalers tend to be more comparable.

Again, however, the size of Australia and its sparse population have produced some differences in the local or regional wholesaler pattern. The most significant of these seems to be the multiple role performed by some wholesale organizations. In a few cases there are organizations that sell the products of a manufacturer who may have some ownership interest; distribute exclusively in some areas for other, non-competitive makers; and act as wholesalers for still more manufacturers and distributors. While concern has been expressed by some principals over the degrees of effort that one is capable of exerting on behalf of one or the other maker, the limitations of the Australian market in terms of population and its enormous expanse in land size present little alternative if the widest kind of coverage at reasonable cost is to be secured. Some changes are appearing and are discussed below.

The Development of Organized Markets

Rail transportation within Australia is a complex affair, made difficult by a variety of gauges. Road communications are relatively extensive but far from comparable with those of the United States, since the population/cost ratio is clearly unfavorable in Australia. These circumstances have combined (and have helped to produce) the large cities, and, as a result, the country presents the picture more of transportation facilities feeding into a few large cities than of an interlocking network with no undue emphasis on any one metropolis.

These large cities tend to be self-contained market areas. While it is true that they are not self-contained industrially, the historical pattern of importing (and Australia was, in terms of manufactured goods, primarily an importer until the end of World War II, with imports still significant in over-all trade) was for agents in each market to import for that market, without too much regard for the centers beyond it. In other words, an agent in Sydney might confine his activities to Sydney and New South Wales; one in Melbourne would do likewise for his city and Victoria; a third in Brisbane would concern himself with that city and Queensland.

Improved communications and the development of industry have altered this picture considerably and tended to diminish the importance of one city over another; manufacturers seek markets well beyond their own center of operation. In agricultural goods, however, the primary central market serving a surrounding area continues important in Australia.

a) The Livestock Market. Specific comparisons with American primary central markets are possible, since the trend of development has been markedly different in Australia. Cattle are still shipped from the ranges in small lots to the primary central market, and feed-lot operations along American lines are nonexistent.

Wages in primary central markets have not risen in Australia to the degree that they have in the United States, so that processors have not been stimulated in this way to develop producing- and shipping-point local markets. Along with this, Australian population movements have been from smaller into larger centers, with much less decentralization than in this country, so that consuming needs tend to support primary central markets.

Finally, freight-rate structures have been so devised as to encourage movement of agricultural goods into rail centers, unlike the situation in the United States, which has made it possible for livestock to be shipped from points west of Chicago to the East Coast, rather than from Chicago, as in earlier days. Even if Australian freight rates had a somewhat different basis, the population concentrations again operate to encourage livestock movements into the central markets in the state capitals, which are the large cities.

b) The Fruit and Vegetable Market. The similarity between Australian and American fruit and vegetable wholesale markets is much more marked, since decentralization has not taken place in the United States to the degree shown in livestock wholesaling. One phenomenon of the American situation has not yet been fully imitated in Australia but shows signs of developing: the improvement in truck transportation, enabling corporate and voluntary chain groups in urban centers to purchase direct from producing regions and also enabling direct shipment from the producing areas to cities which formerly purchased from the larger organized central fruit and vegetable markets.

In Australia, lack of such efficient transportation for perishables has so far tended to prevent direct shipments bypassing the central market. On the other hand, in Australia there are primary central produce markets on a much smaller scale in many of the cities, to some extent a continuing reflection of the isolation and poor communications of earlier days.

EVIDENT TRENDS IN AUSTRALIAN WHOLESALING

Decentralization of Agricultural Wholesaling

During the last few years, Australian retailing has been influenced by the American movement to self-service, supermarket retailing, and stores clearly modeled on the United States pattern have been built. Some of these have been opened by relatively small operators acting only locally; others have been developed by large chain organizations previously essentially in the variety field.

The variety chains particularly have recognized that agricultural marketing through primary central markets with backhauls to smaller markets is costly and that decentralization or direct purchase and shipment from the producing areas offer room for savings. While there has been little sign that either these or other large buyers of food products intend to enter direct growing, through either ownership or contract, some of them have begun direct purchase from growers or brokers in the primary production areas.

Rail communication in Australia has been improved, notably by the standardization of gauge between Melbourne and Sydney, which will eliminate one transshipment point. In addition, government policy now is to encourage industry to move to the smaller centers, and this policy, if effective, will change the traditional market structure. Other factors, as yet intangible but nevertheless likely to be important, are the development of cheap electric power through such schemes as the Snowy River Project, the possibility that oil may be discovered in commercial quantities, and the exploitation of iron-ore deposits in Western Australia. These should support industrial decentralization, and this, in its turn and further supported by improved communications, will probably lead to more and more by-passing of central markets in favor of shorter hauls and relatively local processing and sale.

Bypassing of Wholesalers by Manufacturers

In the postwar period, Australian wholesalers have been affected seriously by two significant changes in the distribution pattern, each of which has been conspicuous on the American scene:

  a) Manufacturers selling direct to large organizations in the capital cities and provincial cities, without setting up a comprehensive wholesale organization.

  b) Manufacturers selling on an even wider scale by setting up their own wholesale organizations. This latter trend means initially the addition of a wholesaler to the marketing structure and not the immediate replacement of the original wholesaler by the manufacturer.

These tendencies for the manufacturer to bypass the wholesaler have had serious consequences for traditional wholesalers and for consumers in small Australian country towns, because of the wide geographical spread and separation of these towns. For example, in the state of Queensland, where smaller provincial markets are very remote from primary central markets, and to a lesser degree in the other states, manufacturers have been concentrating on the profitable, easy-to-sell parts of the market represented by the larger centers, when setting up their own wholesale channels.

This leaves to the traditional wholesaler the job of handling the attenuated lines of supply to the remote areas. Such selling is extremely uneconomic for the wholesaler, unless he can compensate in the form of higher prices which must be reflected in higher retail prices to consumers. In the past, the Australian wholesaler has been able to spread the costs of this uneconomic work over the "easier-to-supply" retailers in cities and large provincial centers. The change in pattern squeezes him between reducing areas of supply and increasing costs.

Changes in Grocery Wholesaling

The development of self-service retailing on a large scale, which may effect the pattern of agricultural wholesaling, has had an effect on wholesaling of other food and grocery products in Australia. The large retail food chains have developed their own wholesale organizations and private brands; under Australian antitrust law or the lack of it, there is nothing to prevent the kind of integration that has been attacked in the United States under the Robinson-Patman Act, in such cases as the A & P.

Australian wholesalers have combated this competition in two ways: by opening their own self-service wholesale centers and by setting up their own manufacturing facilities and retail outlets. Self-service wholesale centers are thriving in Australia, since small, independent retailers regard these as a means of helping them to fight lower prices to consumers in the big chain outlets. It has been reported that the self-service wholesalers have been able to lower the average price of orders by 5 per cent to the independent storekeeper. In addition, they enable the small retailer to buy in small quantities rather than in bulk; he appears to prefer serving himself and thereby eliminating pressure from salesmen; and the warehouses are open for night-stocking, which is the most convenient time for the independent retailer to buy. In 1960, one self-service warehouse was opening each month, and included in their operations were electronic billing equipment.

Trade authorities feel, however, that the rapid growth of self-service wholesalers will fill only a passing need for the small independent retailer, since Australia is following the American pattern and small stores are declining in number. They expand in size or go out of business, and, as they grow, they attract manufacturers who can sell direct, or they join buying groups with other efficient independent operators. The small, self-service wholesaler is also unlikely to increase in numbers but is more apt to decline, working as he does on a net margin of 1.25 per cent and facing heavy competition.

Future trends seem likely to follow the pattern of the co-operative wholesale group in the United States, providing services to large independent retailers. While voluntary chains, wholesaler-sponsored, exist in Australia, they are by no means as strong as in New Zealand. However, a modification of the concept introduced by a Queensland wholesaler in 1960 may have some significance for the future. He selected certain outlets on which to concentrate, provided uniform accounting procedures, advised on store layout, and offered the advantages of large-scale buying through grouped orders, and attained considerable success.

Competitive Activities by General Wholesalers

Some Australian wholesalers have concluded that the single-middleman function is a thing of the past. Typical of a number of old established firms is K. L. Ballantyne of Melbourne, who now operates a large self-service department and, through subsidiaries, is also engaged in manufacturing, packing, and importing of various foods for the grocery and allied trades. Its trade dealings have been diversified to the extent that it now serves independents', chains', and grocers' buying groups.

Thomas Brown and Sons, another large wholesaler, also has several subsidiaries. These include canvas and jute; a packing organization for many grocery lines; millinery; rum; and a retail grocery chain. Like all wholesalers, Thomas Brown faces the problem of increasing costs, which cannot always be offset by a corresponding relative increase in profits. Between 1950 and 1959, Australian wages in the wholesale trade increased by 91 per cent, while wholesale prices moved up by only 53 per cent. Looking at Thomas Brown, an Australian financial journal summed up the situation of the wholesaler in Australia today: ". . . Thomas Brown and Sons, Ltd. is showing signs that it does not intend to sit back and remain exclusively a wholesaler in a world where wholesalers are being increasingly bypassed by manufacturers. . . ." [1] The wheel seems to have come full circle, in that the old shippers who became integrated wholesalers in some fashion set the pattern for today's wholesaler to follow.

[1] *Australian Financial Review*, November 10, 1960.

AFRICA

The proportions of social cause and marketing effect in this paper are the reverse of the usual, and the bulk of the analysis consists of a broad but detailed statement of the Tropical African environment in which the institution of marketing is evolving. The myriad facts concerning social structure, customs, culture, and economic and political systems are replete with inferences which only a trained student of marketing would draw or appreciate. Skillful use is made of an inductive approach to an interpretation of marketing as a social phenomenon.

The range of marketing practices and attitudes in Tropical Africa is as wide as the diversity of stages of civilization there. Because primitive, as well as underdeveloped, conditions prevail, the usual misconceptions about marketing abound. Depreciation of what marketing is and does has excluded the natives in some countries from the work of marketing and has opened opportunity for foreigners to engage in the activity. This transferral of marketing to non-Africans has in the past been accentuated by the colonizing programs of Europeans. Such division of work, however, is now changing, as through education and experience the African nationals come to understand marketing better.

One of the significant developments in wholesaling in Africa has been the creation of Marketing Boards as means of increasing efficiency in distribution and of protecting local producers from exploitation by distributors. These quasi-governmental organizations represent an approach to a universal problem which in other places has been solved by private enterprise or by producers' and consumers' co-operatives. The breaking-up of old customs and practices is a leaven working many such changes in wholesaling.

179

Wholesaling in Tropical Africa

DAVID CARSON *

Tropical Africa affords an excellent example of the relationship that exists between the socio-economic circumstances of a country and its wholesaling system and practices. The nations of that part of Africa represent an amalgamation of primitive traditions, nationalistic aspirations, conflicting group interests, and technical disparities introduced through cultural assimilation. It is an area of wide diversity in geographic, social, political, and economic conditions. Within that environment, wholesaling is technically simple; in contrast to that in many other countries, it is undeveloped. This, however, is but one of several phases of marketing that are unique in Africa.

GEOGRAPHIC FACTORS

A principal determinant of the marketing task and system in Tropical Africa is the geographic character of the continent. Its vast size, the diversity of its climate and vegetation, and the change occurring in its natural productiveness as a result of both physical and human forces—these are some of the geo-economic factors that determine the manner of marketing there.

Tropical Africa is composed of twenty-two sovereign states [1] and

* Dr. David Carson is Professor of Business Administration and Coordinator, Marketing Curriculum, at the College of Business Administration, Boston University. He received assistance in conducting research in this area from the African Studies Program, Boston University, and especially from Professor Mark Karp, Economist for the Program.

[1] Sovereign nations (as of December 1, 1961): Cameroun (republic), Central African Republic (member of the French Community), Chad (Republic of Chad, member of the French Community), Republic of Congo (former Belgian Congo), Republic of Congo (Brazzaville, member of the French Community), Dahomey (Republic of Dahomey), Ethiopia (Kingdom of Ethiopia, or Abyssinia), Gabon Republic (member of the French Community), Ghana (republic), Guinea (Republic of Guinea), Ivory Coast (Republic of the Ivory Coast), Liberia (Negro Republic of Liberia), Mali (Republic of Mali), Mauritania (Islamic Republic of Mauritania), Niger (Republic of the Niger), Nigeria (Federation of Nigeria, member of the British Commonwealth), Senegal (Republic of Senegal, member of the French Community), Sierra Leone (member of the British Commonwealth), Somalia (republic), Sudan (Republic of the Sudan), Togo Republic, Upper Volta (Republic of the Upper Volta).

twenty territorial governments,[2] which are affiliated in varying relationships with the United Kingdom, Portugal, Spain, Belgium, and France. It includes, in other words, the entire continental area of Africa with the exception of the predominantly Arabic-speaking nations skirting the Mediterranean littoral and the Republic of South Africa. Tropical Africa also includes some coastal islands, such as Zanzibar, although not all offshore islands, such as the Malagasy Republic (Madagascar).

Together, these countries have a population almost equal to that of the United States (175 million); it is spread, however, over an area of 8.5 million square miles of land—about three times the size of the United States, excluding Alaska. Africa as a whole is the most land-locked of the continents, for, in spite of its 18,900 miles of coast line, there are only 1.6 miles of coast line per square mile of territory.

The physical conditions of this part of Africa are extremely diverse. Temperatures are generally high, but climatic conditions range from those of the perpetually snow-capped mountains, to the vast temperate plateaus, to the steaming, hot coastal zones. Rainfall also varies considerably from region to region, being much higher on the western than on the eastern coast. Precipitation is markedly seasonal, and its intensity has a wide range. A consequence of great marketing significance is the existence of three basic types of vegetation: forest, grassland, and desert.

The forces of equatorial heat, aridity, and tropical rainfall have combined to produce erosion problems of great proportions. These have been accentuated by human utilization of the natural resources. For centuries a practice of shifting agriculture has been followed. One wooded district after another was burned and its fertile soil used until depleted. Before new forest growth could again cover an abandoned district, former agricultural plots regain their fertility, increas-

---

[2] Other territories: Angola (Portuguese overseas province), Basutoland (British colony, enclosed by the Republic of South Africa), Bechuanaland (British protectorate), French Somaliland (overseas territory), Gambia (British colony and protectorate), Kenya (British colony and protectorate, moving toward self-government), Mozambique (Portuguese overseas province), Northern Rhodesia (British protectorate, member of the Federation of Rhodesia and Nyasaland), Nyasaland (British protectorate, member of the Federation of Rhodesia and Nyasaland), Portuguese Guinea (overseas province), Ruanda (Belgian UN trusteeship), San Tome and Principe (The Islands of San Tome and Principe, Portuguese overseas province), Southern Rhodesia (self-governing British colony, member of the Federation of Rhodesia and Nyasaland), Spanish Guinea (colony), Spanish Sahara (colony), Swaziland (British protectorate), Tanganyika (British UN trusteeship. Achieved sovereignty on December 9, 1961, as a member of the British Commonwealth), Uganda (British protectorate, moving toward sovereignty), Urundi (Belgian UN trusteeship), Zanzibar (British protectorate, moving toward sovereignty; includes Island of Pemba).

ing population sometimes forced a return to abandoned land, although new cropping may have been virtually impossible. Because of intensive evaporation and because of the runoff caused by lack of soil cover, the beneficial effects of the rainfall, though scanty, were lost. In the area bordering the Sahara, the desert is slowly advancing. How to preserve the fertility of the poorly structured and leached soil which covers most of the savannas and the semiarid regions is a problem of no small proportions. In addition to yielding a small assortment of marketable products, these conditions also produce a market limited by want of purchasing power.

ANTHROPOLOGICAL AND ECOLOGICAL FACTORS

Trade in Tropical Africa dates back several millennia. East Indian as well as Near Eastern nations of the ancient world had trading contacts with mid-Africa centuries before the Christian Era, and King Solomon, among others, is believed to have traded with regions as far south as Tanganyika. It was not until the eighth century of the Christian Era, however, that, as a result of the spread of Islam, active colonization was begun in the regions south of the Sahara. This movement was accelerated during the following several centuries, with active trading ties being developed with the Arabian peninsula and with the Arabic-speaking nations bordering the Mediterranean.

Colonization

Modern colonization began with the Portuguese in the fifteenth century with the establishment of forts and trading posts on the west side of the continent, followed by similar developments on the east coast, largely as way stations to India and the Far East. Trade with the natives grew slowly until the seventeenth century, when the demand for slaves for the Americas spurred the growth of trading centers on the west coast, from Dakar to the mouth of the Congo. The Portuguese and other Western European colonizers of the New World purchased slaves from tribal chieftains at these markets, and they occasionally made forays into the interior themselves to capture slaves. Ivory was a side line of these markets. This international trade was generally characterized by barter, although a primitive type of monetary system did make possible an elementary form of market economy in certain regions. With the abolition of the slave trade by the British in 1807, the economic significance of most African colonies declined, and, excluding the British and Dutch agricultural settlements in South Africa, most European interests were centered about unimportant trading posts along the coasts. With the exception of Ethiopia, Tropical Africa was largely a maze of shifting tribal states by the middle of the nineteenth century.

Explorations into the interior during the following decades made the European powers aware of the great potential wealth both above and below the surface of the earth, and, by the start of the 1880's, these powers—with France, Great Britain, and Germany in the lead— were trampling over one another in their race to "fulfill the white man's mission of bringing 'civilization' to the benighted natives." The Berlin Conference of 1884–85 laid down certain "rules" for this colonization. By 1900, the partitioning of the continent was practically complete, with only Ethiopia and Liberia remaining independent. Territories were acquired at various times for different reasons, and some changed hands several times. Frontiers were drawn and redrawn as a result of bargaining among the colonial powers, generally without regard for the natives' ethnic and economic interests. After World War II, a number of independent nations emerged, and other territories continued to strive for sovereignty. The political and economic divisions and exploitations wrought by the European colonizers, coupled with centuries-old ethnic and tribal dissensions, have posed serious problems for these emerging nations.

Population

The character of Tropical Africa as a market is colored by the composition and dispersion of its population. More than one million of Tropical Africa's inhabitants are non-African. The Africans themselves have been classified into ten major ethnic groups and approximately 750–1,000 subgroups. Although language divisions are roughly akin to ethnic divisions, in addition to the Western European tongues at least three African languages serve as *linguae francae* over broad areas: Hausa in the western and central regions, Swahili in the east, and Fula in the west. Amharic is the dominant language of Ethiopia.

Half of the approximately 750,000 Europeans in Tropical Africa are concentrated in four territories: Southern Rhodesia, Angola, the Republic of Congo, and the Republic of Senegal; they tend to reside in large cities such as Dakar, Leopoldville, and Salisbury. Because of past or present colonial interests, almost 90 per cent of these Europeans are of British, Portuguese, French, Belgian, or Italian origin.

The second largest minority group, the Asians, have their origins largely in India, Pakistan, and the Arabic lands of the Near East. About 300,000 of the roughly 400,000 "Asians" live in the British East

African territories, mainly in urban centers. Even though fewer than 10 per cent of the Africans live in urban areas, there are some sizable cities that are entirely African in origin, the largest being Ibadan, a Nigerian city of 300,000.

The population density of about 20 per square mile for Tropical Africa compares with 50 per square mile for the United States, but this comparison becomes rather meaningless when one considers the vast wastelands of Tropical Africa. Yet some districts are actually overpopulated, and there are striking differences in the patterns of dispersion from region to region and within regions. Most economic growth has been concentrated in "islands" accounting for only 4 per cent of Tropical Africa's total area but probably exporting at least 85 per cent of the value of products entering world trade.

Consumption Characteristics

Consumption tastes of Africans have long been influenced by cultural transmission. For centuries, Africans have adopted and adapted customs and habits of foreigners residing in their lands, and even today residual influences of early Arab traders and settlers are evident both in East and West Africa. The processes of cultural change have emphasized Occidentalization, particularly in the manner of living, with Africans of relatively meager incomes purchasing simple Western-style household furniture and perhaps a radio, a sewing machine, a kitchen range, and several electric lamps. The small but growing group of middle-class Africans—civil servants, teachers, artisans, traders, more prosperous farmers—also purchase motorcycles or even automobiles, phonographs, refrigerators, and more diverse household furniture and furnishings. Africans are not blind followers of Western ways, however, as indicated by the Masai tribesmen, who prefer to wear their skins and blankets to shirt and suits, and by the large number of Ghanaian and Nigerian legislators and other august citizens, who prefer their traditional native garb to Western attire.

Public Health

Problems of health and disease reach formidable proportions in Tropical Africa, affecting men, plants, and animals, sometimes in very complex ways. Some progress has been made in introducing more sanitary living conditions and better dietary standards, with widespread spraying and other forms of preventive medicine becoming normal governmental functions. Yet the over-all incidence of disease and the general and infant mortality rate remain high.

SOCIAL FACTORS

Marketing in Tropical Africa is also influenced by a number of social factors. Despite the pervasiveness of traditional social structure and attitudes, social changes have affected every nation, region, and tribe. The family group—bastion of social and economic existence in most rural districts—is rapidly changing, as men, in particular, move to urban districts, plantations, and mines to meet the demands of a more highly industrialized society; as the desire for greater material rewards for their efforts makes men less willing to share their earnings with their family and kinship groups; as indigenous cropping practices and land-tenure systems are cast aside; and as newer forms of transportation and communications open men's eyes and minds to the outside world. Old food taboos are being discarded; traditional trades are falling by the wayside, and new ones are springing up; money is replacing cattle and other possessions as the primary form of wealth and of exchange; pills are superseding panaceas prescribed by witch doctors; and Western-style clothing and homes are becoming more common, even in remote districts. The pace of these changes has been particularly rapid during the past decade.

New Social Pressures

Numerous pressures of marketing significance have accompanied these changes. This migration of men to industrialized districts has brought many social problems, both to the industrialized districts and to the rural "home" districts. Economic changes have caused shifts in the status of many occupations, a case in point being the traditional blacksmith guilds of Nigeria, which are gradually decaying and being threatened with social degradation, whereas unorganized groups of automotive mechanics have arisen, lacking in social solidarity and in standards of craftsmanship. Many Africans employed in the money sector of the economy continue to share their earnings with their families and more distant kin, whereas others prefer to spend their income on eye-catching clothing, trinkets, bicycles, and other personal trappings of material success.

Because of tribal customs, many Africans have refused to become tradesmen, especially retailers, lest their kinfolk help themselves to the merchandise inventories, viewing them as their relatives' personal possessions. Other African businessmen behave as though their enterprises were solely family affairs, refusing to employ outsiders, and distributing business income solely on a paternalistic basis.

Women in Trade

In some regions of Tropical Africa—particularly in Nigeria, Ghana, and Sierra Leone—most retail trades are in the hands of women, referred to as "mammies." Although most of them are petty business women, a few have built up retail and even wholesale enterprises, with sales equivalent to hundreds of thousands of dollars per year. Most of the retail textile business in these countries is in the hands of women. In view of their frequent illiteracy, credit and other operations are often carried on entirely from memory. Some husbands *expect* their wives to support themselves by such enterprises, and often their children and husbands as well!

Minority Groups

In general, the typical African has an antagonistic attitude toward tradesmen; not so much for import-export and wholesale firms, whom he does not contact directly, but toward the thousands of smaller wholesale and retail businesses which serve him. In many West African areas those firms are owned and managed by Levantines— people whose origins lay in Syria, Lebanon, Palestine, Greece, Turkey, Cyprus, the Arabian Peninsula, Egypt, and elsewhere in the Near East and its environs. In East Africa these smaller wholesale and retail tradesmen are likely to have roots in India, in Pakistan, or in the Arabic nations. With the exception of the Arabic peoples resident in these regions for centuries, most of these entrepreneurs (or their ancestors) moved to Tropical Africa during the great period of colonial expansion preceding World War I, some to settle there permanently and others to remain just long enough to build up a nest egg and return "home." Along with the Europeans, they persuaded the African farmer to grow products for export, supplying much of the necessary capital, buying up and shipping the surpluses, and, in general, carrying considerable risks. They organized the distribution of imported and domestic merchandise in many of these countries, with some of the more enterprising Levantine and Indian small-scale traders pushing far back into the "bush," where they still purchase produce from the farmers and, in turn, retail a limited assortment of merchandise to them.

For instance, in Tanganyika an estimated 90 per cent of the export crops raised by Africans is marketed through Asian middlemen, and African hostility toward the Indian minority is therefore increasing. Lack of capital, of interest, and of know-how on the part of Africans has conspired to keep much of this small-scale trading in the hands of non-Africans, though a few nations are taking steps to encourage Africans to become successful middlemen through training programs and the granting of rudimentary financial assistance. Most internal trade in Nigeria has, on the contrary, been in the hands of Africans for centuries.

Throughout Tropical Africa the European, Levantine, and Asian minority groups stand apart from Africans, not only because of the color of their skin, or of their concentrated ownership, and administration of certain types of business enterprises, but also because of their separate social, economic, cultural, and familial ties. In larger cities they tend to reside in their own quarters. Even in many large business enterprises there has been little administrative mixing of races. In recent years, however, some non-African companies have made concerted attempts to integrate Africans into company management. Even so, large numbers of firms owned by non-Africans continue to be conducted as closed family affairs, with their owners and employees living, insofar as possible, as though they were in London, Paris, Beirut, Bombay, Lisbon, or New York rather than in Tropical Africa.

ECONOMIC FACTORS

Subsistence Economy

Some form of money economy is known to have existed in West Africa for at least the last four centuries, but until recently much of this area's livelihood was based almost entirely on a subsistence economy. Under this system the peasant tribesmen obtained from their lands, forests, and waters by their own labor not only the necessities of life, as they viewed them, but also many comforts and even luxuries. It is estimated that 69 per cent of the total cultivated area is devoted to subsistence production today, occupying approximately 60 per cent of the male adult population. For 1950–52, the imputed money value of these activities varied from as high as 65 per cent of the total gross national product of Tanganyika, to 22 per cent in the (Belgian) Congo, down to 3½ per cent in Southern Rhodesia, as against only 1½ per cent for the United States.

Subsistence economies were organized to provide for the economic needs and resources of self-contained rural communities, and they offered a measure of economic security to family and kinship groups. In general, these economies lack specialization on a significant scale, although there are some notable exceptions, such as the production of handicrafts in Northern Nigeria. There is little or no planned production of surpluses for sale, and exchange is viewed as an incidental margin rather than as a primary objective of the economic activity. Technological processes tend to remain stationary. This pattern of economic stagnation is gradually being broken, as small-scale agricultural producers take up the cultivation of cash crops, largely for export; as large-scale agricultural, mining, manufacturing, and other industries provide opportunities for outside employment; as immigrants from more economically advanced nations settle in the area; and as kinship ties are weakened by increasing geographic and social mobility. Today most nations mix subsistence and money economies, with the transition being away from the former and toward the latter. Many farmers, however, still lack confidence in the marketing structure, because early experiences with cash crops, such as cotton, proved unfortunate. Therefore, the movement is not entirely uninhibited.

As a result of the widespread subsistence economy, coupled with large-scale unemployment in industrialized as well as in rural districts, cash incomes are very small by Western standards. The average annual per capita income barely reaches $100 in "wealthy" nations, such as Ghana, Nigeria, the Ivory Coast Republic, and Uganda, and it is approximately half this amount in more depressed countries, such as Angola, Ethiopia, and Somalia. Not all these small incomes can be spent for retail goods, moreover, since rents, taxes, "bride wealth," and other requirements also take their toll. In spite of these low current income levels, they are nevertheless several times higher than the pre-World War II figures in most nations, largely due to price rises in world markets during and after the war for major export commodities, including cocoa, tin, columbite, etc.

Tropical Africa has been only sparsely prospected, and data concerning its natural resources are necessarily rough, tentative estimates. Nonetheless, the physical wealth already known to exist is impressive. Three eighths of the world's total water energy at ordinary minimal flow is contained in this area. Yet barely 1 per cent of the world's total hydroelectric power is being produced, although significant developments are currently either being studied or are under construction.

Agriculture

The mainstay of the economy is the primitive agriculture performed by Africans. There are some important exceptions, notably the large European-run palm-kernal plantations in the Congo, large-scale British farms in East Africa (tea, sisal, peanuts), and Liberian rubber plantations on lease to American companies. Increasing amounts of native produce are also flowing into marketing channels, much of it bound for export. In the West the most important items include cocoa, oil-palm products (for use in margarine, soap, and candles), coffee, peanuts, and cotton. Since these products are generally grown by very small operators, the bulking process is necessarily a very significant economic activity. Commercial fishing is being developed in several coastal areas, and the commercial exploitation of valuable timber stands continues to be important in the Western equatorial forests.

Minerals

A wealth of mineral resources is known to exist in Tropical Africa. Some of the world's greatest known resources of copper lie in the Federation of Rhodesia and Nyasaland; deposits of uranium, copper, cobalt, tin, and other metals are in the Congo; significant amounts of manganese and bauxite exist in Ghana; tin and columbite are found in Nigeria; and commercially valuable deposits of gold and diamonds are posited in several sectors along the West Coast. Iron, coal, and oil deposits are also important, although restricted to relatively few regions. Impressive as it is, this catalogue of known mineral wealth is incomplete. Many deposits lie in remote areas where commercial exploitation so far has been restricted by lack of adequate transportation facilities, but this hurdle will surely be overcome in time.

Manufacturing

Manufacturing is the least developed segment of the economy in most regions. Although some significant expansion has taken place in a limited number of districts during the last 15 years, the growth has occurred from a very low base and is still largely restricted to primary processing of agricultural, mineral, and forestry raw materials supplemented by the manufacture of the more elementary textile, home-building, and household products. Southern Rhodesia, a rare exception, has developed manufacturing in many fields, including the basic production of iron and steel, and the Federation of Rhodesia and Nyasaland, as a whole, processes copper and cobalt ores into metals in modern smelters and refineries. Similar strides have been made in the Congo, particularly in chemicals.

Trade

Apart from the domestic trade within any of the countries of Tropical Africa, the majority of their trade is with Western Europe and North America. Approximately 75–80 per cent of their recorded foreign trade is with those areas, whereas only 10 per cent of it is among the African nations themselves. Transportation and communication difficulties, limited purchasing power, and similarities of products in many of the countries account for the yet small amount of inter-African trade. It is believed, however, that the 10 per cent of foreign trade which is of such character is understated, because of failure to record such transactions as completely as overseas trade.

The tertiary or distributive segment of Tropical Africa's economy is unique because of two institutions: (1) major trading companies and (2) the Marketing Boards. A third institution—co-operatives—though not currently important, is growing rapidly and has considerable potential significance.

Major Trading Companies. Most foreign trade is conducted by a small number of import-export companies of foreign origin, principally reflecting current or former colonial ruling powers, with a sprinkling of Levantine firms in the west and of Asian and Arabic firms in the east. It is estimated that six or seven companies handle between two thirds and three fourths of the entire foreign trade of West Africa, where oligopoly is more characteristic than in East Africa. As a rule, these companies extend their buying and selling activities far beyond foreign trade by collecting produce from farms and from other sources of primary materials and by distributing a wide variety of finished consumer goods at the wholesale level and, at times, at the retail level as well.

Such concentration of trade has been produced by several factors. Non-Africans have made concerted effort to prevent Africans from engaging in this business. One form this has taken has been the reluctance of extra-territorial banks to grant credit and accommodations to African businessmen. Cutthroat competition among European trading companies, as well as their mergers and cartels, has made it impossible for many lesser firms to remain in business. Moreover, the control of trade has been preserved through tight systems of franchising. On the other hand, it is claimed that such concentration merely reflects the farsightedness, efficiency, and entrepreneurial astuteness of those major traders.

The largest trading firm of Tropical Africa is the United Africa Company, an affiliate of Unilever, Ltd. The United Africa Company is reputed to carry on over one billion dollars worth of trade annually, most of it in West Africa from Dakar to the Congo, although its operations in East Africa and in the Near East are also sizable. The firm is said to handle at least one third of the entire import trade of the West African sterling area and only a somewhat lesser proportion of the export trade. Its purchases cover all major primary products exported from the region: palm oil, palm kernels, cotton, sesame seeds, copra, kola, peanuts, hides, skins, rubber, wood, and minerals. Sales of its wholesale and retail subsidiaries include every type of import known to Africa. The largest single retail outlet, the Kingsway Store of Lagos, has over 70 selling departments. The company also owns large palm-oil and rubber plantations, bulking and processing plants for primary products, a huge sawmill, and consumer-goods plants. Because of its size, it has often been a primary target of African nationalists, but in recent years it has been a leader in training Africans to assume managerial positions previously held by non-Africans.

Marketing Boards. Commodity marketing boards are organizations of government-appointed men who regulate the buying and selling of peanuts, palm kernels and oil, cocoa, cottonseed and lint, and small quantities of other commodities. They are found particularly in certain West African territories formerly or currently ruled by Great Britain and are most influential today in Nigeria, Ghana, Sierra Leone, and Gambia.

Before World War II, the trading companies puchased these commodities at low prices, using them as a cheap and convenient means of remitting proceeds to Europe for the purchase of merchandise, which in turn was distributed in Tropical Africa.

Growers were usually obliged to accept the prices offered. As output of these commodities expanded, middlemen working between the trading firms and the growers became important not only as collectors of produce but also as financial agents making loans to the growers against future crops. In time, these middlemen also sold imported merchandise and loaned general funds. Many abuses arose, since the middlemen often held back inventories from the market in anticipation of price rises and, in general, tended to carry on speculative practices profitable to themselves at the expense of the farmers and of the trading firms. With the outbreak of World War II, it became hazardous to ship these crops abroad, and exporters therefore would have decreased their purchase commitments for the following season, thus precipitating a glut of these commodities in the African markets.

The British colonial governments, in co-operation with London,

therefore set up quasi-governmental boards for various commodities
—generally a single board within a territory for each major commodity—to handle shipments and sales of these products. During and following the war, the organization and operations of these boards
became more highly formalized, since the need for stabilization remained great, in order to counteract the effects of weather and of
world-wide fluctuations in volume and in price. Cocoa stabilization
schemes were established in Nigeria, Ghana, and several French territories; peanut controls were instituted in Nigeria, French West
Africa, the Congo, Portuguese Guinea, and elsewhere; and palm-
kernel and oil programs were inaugurated in Nigeria, the Congo, and
Portuguese Guinea.

The Cocoa Marketing Board of Nigeria, for example, is one of four
commodity marketing boards in that nation; the others are concerned
with peanuts, cotton, and palm-oil produce. Formally established in
1947, the Cocoa Board is the sole purchaser of cocoa for export. The
board is responsible for securing the most favorable arrangements for
the purchase, grading, export, and sale of cocoa and is required to
assist in the development of the Nigerian cocoa industry for the benefit of the producers. The board does not purchase cocoa directly from
producers, but it licenses trading firms to act as its agents. These
licensed buying agents purchase cocoa at buying stations at prices
at least equal to those set by the board. They arrange for inspection
and bagging in accordance with board requirements. They finance
purchases and provide storage for the cocoa until it can be shipped.
They arrange transportation to ports and delivery onto ocean vessels.
Finally, they assume insurance against all risks until the commodity
is delivered to the vessels or to board warehouses. Although European firms still dominate the trade, they are steadily losing ground
to Levantine and African companies.

Because of the tens of thousands of tiny producers, these licensed
buying agents generally do not deal directly with the farmers, but
work through middlemen who act as their buyers and who also arrange loans to farmers on the middlemen's own accounts. These middlemen often have sub-buyers working for them, and these sub-
buyers may in turn employ "runners" to bring in the produce from
the most remote areas.

Since the marketing boards fix prices to be paid to the producers
in advance of the gathering of a season's crop, in some seasons these
prices have been lower than the eventual world market prices and in
other years higher. In general, these advance prices have been *lower*

than the eventual world prices, thus augmenting the trading profits accruing to the boards. These operational profits have frequently been used for special governmental health, welfare, and educational projects. Critics of the boards have accused the government-appointed board members of mixing business and politics, particularly in the appointment of licensed buying agents. Proponents of the boards have argued that these boards have stabilized marketing operations to the benefit of producers and of the national populace in general. The performance of marketing boards is still a controversial issue. In some fields, such as sugar, international (largely intercontinental) marketing agreements are gradually supplementing national commodity marketing boards.

Co-operative Marketing. Producers' co-operatives have existed in Tropical Africa for decades, but only during the last 15 years have they shown marked growth. Their proponents insist that they will play an increasingly important role in the future. In size they range from a small co-operative dairy in Ghana to producers' co-operatives in Kenya concerned not only with the marketing of maize, coffee, and other commodities but also with the primary processing of these crops. About one fifth of Ghana's cocoa crop is handled through small-holders' co-operatives, and, in a sense, the commodity marketing boards discussed above are government-sponsored co-operatives. The number of registered co-operatives of all kinds in Tanganyika has grown from 62 in 1948 to 617 by 1959, with most of the increase accounted for by co-operatives of African producers of cotton, coffee, and other products. In addition to their primary function of marketing, many producers' co-operatives also assist members in improving production.

Consumer co-operatives are minor in number and in scope of operation, being restricted largely to relatively small units in British East Africa. Notable exceptions are the two government-sponsored consumers' co-operatives opened in 1961 in the Republic of Upper Volta as a means of driving down the prices of consumers' goods in the general market place. Although initially dealing only with foods, their plans call for expansion to other fields.

Industrialization

Most African nations have made remarkable economic strides since the end of World War II. Rhodesia, a leader in industrialization, experienced a capital formation rate of no less than 30 per cent of gross domestic production during this period. Yet real incomes and money incomes remain pitifully low. Many obstacles must be overcome before Tropical Africa can enjoy a significantly higher level of industrialization: the unsuitability or inadequacy of its economic infrastructure, especially power and transportation; the social structure, institutions, and values inimical to economic growth; a paucity of technical knowledge; and limitations imposed by international conditions, including political and economic colonialism. The domestic supply of funds for private investment is inadequate, not only because of low incomes, but also because many Africans are unaccustomed to dealing with banks and the amounts of profits and savings reinvested in Tropical Africa by non-Africans tend to be limited. Outside incentives are, therefore, needed to spur greater economic growth.

Transportation

The lack of comprehensive and properly integrated systems of transportation is a serious obstacle to the growth of the area's standard of living, particularly in its effect on the system of distribution. Ambitious plans for improvements have been laid in recent years, but, with the exception of British East Africa and parts of French-speaking West Africa, most of these plans have not been implemented. Land traffic from one country to another is poor and uncertain, and the same conditions prevail within individual countries. Air shipments are expensive, and water transportation is slow. Some consumers must travel several days to reach their "local" markets, and primitive means of transportation for goods, such as head porterage and pack animals, are common in many districts. A purchaser may find it easier, more certain, and even cheaper to have merchandise shipped 5,000 miles from Europe by water, or even by air, rather than from an African trading center only 500 miles away.

POLITICAL FACTORS

The influences of forms of government on marketing structures and operations are apparent when one compares marketing in nations possessing relatively free economies, with those practicing total state planning. Evidences of both types of politico-economic systems are found in Tropical Africa. As this area matures politically, marketing is certain to be influenced by the directions taken by the national and supra-national governments. Any study of comparative marketing must thus necessarily consider underlying political factors, especially in the fluid situation currently found there.

Variety is the chief characteristic of governments in Tropical Africa. The 22 sovereign states range from a so-called constitutional monarchy in Ethiopia, bearing little resemblance to the European versions of limited monarchies, to certain former colonies of France and Great Britain which do have fairly broad, effective electorates. Some states prefer to retain close ties with their former colonial rulers, as does the Federation of Nigeria within the British Commonwealth of Nations, whereas others (such as Liberia) are independent republics. Still others (notably the former French dependency of Guinea) are in active opposition to their former rulers. In some instances extreme viewpoints exist side by side within the same nation. The 20 territories ruled by colonial powers also run a wide gamut of self-suzerainty, both nominally and in practice.

Because of the newness of the self-governing nations and the probability that other territories in Tropical Africa will be granted a greater measure of self-rule in the future, some speculation appears to be in order concerning the political directions which these independent nations are likely to take. The following powerful forces will probably shape their trends:

Territorial Fragmentation. The legacy of centuries of strong separatist tendencies, whether by family, by kinship, or by tribal groups, has left its mark in the strong divisive trends found in the emerging nations. Among numerous instances of this tendency toward fragmentation is the Mali Federation, which was granted its independency from France in 1958. Two years later the Federation split up into the Senegal Republic and the Sudanese (Mali) Republic. Still another example is the effectuality of the agreement for federation signed in 1958 by Ghana and Guinea.

Federation. The fact that the Federation of Nigeria and that of Rhodesia and Nyasaland remain in existence despite strong divisive pressures in these areas is a tribute to the viability of federated movements. Even more important for the future are the strong appeals being made by various African leaders—especially those of Liberia, Guinea, and Ghana—for pan-Africanism, either through regional councils and conferences, or by means of more formal, permanent unions.

Authoritarianism. Most tribes in Africa have traditionally been ruled by their chiefs or by their elders in a heavy-handed manner, with strong mixtures of self-centered cupidity and brutality. There are marked signs that this authoritarian approach lives on in the manner in which the governmental leaders of Ghana have muffled their opposition and in the fierceness with which enemy tribes have attacked one another in the Republic of Congo in recent years. The actual powers which tribal chiefs wield today vary considerably from region to region.

Democracy. Western-style democracy has made considerable progress in Tropical Africa both in the independent nations and in territories which are not completely self-governing. In view of the very high rate of illiteracy found throughout the area and the paucity of schools at all levels, it is remarkable that democracy has taken hold here even in a tenuous fashion.

Communism. Although Communism appears to have won over very few governmental leaders so far, there are strong indications that leaders of this movement have assigned a high priority to winning them. The Western powers, increasingly aware of the threat, are forging countermeasures aimed at making these African nations strong enough economically and ideologically to repel this challenge.

Regulation of Business

The areas of business in which some African governments exert influence and power often surprise Americans. As in many European countries, governments in Tropical Africa usually own and operate most public utilities, including railroads, civil aviation, ports, and power utilities, but they tend to consider industrial development as essentially the responsibility of private enterprise. Many territories require employers (including the government) to provide housing for workers below a certain income level who cannot be expected to commute from their usual places of residence daily. In order to stabilize trade, some governments license wholesalers and retailers, Tanganyika and Nyasaland among them. Furthest along the path toward state regulation of distribution is Guinea, where a state trading monopoly imports all merchandise into the country and controls its distribution through 300 state stores and large numbers of private stores.

Numerous barriers to the flow of goods or to the entry of traders into particular districts or trades exist on a less formal level in certain regions. In some parts of Nigeria, Hausa chiefs (the principal dealers in cattle) regulate the number of cattle to be sold and their prices, and in other districts local sellers occasionally try to prevent farmers from selling their produce in town. Guilds or unions of the market "mammies" in Nigeria and Ghana at times attempt to hinder new competitors from entering their districts by the use of force, though such efforts have, on the whole, been ineffective.

The regulation of external trade, especially the export of primary products, has become increasingly important in most territories, with the interests of African buyers and sellers being the paramount governmental concern almost everywhere. In former French territories there are few outright prohibitions against anyone carrying on any legitimate import or export business, controls being based largely on the availability of foreign exchange. Portugal and Belgium also rely heavily on competitive private enterprise, whereas the British tend to place greater stress on governmental or quasi-governmental regulation, including the afore-mentioned commodity marketing boards. On the whole, the new nations tend to adopt policies similar to those held by their former rulers.

CONCEPTS OF BUSINESS AND MARKETING

In common with their counterparts elsewhere, better-educated and more sophisticated Africans usually have a sounder understanding of the positive role played in society by business in general and by marketing in particular than their less fortunate fellows. Since the latter are in the overwhelming majority, most Africans apparently have little regard or appreciation of marketing.

Accumulated wealth is widely thought to be earned solely by the impoverishment of customers and of competitors, and profit margins of tradesmen, especially of retailers, are believed to depend entirely on their personal decisions and desires. An indication of the low esteem with which trade is regarded is the fact that it is often an avocational interest. Many of the more prosperous African farmers, lawyers, and doctors frequently conduct small or large trading firms as sidelines in much the same manner as their peers in the United States carry on stock-market transactions.

There is a widely held conviction among governmental officials that distribution is inefficient, that it is a drain on production rather than an aid, and that it does little or nothing to improve the standard of living. This ingrained view is noted in the lack of pride with which governmental officials and others regard the recent development of several large trading centers, such as Onitsha in Nigeria.

DISTRIBUTION: GENERAL

A considerable amount of trade was carried on in certain districts of Tropical Africa before Europeans entered the area and established their own forms of distribution, and some indigenous trading patterns remain important to this day. A fairly large-scale example is the cattle industry of West Africa, where most cattle are bred and reared by

Fulani tribesmen of Northern Nigeria, Ghana, and sections of what was French West Africa, and sent south—at times 1,000 miles or more —to the principal areas of consumption. Another instance are kola nuts, usually chewed by Africans for stimulative effects, which are grown in Southern Nigeria and shipped to the Hausa tribes of Northern Nigeria and to several of the former French dependencies.

The following are some general characteristics of current distribution in Tropical Africa:

Concentration. Foreign trade and large-scale wholesaling are concentrated in the hands of relatively few firms, ranging in size from giants, such as the United Africa Company, to relatively modest Levantine companies in West Africa or Asian firms in East Africa.

Regional Variations. In general, the scale and scope of trading firms in West Africa are considerably greater than those in East Africa.

Variety of Activities. Trading firms of all sizes tend to carry on a wide variety of activities simultaneously—buying and selling, granting loans, handling many different kinds of merchandise, and performing a wide mixture of wholesale and retail functions.

Assemblers. Middlemen tend to be very important as assemblers where commodities like cocoa or copra must be gathered at frequent intervals in small quantities over wide and remote areas, but they seem to have little or no place where products (e.g., timber) must be moved with difficulty and at great expense or where the products require considerable private or governmental control and protection (e.g., diamonds, gold, and uranium).

Small Quantities. Merchandise tends to be moved in very small quantities at both wholesale and retail levels because of the generally low buying power of the consumer. A natural concomitant is the high markup often found on these goods because of the exhorbitant costs of handling small quantities. A petty retailer finds it natural to sell a single lump of sugar or one cigarette.

Few Records. The myriads of small tradesmen conduct their affairs with few or no formal records or systems. Nevertheless, investigations have indicated that Africans frequently conduct their firms as efficiently as non-Africans with much more formal training and with superior forms of record-keeping and of organization.

WHOLESALING

Just as the major trading firms in Tropical Africa generally work through one or more echelons of middlemen in the collection of produce for export, they also work through one or more echelons of wholesalers in the distribution of imported merchandise and domestic goods. In many instances, the same middlemen carry on both assembling and distribution activities.

Although some foreign manufacturers supply their goods directly to importers in Tropical Africa on the latters' orders, it is more common for major foreign manufacturers to appoint distributors in Africa to sell directly to the public in larger towns and to serve as wholesalers to retail dealers in the more remote areas. In many instances, foreign manufacturers are represented in African cities and towns by agents who display samples, quote prices, and prepare orders for dispatch to the foreign manufacturers. At times these agents act as local wholesalers and also as local retailers for these foreign manufacturers. Because of the high risks involved in doing business on credit, particularly with itinerant retailers, many wholesalers sell only on cash terms. On the other hand, small shopkeepers in remote areas may make all of their purchases from a single wholesaler "in town," which may be several hundred miles away and therefore cannot be visited frequently or easily, in which case long-term credit arrangements may be the rule rather than the exception.

RETAILING

Tropical Africa does have supermarkets, department stores, and other advanced forms of retail distribution, but most of the establishments are affiliated with large trading firms and other European-oriented enterprises. Much of business consists of sales to Europeans and other non-Africans. These outlets account for a very small proportion of the area's total retail sales. Much more representative are the major segments of petty trade—the hawkers, the market places, and the tiny general stores.

Hawkers

Hawkers ply the streets of cities and towns on foot, crying out their wares, or they cycle from village to village, often following a regular route. They tend to concentrate on merchandise that has a high value to bulk, such as medicinal pills, toiletries, and small measures of tea, salt, and sugar. As is true elsewhere in the world, the reliability of many hawkers is questionable.

Markets

African market places have existed for centuries. They have been described as the original supermarkets, with considerable emphasis on self-selection and even self-service. In the larger markets, merchandise is usually grouped by classification. The size of the markets varies considerably, and the frequency with which they are held ranges from sporadic or weekly in the more remote areas to daily in larger cities and towns.

Some remote regions rely entirely on a system of widely scattered markets as a means of distribution. In Northwest Ethiopia, for example, where small local markets serve as places to exchange locally produced goods, as points of distributing goods to consumers from distant places, as a means of assembling regional surplus products for shipment to locales where they are in demand, and as social centers. Bargaining is universal, and bartering is not uncommon. Merchandise consists mostly of domestic products, except for razor blades, needles, thread, cloth, soap, and spices. Itinerant artisans, such as makers of earthenware pots, often set up "ateliers" at these markets by making goods to order on the spot.

At the other end of the scale there is the market of Ibada, Nigeria, containing about 3,000 small stalls. Large assortments of foods and nonfoods are available and sizable selections of both foreign and domestic manufacturers. Larger markets are generally administered by the government, with sellers being obliged to pay an entrance fee. Some markets have areas of permanent stalls and shops, together with so-called "bartering" areas for itinerant traders, where much of the business nevertheless consists of *cash* transactions.

Numerous mutations between the itinerant hawker and the markets are also found. Often in cities, towns, and crossroads, petty retailers set up "shop" on a mat under a shade tree or in front of their homes.

General Store

Although town stores tend to be specialized and run in a manner similar to those found in urban areas of similar size and wealth in the Western world, it is the village store that is really typical of Tropical Africa. These crude, tiny general stores are often located at mere crossroads and are frequently run by non-Africans or by Africans not native to the particular district. The proprietors buy and sell a bit of everything in demand pertaining to the person, the home, and the farm. The stores are often open all hours of the day and night, serving their communities as social as well as trading centers. Credit is sometimes offered at usurious rates, inasmuch as risks tend to be inordinately high. Since many of these shops have monopolies in their districts, price abuses are not unknown. In spite of their current importance and ubiquity, these small shops are gradually losing business to company-run stores affiliated with plantations, mines, and other large-scale enterprises; to stores and markets located in cities and towns; and, on a lesser scale, to consumer co-operatives.

FACILITATING MARKETING INSTITUTIONS

Advertising

In view of the fact that over 90 per cent of the Africans in Tropical Africa are illiterate, advertising directed to them must stress symbols, especially by the use of trade-marks and of point-of-purchase media placed in the larger shopping centers. Most periodicals—which consist mainly of newspapers—tend to be segregated for either Africans or Europeans, in terms both of orientation and of readership. These are supplemented by a smaller specialized press for Asians in East Africa. There are over 50 newspapers in the British Commonwealth regions of West Africa, including about 30 in Nigeria alone. Circulation is small by Western standards, but their influence is sometimes great. Advertising accounts for 25 to 50 per cent of total space, with emphasis on branded merchandise steadily becoming more important. There are well over 80 radio transmitters in Tropical Africa and at least 600,000 receivers, with their numbers growing rapidly as programing is being increased in length and in orientation toward African listeners. As in most European nations, radio stations usually do not accept advertising.

Banking and Credit

In the past, most European banks located in African territories favored their own nationals in extending credit, and even today European firms, along with Levantines and Asians, can obtain credit fairly readily, even though such loans may be on usurious terms. Short-term credit for retail and wholesale companies is inclined to be particularly tight, and Africans, often unable to produce negotiable securities, tend to be last in line for what is available. Other reasons for the difficulty in securing bank credit are that African businesses are frequently too small to make such transactions worthwhile for the lender, and these small firms often do not maintain adequate records. Moreover, experience has taught the lenders that these customers do not always appreciate their obligations. Many governments are encouraging improvements in credit facilities. In Nigeria, for example, a well-developed group of indigenous banks has been placing particular stress on meeting the credit requirements of African businessmen.

MARKETING PRACTICES

In view of the low incomes found among Africans, the area is essentially a poor man's market, even though consumers are hardly unsophisticated as to what they want, nor are they bashful about expressing their wishes. Women often become very much attached to a certain style of fabric, garment, and/or color, refusing to consider innovations; and brand loyalties and prejudices are frequently deeply ingrained. Spending habits may at times be channeled to surprising extremes, as was revealed in a study of mine workers in Northern Rhodesia, who, over a period of several months, spent 90 per cent of their disposable income on clothes.

Merchandising often takes strange turns, in the eyes of Western observers. A run on a certain brand of soap in one district upon investigation revealed that the product was in demand primarily as fish bait! Merchandise containers, such as gasoline cans, are frequently put to a multitude of unorthodox uses in homes and on farms. Tractor seats sent to certain districts must be small because of the generally smaller posteriors of the local African users.

The metric and British systems of weights and measures are widely accepted in the various territories for foreign trade, but internal trade within the African nations often suffers because of the great diversity and uncertainties of weights and measures. Some commodities are quoted in such vague terms as bundles or heaps, and their meanings vary greatly from region to region.

Prices in Western-type wholesale houses, department stores, specialty shops, and chains are usually fixed, but the great majority of trade at all levels of distribution is transacted on the basis of haggling and bargaining. Original prices are often set by sellers entirely on the basis of appearance; e.g., if a seller believes that fabric "A" is more attractive to the prospective buyer than fabric "B," the seller will ask a higher price for fabric "A," even though he may have paid the same price for both fabrics. The African consumer is likely to be a very careful shopper, taking great care to inform himself about the quality and value of merchandise, to the annoyance of those sellers who still believe that Tropical Africa is a place to "dump" unwanted and shoddy goods.

CONCLUSIONS

There are few areas of the world in which social, economic, political, anthropological, and historical factors are interwoven as complexly with marketing as in Tropical Africa. As this great area continues to develop, the interactions of these fundamental factors with marketing should be a most important learning experience for marketers and for marketing students. The rest of the world should be able to contribute much toward this development, and, in doing so, much is to be gained by all.

LATIN AMERICA

Central America

CENTRAL AMERICA

This account of wholesaling in Central America is evidence that wholesaling is characterized more by the character of the economy than by the mere size of the country. Other small agricultural countries have more developed wholesaling systems than some of those in Central America, because of differences in volume of production, degree of specialization, concentration or dispersion of markets, literacy and productivity of the population, etc.

Wholesaling in Central America follows simple patterns. The importance of lack of capital is shown in the activities of various manufacturers and agents who advance funds to producers in the form of seeds and materials. Likewise, the importance of large-scale activity in exporting is also shown, demonstrating the economies which must be effected in moving bulky goods long distances.

The author of this chapter also discusses the possible impact of common market agreements among the countries of Central America.

Wholesaling In Central America

DONALD F. MULVIHILL *

The countries of Central America are Guatemala, El Salvador, Honduras, Nicaragua, Costa Rica, and Panama. The latter is included for purposes of this study because of the similarity of its market situation (outside the Canal Zone) to the other countries and because of its possible inclusion in the common market with Nicaragua and Costa Rica.

All six of these countries were at one time part of the Spanish sovereignties and of the brief Republic of Central America. They have similar physical geography and climate. They are also alike in having but little manufacturing and in continuing development of their agricultural production. Their rugged terrain, with luxuriant vegetation on the coastal plains and with volcanoes and forbidding mountains on the central plateau, has made transportation and communication difficult. Rivers are unnavigable for even the smallest vessels. Not until the last few decades has it been possible to traverse most of the countries except on foot or pack animals.

Such conditions, coupled with the lack of surplus items to barter or sell, have made for simple marketing institutions and channels of distribution.

Population. Marketing is affected also by the size and concentration of population. The countries of Central America are small in land area with relatively large populations. Table 1 shows the areas, official population figures for 1950, and estimated population for 1960. The six countries occupy an area slightly larger than the combined states of Ohio, Michigan, Indiana, and Illinois, with a population that is approximately 37% of that of those states.

Further evidence of population trends is found in the rates of population growth. In Table 2 that of the Central American countries is compared with that in Latin America and the United States. All the countries of Central America have a population growth rate greater

---

* Dr. Donald F. Mulvihill is Professor of Marketing at Kent State University, Kent, Ohio.

208

TABLE 1

AREA, POPULATION, AND POPULATION DENSITY
OF CENTRAL AMERICAN COUNTRIES

Country	Square Miles Approx.	Population 1950	Population Density 1950	Estimated Population 1960 *	Est. Pop. Density 1960
Guatemala	42,042	2,790,686	66.4	3,658,000	87.0
El Salvador	8,060	1,855,917	232.6	2,521,583	312.9
Honduras	43,278	1,428,089	33.	1,949,858	45.1
Nicaragua	57,145	1,057,023	18.5	1,525,000	26.7
Costa Rica	19,328	800,875	41.6	1,150,000	59.8
Panama	28,576	805,285	28.2	1,053,110	36.9
Total	198,339	8,737,875	44.1	11,875,551	59.9

* Estimated by governmental agencies and published by Caribbean Networks, Inc.

TABLE 2

POPULATION INCREASES AND RATE OF GROWTH, 1953–60

Central America	Estimates of Midyear Population (Millions)			Annual Rate of Increase in Population 1953–1958 (%)
	1953	1958	1960	
Guatemala	3.1	3.5	3.7	3.0
El Salvador	2.1	2.4	2.6	3.5
Honduras	1.6	1.8	1.9	3.3
Nicaragua	1.2	1.3	1.4	3.4
Costa Rica	0.9	1.1	1.2	4.0
Panama	0.9	1.0	1.1	2.9
LATIN AMERICA	167.0	188.1	197.3	2.4
U.S.A.	160.3	174.8	180.5	1.7

Source: *United Nations Demographic Yearbook* (1959).

than all Latin America and approximately twice or more as great as that of the United States.

There is marketing significance not only in the expansion of the population but also in its concentration and density. Because a census of population is not taken regularly, it is difficult to know exactly where people are. However, it is a fact that population is usually concentrated in the capital city and in a few large towns near the capital. With the exception of Nicaragua, the bulk of the population is found on the central plateau or in the mountainous region that runs through Central America and is an extension of the western mountain chains in the United States. In 1960, the population density of the United States (50 states) was 50.5 persons per square mile. The density for the Central American countries and of states which are comparable in size is shown in Table 3.

TABLE 3

POPULATION DENSITIES OF STATES OF COMPARABLE SIZE, 1960

Country	Comparable State	State Pop. Density	Country Pop. Density
Guatemala	Tennessee	85.4	87.0
El Salvador	Maryland	31.4	312.9
Honduras	Tennessee	85.4	45.1
Nicaragua	Iowa	49.2	26.7
Costa Rica	Vermont–New Hampshire	54.6	59.8
Panama	South Carolina	78.7	36.9

The major political subdivisions in which the capital city is located contain from three fifths of the total population (Costa Rica) to one sixth (Honduras). There are some developing areas around the port towns, particularly on the Caribbean side of the countries. Because of the high degree of concentration along the central plateau with sparsely settled areas elsewhere, there are many portions which contain no stores or trading establishments. The population densities will undoubtedly continue to increase, since public health and welfare programs under governmental sponsorship and United States aid are providing the basis for a "population explosion" in Central America as elsewhere. Coupled with the high degree of concentration of population around the chief city, this growth rate presages a greater need for assembling supplies, transporting and storing them, and dispersing them throughout the cities, activities usually considered in the domain of the wholesaler.

Economic Situation. Some measure of the economic situation may be seen in Table 4, which indicates the Gross National Product of these countries.

TABLE 4

GROSS NATIONAL PRODUCT OF CENTRAL AMERICAN COUNTRIES

Country	GNP Total ($ Million)	GNP per Capita (Dollars)
Guatemala	679	180
El Salvador	490	188
Honduras	384	197
Nicaragua	310	210
Costa Rica	402	343
Panama	418	396

Source: Statistics and Reports Division, Agency for International Aid, March 22, 1962.

In comparison, the per capita GNP for Africa is $129; that of the Far East, $186; Western Europe, $917; and the United States, $2,791. Puerto Rico has a per capita GNP of $719, while Latin America as a whole has $296. Latin-American countries range from Bolivia with $62 to Venezuela with $1,066. Thus it can be seen that the Central American countries are not in the best position economically, but neither are they the poorest.

Central American countries have been heavily dependent on single commodities for export. Although this tendency may be lessening, the percentage of total export earnings derived from one commodity, based on the 1957–59 average were as follows:

	Per Cent	
Guatemala	72	(coffee)
El Salvador	72	(coffee)
Honduras	51	(bananas)
Nicaragua	39	(cotton)
Costa Rica	51	(coffee)
Panama	69	(bananas)

Source: International Monetary Fund, *International Financial Statistics*, November, 1960.

Most of the labor force is in agriculture, as might be expected in developing countries that are just beginning to industrialize. In the period from 1947 to 1953, the percentages of labor so engaged were as follows (no comparable figures are available for Guatemala):

	Per Cent
El Salvador	56–65
Honduras	76–85
Nicaragua	66–75
Costa Rica and Panama.....	46–55

Source: United Nations, *Statistical Yearbook* (1957).

These compare with an average of 12.2 per cent for the United States. Another significant economic measure is the cost-of-living index. For selected years, Table 5 shows a comparison of the Central Ameri-

TABLE 5

Cost-of-Living Indices for Selected Countries of Latin America (1953 = 100)

Country	1950	1953	1955	1957	1960
Guatemala	95	100	105	104	104
El Salvador	82	100	104	102	107
Honduras	91	100	114	108	110
Nicaragua	74	100	123	114	114
Costa Rica	95	100	106	110	114
Argentina	51	100	117	165	590
Bolivia	30	100	404	2,498	3,350
Brazil	62	100	142	206	433
Mexico	79	100	122	135	161

Source: International Labour Office.

can group with certain other Latin-American countries, indicating a higher degree of stability for them than for other Latin-American countries (Panama is omitted because figures are available only for Panama City).

Although the absolute amount of cost of living has significance, the relative index shows a shifting situation that may have even great bearing on marketing activity, in both magnitude and structure.

Another aspect of economic life may be seen in the balance of trade between exports and imports. Table 6 shows the balance of

TABLE 6

Excess or Deficit of Exports as Related to Imports for Selected Years
(Value in Million U.S. Dollars)

Country	1950	1953	1955	1957	1960
Guatemala	8	19	1	−31	4
El Salvador	20	19	8	8	20
Honduras	16	6	−12	−14	....
Nicaragua	−2	−5	2	−17	−6
Costa Rica	10	6	−6	−7	−11
Panama	−46	−56	−52	−82	−95
Latin America	1,176	1,079	452	−679	....

Source: International Monetary Fund, *International Financial Statistics*, February, 1961.

trade for the Central American group compared with each other and all Latin-American countries for selected years.

Only El Salvador has a surplus balance of trade, while the others tend to have a continuing deficit position. These years may be a transition from the wholly agricultural economy to the mixed agricultural-industrial one.

Education. Central American countries have been faced with a high rate of illiteracy, which is slowly being lowered. Measures of this are not too precise. In 1950, in all the countries but Panama, 95 per cent or more of the population had only a primary education or less. United States figures are also shown in Table 7.

Although not strictly comparable, a 1957 estimate from the same source shows that, in the first four countries, 76 per cent of the people were unable to read or write. Costa Rica and Panama were in a better position, with only 14 and 30 per cent in this condition, respectively.

With such lack of education, the marketing information function must usually be carried out through the oral media or simple pictorial visual media. No sophisticated copy can be used in newspapers or magazines except to reach the very small percentage of highly literate groups. The manufacturer-wholesaler has to depend on radio, outdoor, and point-of-sale advertising to carry his message.

TABLE 7
EDUCATIONAL ATTAINMENT IN CENTRAL AMERICAN COUNTRIES, 1950

	Percentages Having Completed		
Country	*Less than Primary Ed.**	*Primary but Not Secondary Ed.†*	*Secondary or Higher*
Guatemala	87	11	1.8
El Salvador	85	10	4.1
Honduras	88	11	...
Nicaragua	84	14	...
Costa Rica	62	33	4.9
Panama	55	38	5.9
United States	12	55	32.3

* In general, persons having completed less than four years of primary education.
† In general, persons having completed four or more years of primary education but less than four years of secondary education.
Source: United Nations Educational, Scientific, and Cultural Organization, *Basic Facts and Figures, 1959* (1960).

Summary of Economic Environment. The Central American countries are similar in many respects. They are small in size, with their people clustering around their capital cities. Their populations are increasing more rapidly than in many other countries. In terms of per capita gross national products, these countries are not the poorest but are well below Western Europe or the United States. Highly dependent on one commodity for export, their labor force is predominantly in agriculture. Costs of living are rising, but not at the rate of many other Latin-American countries. Nearly all have a trade-balance deficit. Illiteracy is high, with the great majority of people having little schooling.

These conditions result in a simple marketing system. This may change in the future, however, as industrial production becomes a more important phase of each nation's economy.

WHOLESALING OF FARM PRODUCTS

Under such circumstances, it is natural that wholesaling would not have become highly specialized. A great deal of wholesaling is done directly by the producer or grower, who may also do his own retailing in the market of the town nearest him. Since World War I, there have been an increasing number of importers, representing groups of firms in the United States, Germany, or Japan. They are in some instances agents of these companies, but most often they are independent merchants. Where production is specialized, either because of natural resources or because of the establishment of particular crafts, specialized wholesale middlemen may be found.

Fruits and Vegetables. Farmers who grow fruits and vegetables often move their produce directly to the nearest large town in their area. They move it by cart, automobile, truck, or on the backs of the growers; or they may hire a truck driver to take the crop to market for them, sometimes accompanying him or having him sell it for them on a commission basis. Farmers also sell to truck owners, who move the produce of several growers to the market.

Truckers sell in the wholesale market from their truck or from rental space. They sell to retailers, who have stalls or positions in the retail market, or to wholesalers, who in turn carry their wares to the retailers' stores.

Such transactions are nearly always for cash, and, when the trucker is receiving a commission, he will pay the farmer on his way back from the market.

The following diagram represents the channels by which fruits and vegetables move to the market:

Beans may be stored and dried by the farmer, so that they may get a better price than for the newly harvested beans. Since this may be a sizable crop, they will take samples of it to the wholesalers or retailers in the local market and agree upon a price prior to delivery. The merchant in turn may send his trucks to pick up the beans and transport them to the market.

Eggs and Chickens. Although some farmers raise chickens for market, many of them raise hens for eggs and sell the chickens only after they have ceased to lay. The eggs are washed, classified sometimes by eye (and in a few cases by candling), and packed in various kinds of containers. Eggs may be sold in the same manner as fruits and vegetables or from door to door by farmers to regular customers. Some farmers take their eggs to feed houses, which market them for the farmer, who may have been furnished by them with feed, on credit, for raising his chickens. The difference between the cost of the feed the farmer has been given and the price obtained in the market is his only cash return. In some countries this type of marketing, tied in with the purchase of feed, is carried out by an egg cooperative. Some wholesalers and retailers may have a route which is followed periodically by truck, and the farmer sells directly to these truckers, who, in turn, may sell in the local market or through their store.

When hens stop laying, the farmers sell them to wholesale or retail truckers, to the co-operative, or as they sell fruits and vegetables. The wholesalers who buy hens for slaughter clean them and sell them unpacked in their retail or wholesale outlets. Farmers who raise hens exclusively for slaughtering may also dress and package them. Sales are made through the following channels:

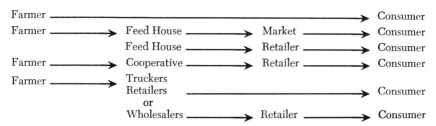

Milk and Milk Products. The production of pasteurized milk is encouraged by the establishment of autonomous co-operatives subsidized by the government, although farmers and processors themselves may participate in forming co-operatives. The price of both raw milk and milk at retail is usually established by a government agency.

Farmers may transport milk to wholesalers or to regular processers, such as cheese makers, who, in turn, will sell to wholesalers and retailers distributing into the local markets.

Grains. Rice is taken by farmers, in their own truck or in one hired, either to the nearest processing point or to a national or producers' co-operative. Rice processers either buy it outright or charge the farmer a fixed price for preparing it for market. If the latter, the processer keeps the semolina without reimbursing the farmer for it, which is then used for feed or other purposes because of its high nutritional value. In some of the larger towns, there is a special market place for the sale of rice; there both wholesalers and retailers are to be found.

Corn is sold by the farmer to wholesalers, retailers, and to a national or producers' co-operative.

Tobacco. Farmers usually grow tobacco for a factory which is producing cigarette or pipe tobacco. Tobacco rejected by the factories may be sold to small fabricators of cigars and chewing tobacco. The bulk of the crop is taken, however, from the farmer by the tobacco factories, which may be autonomous institutions. The price is fixed by a governmental agency. The tobacco companies, in turn, sell finished products to wholesalers and retailers.

Coffee.   Coffee, after it is picked by hand, is usually taken by the grower in whatever type of vehicle he has available to the *beneficio.* This processer may export some or all of the coffee or may offer it for auction, on certain days and in certain places, for purchase by local roasters. The *beneficio* does not buy coffee from the farmer but advances money to him for making the crop, in a procedure and at rates usually prescribed by the government. The amount advanced to the farmer is offset by the rates which his coffee brings to the *beneficio* upon its sale.

The price to the farmer is determined for a particular period on the basis of the total crop, and not just the individual farmer's production. Usually the country's national bank finances the *beneficios* by advancing money to them, as well as underwriting the expense of exporting processed coffee.

Coffee sold to local roasters is processed, packaged, and marketed by them either through a sales force, who may call upon retailers and industrial users, or through wholesalers.

At present, the better coffee is being exported throughout the world, particularly to Western Germany and the United States. Very close control is maintained over the price structure at all stages of the exchange of ownership in the coffee.

Sugar.   Cane is both processed by farmers and sold in local markets or processed at a nearby *ingenio.* Farmers press the juice from the sugar on their own farms with special equipment and boil it into a crude brown sugar, which is molded. In this form it is taken to special markets, where, on certain days, it is bought by wholesalers and retailers. Crude brown sugar is also sold directly to liquor factories, which are usually autonomous institutions.

The ingenio sells the molasses to cattle raisers for feed or to the liquor factories. The refined sugar must usually be sold to a voluntary association to which the ingenio and the producers belong. Minimum prices are fixed by the government. This affects the price fixed by the voluntary group to control the sales to the farmer. The farmer is paid once a week for the shipments he has brought to the ingenio.

Refined sugar which has been inspected and cleaned is delivered to the voluntary associations' warehouses, where it is sold to wholesalers or retailers. The buyers, who must purchase a minimum quantity, arrange to do so through a bank or the warehouse.

The association determines how much sugar to export and moves it from the warehouse to the port. The association notifies prospective importers or their agents of the sugar's availability. The price for this sugar is determined by the New York market price.

Meat and Poultry. There has been a considerable increase in the amount of cattle grown for meat, but the slaughterhouses have not kept pace with production. There are some modern yards and houses, but many others are still crude and wasteful. The farmer often drives a single head or herd of cattle to the nearby market town which contains a slaughterhouse. Only recently has stock been transported by truck, and very little fattening or grazing is done in the process of taking the stock to market. The animals are often too lean, and the slaughter process, because of its crude methods, often decreases the value of the meat. Farmers sell to wholesalers in the market or offer their stock in auctions which occur several times each week. Fresh meat, often sold "hot," is bought by retailers and institutional buyers from the processer in the stockyards. Some meat is dressed in accordance with European or American customs, and some is quick-frozen and prepared for sale in the new self-service supermarkets that are beginning to appear.

A specialty trade in chickens has been encouraged on a small scale either through quick-freezing or by rapid movement in the market by planes from rural areas to the larger cities. At least one attempt has been made to break into the New Orleans market in this way.

Bananas. Bananas are marketed primarily through the fruit companies, but some are grown for local consumption and are marketed as are other fruits and vegetables.

WHOLESALING OF MANUFACTURED PRODUCTS

Although many manufactured products are imported, there are some light industries in each of the Central American countries. For many of them, the raw materials and parts are imported. In certain of the countries—for example, Costa Rica and Honduras—the importer of raw materials must make an assignment of cash to cover the import bill, either to the national bank or to the governmental import agency. This means that the importer of raw materials must be a financing institution as well.

Parts or finished manufactured products may be imported, with payments made in the usual fashion to the manufacturer abroad. The importer, for this reason, often is a manufacturer's agent rather than a merchant-wholesaler in his own right.

If goods are manufactured in one of the countries for local use, the manufacturer may serve as his own wholesaler, and quite often he has at least one store of his own in the capital city. For example, one manufacturer of paints in Costa Rica has his own retail outlet in San Jose and certain other larger towns. In addition, the company sells to retailers in smaller towns through a sales force. The same company also has a manufacturing plant in Nicaragua and follows the same pattern there. The company has two qualities of paint which are sold to retail outlets without restriction, so that the company finds itself competing for sales not only through its own retail stores, which handle only the higher-quality paint, but also through other establishments (see Fig. 1).

FIGURE 1

Manufacturing and Selling Activities of Firm Operating
in Two Countries under Bilateral Agreement

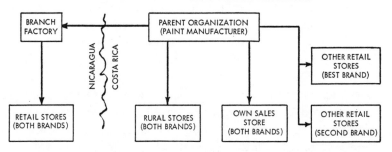

As another example, a furniture factory is a part of a complex grouping of activities under one management. The furniture is sold through its own store, which also is an outlet for imported household appliances, chinaware, flat silverware, and other furniture. This company also serves as a wholesaler for these products and even for an internationally distributed brand of hair tints. The last product, of course, is sold to an entirely different set of retail stores than are the first and is still in the company's line because it was one of the first items it imported and has an extremely high profit. In addition, this company is a leading importer of Japanese-made motorcycles and scooters and has a separate retail outlet for the sale of these, since it is thought that they do not appeal to the same type of customer as do the other products (see Fig. 2).

As is the case in many companies, it is difficult to distinguish clearly where the wholesaling activities begin and where the retailing functions start. No separate divisions have been established except for the cosmetic product and the motorcycles. As a further complexity, since the furniture manufacturer includes metal tables,

FIGURE 2

MANUFACTURING, IMPORTING, WHOLESALING, AND RETAILING
ACTIVITIES OF ONE COSTA RICAN BUSINESS

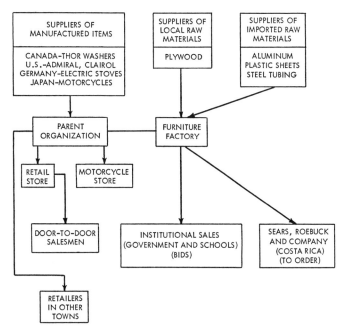

chairs, and office furniture with plastic tops, a great deal of the capital of this company must be invested in imported raw materials.

The two examples cited above are not unusual. They are relatively simple examples of the complexity of trade in countries where there is a relatively low per capita income and, until recently, very few credit transactions.

EXPORTING

Not much exporting is done by individuals. The volume exports, such as coffee, cacao, sugar, bananas, etc., are usually grown, processed for shipment, and exported by large companies who control the process from the planting of the plant or tree until the product is sold in some foreign country.

What little exporting is done by others is in specialized fields, such as textiles, art objects, and national specialties. These are sold to individuals or to retail outlets in the United States and a few European countries. The exporting of items into other Central American countries will, of course, increase when the common markets are established. Reciprocal agreements have already been signed between neighboring countries which permit noncompeting manufactured products to enter at very low rates or duty-free. Presumably, this trend will be accentuated in the next few years, as the details in regard to the common-market procedure are worked out.

COMMON-MARKET ACTIVITY

No discussion of marketing and wholesaling in Central America would be complete without a reference to the activity taking place in regard to common markets. In June, 1958, five countries (Panama not included) signed the Multilateral Treaty of Central American Free Trade and Economic Integration, which provides for the gradual establishment of a common market. Also agreed to was the Convention of Central American Integrated Industries, setting up a commission to determine which industries are to be considered as "integrated." Both of these provide for a ten-year period to attain their objectives. Later conventions were ratified as to import charges and tariff preferences.

In February, 1960, Guatemala, El Salvador, and Honduras signed a Treaty of Economic Association aimed at speeding up the economic integration process by five years. Nicaragua became a party to this agreement in December, 1960. Costa Rica has been reluctant to join wholeheartedly in the common-market activity for, under previous bilateral trade agreements, she already had several advantages for the movement of some of her manufactured products into other Central American countries. In some respects the poorer, more agricultural countries such as Honduras and Nicaragua, look on the changes with apprehension, fearing their inability to match the more rapid industrialization of El Salvador and Guatemala.

The future development of the common-market items and the extension of the area to include other nations will be worth noting. Probably it will be some time before there will be any fusion of the Central and Latin-American free-trade groups.

WHOLESALING FUNCTIONS

The wholesaling functions are carried out in the Central American countries by growers and processers of farm products and by manufacturers and importers. Since these are lands of relative scarcity, little risk is borne by dealers in food products, particularly since basic farm prices are quite often fixed by some governmental or autonomous agency. The importer bears little risk, as he has chosen his imports in terms of the local demands. Transportation and storage are provided by the wholesaler himself, although some equivalents of public warehouses are appearing. One of the difficulties besetting the importer of raw materials is the lack of space for holding the vital imported materials in such a manner that the goods may be withdrawn as soon as cash has been accumulated to set up the sale. Whatever standardizing and grading take place is usually performed by the processer-wholesaler, although sometimes a governmental agency establishes grades and the autonomous institutions or co-operatives apply these standards during the inspection of the items.

Relatively little advertising is done except in the case of manufactured goods, and marketing research is just now being thought about.

The basic buying and selling functions of the wholesaler are the most important aspects of his work. He does, under the circumstances in which he finds himself, all of the marketing functions that are necessary in the developing economy in which he is located. As per capita incomes increase and as manufacturing becomes a larger part of the economy, the other functions will become more important, and the wholesaler will more nearly approach the performance levels to be found in countries where marketing procedures are more firmly established.

CONCLUSIONS

The developing countries of Central America present proof of the fact that marketing systems and institutions are dynamic, changing as is necessary in terms of the economic situation which prevails at the time. Basically, wholesaling in Central America is still simple, as might be expected in an economic environment characterized by low productivity and income per capita with little surplus to be exchanged.

The increase in productivity and income, spurred on by population growth, increased literacy, and attempts at more democratic governmental controls, causes changes in the institutions and systems for the distribution of goods. Both wholesaling and retailing activities are showing signs of change.

The introduction of the common-market concept and its adoption will probably have an influence leading to greater regional specialization and the introduction of new proceses and products, resulting in further increases in productivity and income. This has set in motion the "snowballing" effect that will continue the development of Central America.

COMMUNIST COUNTRIES

U.S.S.R.

Communist China

Yugoslavia

U.S.S.R.

The wholesaling system in the U.S.S.R. represents the application of a different ideology to the distributive task that falls to the wholesaling mechanism in any country.

In this chapter are found some perceptive interpretations of what wholesaling is. It is called an "intermediate activity," a sphere of circulation of commodities, and the area of the economy in which planning takes place. The necessity for wholesaling is attributed to social division of labor, the ultimate need for an assortment of commodities, and the separation of production and consumption both by space and by time.

The wholesaling organization is charged with implementation of the planning upon which much of the success of the Communist economy depends. Wholesalers do market research concerning consumer goods; they determine and transmit details for the broadly conceived government economic plans; they match market demand with potentialities of industry; they facilitate the allocation of products to various areas; and they supplement the product quality-checking function of governmental inspectors.

Throughout the various Five-Year Plans, wholesaling has alternately been more and less centralized. In general, the great bulk of the wholesaling function has been placed under the control of the Ministry of Trade, thus minimizing the "interference" with proper shipment of goods to consumer markets resulting from the presence of regular wholesalers, and at the same time exemplifying Lenin's dictum that the government must become a careful wholesale trader.

Some discussion is given also to the problems of transportation which arise as wholesaling problems in a planned economy.

To aid the reader who may be unfamiliar with marketing in a Communist country, some tables of organization have been provided to indicate the setting for wholesale activities in the Soviet Union. The bulk of wholesaling today takes place within the jurisdiction of the Ministry of Trade of the various republics (see Table 1 and Fig. 1 at the end of this chapter). The relation of the Ministry of Trade to other organizations concerned with the distribution of consumer goods is shown in Figure 2. These tables and figures are taken from Marketing in the Soviet Union, by Marshall I. Goldman, published by The Free Press, 1962.

Wholesaling in the U.S.S.R.

V. I. GOGOL *

THE ROLE OF WHOLESALING IN THE DISTRIBUTION OF GOODS

Introduction

The distribution of consumers' goods ends with the exchange of goods between the trade enterprises and the consumers. This process is usually known as "retailing." However, before such a transfer of goods can be made, there are some preliminary transactions. This stems from the nature of production and distribution. Upon leaving the producer, it is usually necessary for industrial and agricultural products to pass through certain intermediate links—industrial sales organization, procurement units, and Ministry of Trade distributors. This intermediate activity between government and co-operative organizations and retail enterprises is known as "wholesaling."

Wholesaling precedes retailing. If, in retailing, the process of distribution is completed, then, in wholesaling, commodities continue to circulate in the sphere of distribution or are directed to industry, so that the production process may continue until the goods are again directed into the distribution channels.

In a socialist society, it is through wholesaling that the planned commodity exchange of goods is conducted between different branches of the national economy, between economic regions of the country, and between the government and collective farm sectors of production. Wholesale trade brings the goods to the retail sales network, thereby providing the population with a supply of necessary consumer goods.

Wholesaling in a socialist society is significantly different from

---

* V. I. Gogol is one of the leading Russian authorities on marketing in the Soviet Union. In addition to his position as cheif editor of the monthly journal *Soviet Trade* (*Sovetskaia Torgovlia*), he is on the staff of various marketing institutes. He has written numerous articles and edited several books. This article was originally written as part of his textbook, *The Economics of Trade in the Soviet Union,* which was designed for use in Soviet universities and marketing institutes.

Dr. Marshall I. Goldman, Assistant Professor of Economics, Wellesley College, is the translator of this article.

wholesaling in a capitalist country. Capitalist wholesalers conduct their operations with the sole purpose of making a profit. Therefore, they are not interested in the real movement of goods or the full needs of the market or the most rational organization of marketing links. Wholesaling does not bring about the best organization of retailing. It is very often in conflict with retailing in the competitive battle for a share of the profits.

"Distribution [exchange between businessmen] and the fulfillment of distribution [exchange between businessmen and consumers], even though they must ultimately be mutually related are nonetheless affected by completely different laws and motives. This may lead to great conflict." [1] In this passage Marx indicates the division between wholesaling and retailing under capitalism contains the seeds of marketing crises.

In capitalism, wholesaling is characterized by excessive transfer of commodities; in many instances, the goods themselves do not move, only "the title of the goods" is transferred, such as deals on the commodity and future markets. Under such conditions the process of buying and selling can also become a "commodity," even though the real goods do not as yet exist (the sale of a future harvest or of an unmined mineral, etc.). The relationship between demand and supply is completely perverted.

A fictitious demand is created in wholesaling. Frequently this stimulates an increase in production. However, in final accounting, this may lead to a still greater intensification of the impending crisis. The trouble will not break out in the retail sector but in the sphere of wholesaling and banking, which has financial capital at its disposal.

The superiority of socialist wholesaling is reflected in its planned organization, its rational movement of goods, and its sharp reduction of labor and capital costs. Wholesale trade brings about the successful development of the socialist economy and the best satisfaction of the growing demand of the people.

The necessity for wholesaling under socialism stems from the social division of labor and the presence of commodity production. Enterprises of one branch need products produced by other branches of the economy. Some economic regions of the country need production of other regions, etc. In an era of commodity production, the transfer of products from one socialist enterprise to another can be carried out only by buying and selling goods.

In the majority of cases, the movement of goods to the retail net-

---

[1] *The Archives of Marx-Engles,* Vol. IV, p. 71.

work also requires intermediary or wholesale links. This is because (1) the trade network needs a commodity assortment drawn from not one enterprise but many; (2) a large part of the goods are sold in areas other than where they were produced; (3) for many goods, the time of their sale to consumers does not coincide with the time of their production. This, therefore, necessitates accumulation and storage of inventories. There are three types of wholesale trade.

1. Sales of the means of production between government enterprises and organizations (raw materials, materials, fuel, machinery, etc.).

2. Sales between the state and the collective farms (purchases of agricultural products, raw materials, and sales to the collective farms of machinery, fertilizer, fuel, etc.).

3. Sales of consumer goods, as they move to the retail network and restaurants for sale to consumers.

The different forms of wholesale activity are carried out, as a rule, by special industrial sales organizations, procurement units, and Ministry of Trade distributors. However, there are occasions when one of these organizations will perform more than one type of wholesale activity, especially where some goods have several uses.

In this paper, we shall study wholesaling of consumer goods and the activities of those wholesale organizations that carry out this particular type of wholesale work.

The wholesale trade of consumer goods fulfills a series of important functions. Its main task consists of the shipment of goods to areas of consumption and the provision of the retail network of those goods that are necessary to satisfy the demands of the population. To do this, wholesale organizations and enterprises must conduct market research and encourage industry to produce the necessary items in the proper assortment and quality.

Wholesalers are called on to gather products which frequently are produced by thousands of large and small enterprises, put these items into circulation, stimulate the production of new goods, insure their sale on the market, and facilitate the maximum use of local sources of raw materials. Wholesalers should also seek new sources to obtain supplementary supplies of goods needed by consumers.

The work of wholesalers in forming the assortment of goods produced is very important. Because of specialized production, each enterprise prepares goods in a relatively narrow assortment. Moreover, each enterprise seems to prepare only one definite size, color, and fashion in a given period (a shift, a day, a week). But the retailer will demand an assortment that will provide a varied selection of goods. By collecting the products of many enterprises at various times, the wholesale organizations are able to sort the goods and form complete assortments which the retail network needs.

Wholesale trade organizations deliver goods from one economic region to another, thereby facilitating the economic development of each region and satisfying the demands of the population for various goods. For example, the trade organizations of the Ukraine warmly accept prefabricated homes, carpeting, clocks, and television sets from other republics. Eighty to 90 per cent of the Ukranian consumption of fabrics, stockings, sewing machines, and a series of other goods is satisfied by means of imports from other republics. Simultaneously, the Ukraine ships a significant quantity of sugar, knitwear, furniture, and many other goods to other republics. In 1960, the volume of interrepublic trade of 150 commodity groups (fabrics, clothing, shoes, cultural and household goods, perfumes, haberdashery, and groceries), will reach 22 per cent of total production. For example, 34 per cent of cotton textiles, 38 per cent of the radios and television sets, 42 per cent of the sugar, 26 per cent of the dishwares, and 34 per cent of the sewing machines are interchanged between republics in this manner. Moreover, inside each republic there is a considerable amount of interregional trade.

Furthermore, it is necessary for wholesalers to concentrate their stocks of goods so that the inventories of retailers may be refilled and so that goods produced or consumed seasonally may be stored in the interim (i.e., bread, vegetables, potatoes, fruits, sugar, furs, winter and summer sporting equipment, bicycles, etc.). It is also necessary for wholesalers to maintain reserve stocks in case of unforeseen shifts in demand or changes in production or transportation schedules. The concentration of a large mass of goods at the wholesale level is usually more expedient economically because it permits the manipulation of resources and regularity in retail delivery schedules and provides the best facilities for storage with low cost and waste.

Wholesale outlets work actively with manufacturers, in order to increase the output of commodities, widen and renovate the assortment, and improve the quality of goods. Wholesalers also sort, pack, and wrap. This improves service (*kul'tura*) and the quality of the goods.

Plans and Orders

In the socialist economy, the production of goods is developed according to plan. Wholesalers play an important role in this. Wholesale bases and offices present their order (*zakazy* and *zaiavki*) to industry. They also participate in the discussions about planning the assortment and designing fabrics, clothing, and shoes. In order to select the best model of a good, wholesale organizations periodically have trade exhibitions, consumers' conferences, and interregional and interrepublic wholesale trade fairs. They also perform a series of other activities related to market research.

The government plans which outline industrial production cannot specify all the varied goods by title, color, design, fashion, model, style, size, and other quantitative designation. The majority of these questions are decided in the course of dealing between wholesale organizations and regional economic councils (*sovnarkhozy*), their industrial enterprises, the organizations and firms of local and co-operative industry, and state and collective farms.

Wholesale organizations must encourage the production of the most varied goods with the most rational use of productive capabilities. This means creating new products, utilizing local sources of raw materials in the most effective manner, and mobilizing internal reserves. To a large extent, canceling the production of outmoded and no longer desired goods, anticipating seasonal demands, and improving packaging and wrapping depend on the pressure exerted by the wholesale organizations.

The 1957, reorganization of industrial administration, the organization of the *sovnarkhoz* for economic and administrative regions, and the subsequent transfer of production-planning and wholesale-trade responsibility to the union republics has increased the prospects for fuller provision of goods. As the wholesalers were given more authority regarding the production, assortment, and quality of goods, it was expected that the needs of the market would be more fully satisfied.

The delivery contract is one of the most important means of influencing production. Contracts are used to establish the proper relationship between wholesalers and manufacturers and between wholesalers and retailers. The contract is an instrument of the plan; it insures the planned delivery of goods and establishes the material responsibility of the supplier for the proper assortment, quality, and time of delivery.

A procedure for assuring unified contractual practice was worked out in our country as early as the 1930's. This was achieved by establishing Basic Conditions of Delivery (*Osnovnoe Uslovoe Postavki*), which outlined the basis for concluding contracts, Recently, however, the quantity of these model documents has increased inordinately (there are now more than 100 of these Basic Conditions of Delivery for consumer goods), and their excessive detail has begun to hinder independence and initiative. Therefore, as of July 1, 1959, a single Regulation for the Delivery of Consumers Goods was introduced with supplemental Special Provisions for various goods. This new regulation sets forth the basic contractual responsibilities of the supplier and buyer and all the obligations of the government and co-operative organizations and enterprises of the country.

The contractual agreement as to assortment, quality, and cost is very important. Underlying such an agreement are the requests (*zakazy*) of the trade organizations for goods, design conferences with the textile and other industrial organizations. These negotiatons make it possible to match the demands of the market with the potentialities of industry and to determine the proper output assortment.

The issuance of requests (*zakazy*) by trade organizations to industry is a basic method by which trade affects industry. The system of preliminary requests was introduced in the prewar period (1931–36); however, it was not widely adopted. In 1951, the system of preliminary requests was reintroduced for a selected number of goods and by certain trading organizations. In recent years this method has spread and is now used by all trade organizations.

At first, the system of preliminary orders was heavily centralized. All orders were concentrated in the central (*Glavky*) administrations of wholesale trade, and only through them were the orders transmitted to industry. The influence of the local trade organizations on the work of the factories was hindered. Beginning in 1955, the system was decentralized. Local trade organizations and wholesale organizations were allowed to place their orders and decide on the assortment directly with factories located within the borders of their republic, region, or area. Orders were centralized only if items were to be shipped from other republics or regions. This has simplified the method of ordering, strengthened the rights and responsibilities of local organs, and also facilitated the production of items needed in the local market. It has also reduced shipping distances.

Recently, measures have been taken to widen the direct contacts of government and co-operative organizations with industrial enterprises. Now it is even possible to make direct contracts (*priamye dogovor*) if both parties are within the same city or region or some of the smaller republics.

As it works now, the wholesale organizations order goods and make contracts with the industrial enterprises on the basis of models and samples shown by industry at the beginning of the year. In turn, the wholesalers sell these goods to the retail organizations based on the latters orders. To become very common, and, as of 1959, all–Union wholesale fairs were inaugurated. To these fairs come representatives of wholesale bases, industrial enterprises, and retail organizations.

Quality

Assurance of high quality in the U.S.S.R. is a matter of general government significance. The production of goods is permitted only if the established government standards (*Gosty*) are observed. The law prohibits the production of poor-quality merchandise. Government standards are revised and upgraded as production develops and improves.

The government inspectors are under the jurisdiciton of the ministries of trade of the various republics. Quality control is also maintained by the wholesale and retail enterprises, which check the goods as they arrive. If the goods are of poor quality, some are downgraded and sold at a lower price, and some are returned to the factory for repair. If a factory produces a large percentage of poor merchandise, there may be financial sanctions and penalties of as much as 100 per cent of the value of the goods. In certain instances, an order may be given to ban all goods from the guilty factory until a basic improvement has been made in the quality of the affected items.

On some goods, better quality is assured because the factory is required to guarantee the goods for a certain period of time. This is done on television sets, radios, refrigerators, clocks, etc. Within the warranty period, consumers have the right to have the goods repaired free of charge or have the goods exchanged. On many other items (clothing, shoes, fabrics, etc.), the customer also has the right to return the products to the stores within 7 days after finding any production defects.

The order of the Communist Party and the Council of Ministers, "Measures for the Further Improvement of Distribution," prohibits trade organizations from accepting merchandise from manufacturers that does not correspond to assortment, quality, and appearance of the original orders.

Delivery

Wholesalers provide merchandise for the retail network. This allows the wholesaler to influence the level of service at the retail level and how it is organized. One of the ways in which the wholesaler does this is by the centralized delivery of goods to the retail network. This means that the wholesale base assumes responsibility for the regular shipment of goods in the requested assortment directly to the store, restaurant, village shop, or other trading enterprise. Centralized delivery makes possible the creation of consolidated warehouses by the wholesale base, and it frees the retailer from the necessity of running his own transshipping and distributing warehouse.

Wholesalers carry on their work in a spirit of harmony with manufacturers and retailers. They subordinate themselves to the general goal of providing the fullest and best satisfaction of the growing demands of the population. This unity of interests and goals is brought about by the socialistic nature of industry and trade and by the concept of social property on which it is based. Anarchy and the competitive battle are replaced here by planned agreements, which co-ordinate the activities of the different branches of the economy and the links of the marketing system.

THE STRUCTURE OF THE WHOLESALE TRADE NETWORK OF THE MINISTRY OF TRADE[2]

History and Functions

The organization of Soviet wholesale trade dates from the first days of the socialist revolution. By late 1917 and early 1918, syndicates and large wholesale enterprises were nationalized. The wholesale trade of bread, textiles, agricultural machinery, and matches was taken from the hands of private businessmen and taken over by a state monopoly. With the beginning of the New Economic Policy (NEP) in 1921, the stubborn battle for the mastery of wholesale trade began. Wholesaling was considered to be the commanding height on which the success of regulating all market relationships depended. This was also the means by which the exchange relationship between the city and village was to be restored and developed. Wholesaling was also to be used as a lever to force the private businessman out of existence.

Lenin taught that "the proletarian government must become a sharp, zealous, daring manager, a careful wholesale trader."[3] The government created syndicates, trusts, and various other organiztions, including commodity markets and exchanges. Periodically, trade fairs were held in their historical locations. Gradually the government forced the private businessman out of wholesaling. If in

---

[2] This is in contrast to the co-operative wholesaling network (MIG).
[3] V. I. Lenin, *Collected Works*, Vol. XXXIII, p. 36.

1923–24 the percentage of private trade was 22 per cent, by 1925–26 it had fallen to 9 per cent, and by 1929 it was 0.9 per cent. Shortly thereafter, all wholesaling was taken over by the government and the state co-operatives. The complete socialization of wholesale trade and the transition to planned government stocks and shipments brought about changes in wholesaling. In 1928–30, the trade fairs were abolished, and, in 1930, commodity exchanges were closed.

From the end of 1929 to June, 1953, the majority of wholesale operations were under the control of the central (*glavky*) administrations of various industries. Attached to these central administrations were separate industrial sales departments with sales bases and offices. Initially, the Commissariet of Trade(created in 1934 and retitled Ministry of Trade in 1946) controlled only a few wholesale organizations. Thus only a limited number of goods, such as haberdashery, certain household items, jewelry, and some groceries, were under the direct control of trade officials. While this table of organization was successful for a time, it was soon found to hinder the further development of marketing. In matters of quality and assortment and shipping procedure, the attitude of the wholesaler coincided with that of his superior, the manufacturer. Not having their own wholesale organization for most goods, the Ministry of Trade was unable to insure that the right goods were shipped to consumers in the most efficient manner.

To correct this situation, most wholesaling operations were subsequently transferred to the Ministry of Trade of the U.S.S.R. In the process of decentralization which took place in 1957 and 1958, the All Union Ministry of Trade was abolished, and the wholesaling function was assumed by the Republic Ministries of Trade. Now the various Ministries of Trade handle 60 per cent of the total wholesale trade of Russia's consumer goods. This included goods produced by enterprises of various *Sovnarkhozy* and local and co-operative industry. Trade organizations of the Ministry of Trade now make deliveries to retailers and to some industries, as, for example, when they supply fabrics to garments industries and sugar to candy factories.

For certain basic commodities like fabrics, clothing, shoes, soap, and fish products, the wholesale organizations of the Ministry of Trade make deliveries to both urban and rural trade networks. The consumer co-operative trade organization handles the wholesale rural trade of certain other goods (haberdashery, household items). In these instances, the wholesale offices of the Ministry of Trade supply the urban outlets.

More than 10 per cent of all wholesale trade is carried out by agencies of the Ministry of Bread Products in the various republics. This includes the sale of grain, flour, groats, and other grain products. Much of this is sold to bakeries and confectionary factories for further processing.

The Industrial Sales Organizations of the Gosplan units of the Republics also account for about 15 per cent of the wholesale trade of consumer goods. These units were formed in 1957 after the industrial ministries were liquidated and the administration of industry reorganized. The majority of their sales are to other industries, but they do carry some goods intended for consumers, such as petroleum products, electrical appliances, and hardware.

Other wholesale operations are conducted by All Union Book Publishers, the Drug Administration, and factory commissaries. On the whole, about 95 per cent of the wholesale trade volume of consumer goods is handled through government trade organizations.

Wholesaling Units

The main link in government wholesaling is the wholesale base. Depending on the function it performs, there are trade, trade-procurement, and shipping bases.

Trade Bases. Most bases are trade bases. They are located where the goods are to be consumed, and they supply the retail network. Trade bases are usually specialized as to product. The creation of unspecialized bases for the supply of several unrelated goods is usually not justified. Trade bases may be republic, regional, or inter-regional. They are usually located in population centers or at other places having good transportation facilities.

Trade-Procurement Bases. These bases are situated in industrial areas where the consumer goods are produced. Their function is to buy and accumulate goods for shipment to areas of consumption.

Shipping Bases. This last type of base is generally located near large industrial enterprises. The function of a shipping base is to make qualitative checks of goods it receives. It then sells and ships its products to consumer areas throughout the country.

The various wholesale bases have their own warehouses. Here they sort, pack, and ship the goods, but a wholesale base has other functions as well. It is, above all, a link in the movement of goods, and it has the responsibility for facilitating the most expenditious arrangements between industry and distributors, between republics and regions of the country, and between different branches of the country's economy. To do this, wholesale bases must perform a series of important marketing functions. They accumulate orders and requisitions of retail organizations, and they study demand and conduct market research. With this information, wholesale bases and their parent organizations (*Kontory*) order goods from industry in the indicated quantities, assortment, and quality. Once this is done, it is also necessary to draw up shipping plans and specify interrepublic and interregion business relationships.

As an intermediary between producer and consumer, wholesale bases facilitate the introduction of new goods and improved models. They also collect scattered commodity resources, direct them to where the demand is, and check qualitative standards. In doing all of this, a significant portion of the goods is shipped to retailers in transit, that is, they bypass the warehouses of wholesale organizations.

Several wholesalers have not only wholesale bases but manufacturing enterprises as well. Thus the offices of the Meat and Fish Trade Organization has a large network of cold-storage plants, which freeze products, clean fish, and pack butter and meat. The offices of the Delicatessen Trade Organization has a series of packing factories for packaging salt, sugar, and other products. The offices of the Jewelry Trade Organizaton have firms which produce jewelry.

By the beginning of 1958, administration of the Ministry of Trade of the U.S.S.R. had 620 trade and 35 shipping bases. The majority of the trade bases (88 per cent) were located in urban centers of the republics and the regions and the remainder in local centers and at major railroad junctions. As as rule, three quarters of all bases serve a region or part of a region, and the remainder are interregional and serve from 2 to 12 regions (*oblast*).

Government wholesale bases are important marketing enterprises. Bases with sales of from 100 to 500 million rubles a year constitute 65 per cent of the total.[4] Only 18 per cent of the bases have sales volume of less than 100 million rubles, and their share in total government sales is only about 4 per cent.

Offices of the Government Trade Intermediaries connected with the Republic Ministries of Trade also have a certain role to play. These offices render middleman services for wholesalers and other organizations who have surpluses of goods and wish to resell them. Such units help to redistribute inventories to fit the demands of the

---

[4] All ruble figures are in terms of pre-1961 rubles. The official exchange rate was 4 rubles to $1. As of January, 1961, it was 10 old rubles to $1.10.

population. They also strengthen interregional trade connections and facilitate better market research. Sale volume of the Government Trade Intermediaries of the Russian Republic (RSFSR) grew from 1.5 billion rubles in 1954 to 10.4 billion rubles in 1959.

THE WHOLESALE ORGANIZATION OF CONSUMER CO-OPERATIVES

The wholesaling activities of the consumer cooperatives largely duplicate those of the Government Trade Organizations operated by the Ministry of Trade. There are certain differences, however. These are largely predicated by the nature of rural marketing in the Soviet Union, which is the task of the Consumer Cooperatives.

Of necessity, many small and remote warehouses are needed to supply rural Russia. In 1958, these smaller units handled more than 102 billion rubles worth of goods. This is equivalent to 52 per cent of rural retail trade. Recently, the share of these smaller warehouses has fallen, as large consolidated warehouses have been built in the rural centers.

In addition to the usual local and regional warehouses and wholesale organizations of the consumer co-operative, normal wholesale activity is supplemented by mail-order service. In this way, small orders of goods can be provided directly by mail from larger mail-order bases. Given the remoteness of many rural retailers, such service is a necessity. The Central Organization of Consumer Cooperatives maintains the Cooperative Mail-Order Trade Administration for this purpose. By 1965, this type of mail-order activity will expand to 6 billion rubles worth of goods.

Occasionally, unnecessary parallelism develops between the work of the wholesale bases run by the government and those of the consumer co-operatives. This complicates the movement of goods and increases the wholesale costs of distribution. Such a situation demands that additional work be done in order to improve the organization of wholesale trade in the country.

THE FLOW OF GOODS AND THE PLAN OF THEIR SHIPMENT

The Structure of Soviet Transportation

The movement of goods from the point of production to the point of consumption is the task of the wholesaler. Karl Marx indicated that the product is ready for consumption only when it has reached its ultimate destination. Given the modern-day division of labor, the manufacturer is usually separated from the consumer, as to both time and distance. A transportation program is thus a necessity.

Whereas the economic necessity for shipping goods arises in all societies with the division of labor, the form and organization of this movement is determined by the method of production. In a capitalist society, which is characterized by anarchy and competition both in production and in distribution, it is impossible to organize transportation rationally. Lenin taught that, in capitalism, all work is for naught because of the disorder and chaos in capitalistic production. "So much time is lost transferring raw materials through hundreds of speculators and brokers amid market uncertainty. Not only time, but the product itself is misdirected and wasted. Moreover, the loss of time and labor on the delivery of goods to the consumer through an abyss of small middlemen who also are ignorant of the market conditions creates both superfluous shipping and excessive buying."

In capitalist markets, commodities must follow a long and tangled route through tens of middlemen. However, Frederick Engles pointed out more than a hundred years ago that the situation in socialism is entirely different. "In due time and without excessive frills the proper quantity of each good needed to satisfy the population is determined. Excess middlemen will be unnecessary. Goods will be delivered directly to where they are needed. Delays and reshipping will be eliminated and shipments will be made with no waste. It will no longer be necessary to pay profits to speculators and big and small businessmen."

The socialist method of production makes possible the rational and planned organization of commodity shipments with a minimum expenditure of time, labor, and material resources. This type of planning in a socialist society is based on the predetermined balance of production and consumption (supply and demand) and the planned sale of an enterprise's products as specified by a locational plan. This involves the determination of the marketing and intermediary links through which goods will move and the planned dispatch of shipping equipment.

By determining the location of production resources, developing particular sectors of the economy, and improving transportation connections, the prerequisites are provided for further improvement in the commodity flow. For example, the creation of a major textile complex in Western Siberia and Uzbekistan brought production to the sources of the raw material, fuel, and to the consumers of the fabrics. Previously, all fabrics had to be shipped from the central regions of the country. The construction of a sugar factory in the Kuban region, in Kazakhstan, and in a series of other regions permitted a curtailment of sugar shipments from the Ukraine. The opening of candy factories in the east and several other regions of the country sharply reduced the shipment of these goods from Moscow and Leningrad. The latter's share of confectionary production fell from 72 per cent to 23 per cent.

The creation of state farms for the purpose of growing potatoes and vegetables around major cities and industrial centers is of considerable importance. These state farms, along with the formation of specialized collective farms, means shorter shipping distance for potatoes, vegetables, milk and other products consumed by cities.

The organization of *Sovnarkhozy* and the decentralization of industrial administration permits a fuller use of local resources, a more rational location policy, and more rational ties between and inside regions. The present Seven-Year Plan for 1959–60 calls for further moves in this direction.

Transportation is one of the basic factors affecting the commodity flow. Freight turnover of all forms of transport increased by more than 2.2 times from 1950 to 1958 and amounted to more than 1,600 billion tons/kilometers. With the rapid development of highway transportation and pipelines, the share of the various forms of transportation in total freight turnover fell. The share of railroad freight was reduced from 85.1 per cent in 1940 to 81.2 per cent in 1958 and will continue to fall somewhat in the current Seven-Year Plan. Nonetheless, railroad transportation remains the main method of shipping goods to all the most important regions of our huge country. Freight turnover of the railroad in 1965 will reach 1,800–1,850 billion tons/kilometers.

A wider and more efficient use of automotive transport is of major importance in the rationalization of the commodity flow. Automotive transport is used primarily for short shipments. While the average shipment by railroad in 1958 amounted to 805 kilometers and river transport amounted to 480 kilometers, automotive transport amounted to only 12 kilometers. Trucks are used primarily within the city, around the city, and for interregion shipments. In 1958 an average truck carried 6,474 million tons of goods, while an average freight car carried 1,617 million tons—that is, one fourth as much. Trucking has many advantages and is being used more and more for longer hauls.

There is great efficiency in centralizing transport facilities. This means that all the supply points in the trade network ship their goods via one trucking organization. This frees the stores, restaurants, and other recipients from having to order, route, and deliver. Normally, deliveries are routed along circular routes. This permits a more efficient use of the trucks and their shipping capacities. Costs are lowered, time saving and goods delivered regularly according to schedule. This system is widely used throughout the country, and more than half the shipments of many products are made this way. Nonetheless, there are still too many warehouses scattered about. This increases costs and leads to duplication in delivery routes. It is necessary to improve this situation and use centralized deliveries more widely, in both urban and rural areas.

Soviet river transportation covers more than 120,000 kilometers. It is especially suited for bulk loads. Shipping by sea is also important, and where there are suitable ports, goods can be shipped faster by sea than by river.

It is often necessary to use several forms of transportation. It is important to use the right combination. Bulk shipments can be moved either by truck or by freight car if the distance is 26–31 kilometers. Broken-lot shipments may be sent by truck or train if the distance is 32–59 kilometers. If trailer trucks are used, trucks may be sent over greater distances.

The unbalanced location of our industry and its specialization, as well as the significant territory of our country, mean that some goods are sent long distances. The increasing role of the eastern portions of the country intensifies the problem. Thus, while the average haul by railroad in 1940 was 700 kilometers, it had increased to 805 kilometers by 1958. For some goods, such as cans, the average shipment amounts to 2,200 kilometers.

Under such conditions, irrational shipping procedures must be eliminated. In some instances, there are sources of supply closer at hand, and cross-shipments actually take place. This arises when the assortment of goods is too narrow in various regions of the country and there are deficiencies in the planning and organization of transportation. Given proper organization and co-operation, these deficiencies can be remedied. The importance of undertaking cost-reduction programs is underscored by the fact that the total amount spent on transportation in the Soviet Union amounts to 80 billion rubles yearly. Of this, 12 billion rubles is spent for wholesale and retail trade. A reduction of total transportation cost by 1 per cent will yield a saving of more than 800 million rubles. A similar reduction in the transportation necessary for marketing would amount to 120 million rubles.

The proper organization of freight rates is also important. In railroading, rates are divided into the following categories: general, exceptional, privileged, and local.

General. These are the normal rates set for most goods throughout the country.

Exceptional. These apply for certain goods when they are shipped between specified points. Depending on what is desired, these rates can be set higher or lower than the general rates.

Privileged. These lower rates are granted to certain organizations or firms or goods which have a special designation.

Local. These rates are set by various lines for the rendering of special services, such as disinfecting the car, etc.

Freight rates also depend on the character of the shipment. Thus rates are also classified as main line, by the carload, and broken lot.

Main Line. These are the lowest rates and apply because mass shipments mean lower costs. For instance, such rates are set on fish sent from seaports and sugar sent from sugar-producing areas.

Carload. This is the rate used for a carload shipment.

Broken lot. This is higher than the carload rate and applies to less than carload shipments.

Rates also differ according to the distance of the shipment. If the destination is farther than the normal shipment, then rates may be raised unless it can be shown that there is no more rational method of shipping. Such methods of rate making promote the most efficient shipping and use of railroad transportation.

Trucking rates are divided by type of shipment (there are 4 classes). Payments are made by the ton/kilometer and in some instances are paid by ton or number of days a truck is required.

To improve the use of all transportation resources, fines are levied if established norms are not fulfilled, and premiums are awarded for rapid release of transportation equipment and consolidation of small shipments.

Forms of Commodity Flow

There are two methods of moving goods from the producer to the retail network: direct transit and warehouse storage.

In the direct-transit method, the goods are sent from the producer (through an expediter or shipping base) directly to the retail trade network. This is used mostly for goods that do not require sorting or that are produced by several firms in one city. For example, bread is shipped directly from the local bakery. It is a bit different when goods must be shipped from out of town. Then only the largest stores (and only for certain goods) will receive direct-transit shipments by the carload or in a shipping container.

There are many locally produced goods which cannot be shipped without preliminary sorting in a wholesale warehouse. Furthermore, it is often necessary to package and stock replacement merchandise in warehouses because these things cannot be done efficiently by the retail organization itself.

When goods cannot be sent direct, the warehouse form of shipment is used. This simply means that when the goods are produced, they are processed through one, two, and sometimes three warehouses before they reach the retail outlet.

Thus there are various intermediary links between producer and seller. The number of such links is an important problem in the commodity flow. This affects the amount of time a good must stay in circulation and the size of inventories since each extra link means a delay in the flow of goods. An increase in the number of links means that more spaces must be provided, more labor effort expended, and more equipment and transportation required. This all increases the cost of distribution.

From what has been said above, it is clear that efforts should be made to increase direct-transit shipments and reduce the number of trade links. This can be accomplished by the following measures:

a) Provide the trade network with as many locally produced goods as possible and reduce the shipment of goods from distant regions

b) Increase containerization

c) Consolidate the shipment of odd lots or use mail-order shipments [5]

d) Enlarge the size of trade outlets so they will be able to handle goods sent by direct transit.

Containerization holds great promise. It means more direct transit, greater use of material-handling equipment, cheaper packaging costs, faster service, and less waste. By 1965, the number of loading platforms for containers will be 1,100 in comparison with 850 in 1958. The number of containers will grow to 621,000 as opposed to 347,000.

Many manufactured goods are shipped wholly by means of direct

---

[5] This may very well increase total costs of distribution and simply shift the work to the transportation sector (MIG).

transit. Numerous, small, and remote trade links are usually required for the movement of agricultural products. Yet a large portion of such goods do move in direct transit. It must be understoood that direct transit frequently means that the goods are sent from the factory to the parent retail organization and then to the retail store or restaurant. This is not direct transit in the true meaning of the word, since there do exist intermediate retail warehouse links.

The presence in one city of both wholesale and retail warehouse leads to a dispersion of warehouse activity, excessive expenditures, and needless transshipment. Consequently, the consolidation of warehouses and their transfer to wholesale organizations has important significance. By consolidating warehouses in Talinin, Kazan, Kuibyshev, Sverdlovsk, and Tashkent, storage space has been increased by an average of 34 per cent, and the amount paid yearly to warehouse employees has been reduced by more than 2 million rubles. Moreover, servicing the trade network has been improved, and inventories have been reduced.

Technically, the consolidation of retail warehouses with wholesale warehouses means that goods formerly sent by direct transit are now sent via storage warehouses. But, because this in fact means that one marketing link has been eliminated, a fall in the amount of direct transit because of such consolidations is not considered to be a bad thing.

The formation of larger consumer co-operative societies and a consolidation of their resources into intercounty wholesale bases also permit more direct-transit shipments and a bypassing of the warehouse of the county consumer co-operative. This eliminates one link of the commodity flow. In the old system goods moved in the following manner:

Factory—Wholesale base of the—Warehouse of—Retail outlet
Ministry of Trade or   County Co-op.   of co-op.
Regional wholesale
base of the co-op.

With the organization of intercounty bases, the movement takes the following form:

Factory—Intercounty base—Retail outlet of co-op

The elimination of superfluous links and the increase in direct-transit freight are very important. Yet it must be remembered that overemphasis on direct-transit freight, especially for goods that come in a complicated assortment may hinder more than it helps.

The Planning of Shipments (Delivery and Dispatch)

The shipments plan is drawn up after consideration of the rational intercounty connections, the proper distribution of the freight load between the various forms of transportation, and the best use of transportation facilities.

In essence, the shipment plan depends on the balance of production and consumption of consumer goods in each economic region of the country. This is also called the "transportation economic balance." The following factors must be balanced:

Input	*Output*
1. Stocks of goods in industry and wholesale bases at beginning of period	1. Fund of goods (i.e., those subject to planning) which are to be consumed within the given region
2. Production in the period within the economic region	2. Funds of goods destined for institutional consumers in the region
3. Delivery of goods from other regions	3. Goods are to be shipped outside the region
	4. Stocks and inventory at end of planning period

By deriving this balance, it can be determined what must be brought in from other areas or what is available for shipment elsewhere. Such a balance is made for all basic commodity groups. Moreover, the intergroup assortment of goods must be considered and also how the balances work out on a quarterly basis within the year.

The importance of interassortment balance was seen in Estonia in 1957. It looked for a time as if they could export to other republics about 502 million rubles worth of fabrics. This would have left 213 million rubles worth of consumption within the republic. It was found, however, that 115 million rubles of the fabric set aside for local consumption was not suited to local tastes. Instead, another 115 million rubles worth of goods had to be imported from other republics. This also meant, of course, that the original 115 million rubles of fabric could in turn be exported outside Estonia, along with the original shipment of 502 million rubles.

It is clear from the above example that planning the balance of shipments is a complicated affair. Moreover, it is not enough just to put the goods where they are desired; it is also necessary to keep shipping distances down as low as possible. To do this, wholesale bases must actively promote production assortment in the *sovnarkhozy,* factories, local industrial firms, and co-operative workshops so that the area will become more self-sufficient. Yet specialization and division of labor are to be encouraged so that enough will be produced for shipment outside the immediate area. Thus on occasion it is even permissible to promote specialization and production of a narrow line of goods because the growth of output and reduction of production costs offset the transportation expense. Despite the fact that this increases the number of goods that must be shipped, this may be the best solution, although there are many occasions when too much specialization is not justified.

Clearly, this is a complicated matter and must be balanced in the optimum manner. Thus, when deciding whether or not to produce or bring in shoes, it usually is more expedient to ship in the leather and other raw materials rather than the finished shoes. If the shoes are shipped in, they are subject to damage in shipment, and shipping charges are significantly higher for the finished product.

This whole question of proper balance is vitally important to the nation's economy. For example, in the period from 1955 to 1957, thanks to the rational planning of bicycle shipments, the annual use of transportation was reduced by 10,000 freight cars, which meant a saving of 15 million rubles.

Interregional and interrepublic shipment are very important in our country and require up to a million freight cars and several million containers yearly. Almost one third of the output of 32 of the most important industrial goods enter into interregional trade. Some republics receive almost the entire supply of certain goods from other republics.

After the pattern of shipments and deliveries has been worked out, a scheme to link regions of consumption with regions of production is prepared. In doing this, a whole complex of questions is considered regarding the distance of deliveries, the presence of suitable transportation facilities, the assortment of goods to be shipped, the value of deliveries, the existence of business ties, etc. When the various regions are linked together, a plan of interregional shipments is compiled in the form of an input-output table. The productive regions (the factory or wholesale base) are arranged in rows, and the consumption regions are enumerated in columns.

The railroads, having received detailed plans from wholesale organizations, industrial sales offices, procurement bases, and other organizations, work out for themselves a general scheme of interline switching, which specifies the receipt and delivery of shipping loads of the basic commodities. Based on these plans and a study of the average shipping distance, the general volume of freight turnover in

ton-kilometers can be estimated. The plans linking consumption regions are carried further in the linking-up of shipping points and
receiving points for each good. To derive a shipping plan in which
the distances traveled are the smallest possible, one should use a
graphic-analytical method or compare the differences in distance. By
finding the least possible shipping distances, costs of distribution are
lowered, and there is no waste of manpower or time.

Also important in fulfilling the plan is a smooth flow of goods to
all regions on a quarterly, monthly, and 10-day basis. To do this, the
manufacturer must work continuously, the wholesale base must ship
regularly to all customers, and the transportation agencies must make
their deliveries on time. Irregular shipments of goods disrupt trade
and lead to excessive inventory formation, unfilled plans, and poor
service. A steady flow of deliveries is one of the main criteria of efficient wholesale trade.

Thus the tasks of wholesale trade are to rationalize the commodity
flow, curtail the number of handling stages, and assure the smooth
and timely delivery of the proper assortment of goods.

WHOLESALE TRADE AND ITS PLANNING

It will be remembered that sales are made in two ways in wholesale
trade, from the warehouse and by direct transit. Gross wholesale
trade of the country consists of the aggregate sales of all wholesale
organizations and firms. The general sum of wholesale trade will inevitably include so-called duplicate trade, that is, the double counting
of some goods as they move between wholesale organizations. In addition, the general sum of wholesale trade includes the sale of some
goods that are not planned by the government authorities. The end
result is that the general volume of wholesale trade usually exceeds
the country's retail sales volume.

While one can judge the tempo of consumption by the dynamics
of retail sales volume (in constant prices), the volume of wholesale
transactions has no such meaning. An increase in wholesale volume
may be due to an increase in goods or an increase in the number of
trade stages or links within the wholesaling operation. Because of
this, no attempt is made to determine a goal for wholesale transactions, nor is there any effort to increase wholesaling activity in the
country's economic plan.

Wholesale trade volume is planned by each separate trade system
where necessary. (This includes the various republic ministries of
trade, the consumer's co-operative, and industrial sales offices of the
republic gosplans.) Underlying the plan of the shipping bases is the

retail plan of sales of the organizations served by the bases. It is also necessary to consider the shipment of goods which must be made to institutional consumers. The shipping routes for various goods, the sources of supply, and inventories at wholesale and retail warehouses are also important. The wholesale trade plan must balance the commodity stocks assigned to a given region with the requisitions of retail organizations, which, in turn, are needed to conduct retail trade.

The wholesale base must conduct market research and study the stage of the cycle of the given region, determine what production opportunities there are at local factories, ascertain what other wholesale bases in other areas are willing to exchange, and also study the volume of shipments for interregional and interrepublic deliveries. Before wholesale trade plans can be drawn up, it is also necessary to study the sales of the preceding period, the sources which provided the supplies, and the extent to which the shipping and receiving plan was fulfilled. This must be done for each commodity assortment, for various time periods, and for both institutional and noninstitutional consumers. It may happen that the over-all sales plan was fulfilled but that the quota of direct-transit shipments was too low. This may cast a different light on the results of the plan because less direct transit means that more warehouse space, labor, and transportation will be required, that costs of distribution will be increased, and that deliveries will be slower than intended. On the other hand, it may be found that direct-transit shipments to villages will exceed the plan. This is undesirable because of the minuteness of most retail outlets in rural areas. By making a breakdown of transportation activity in past periods, it may also develop that shipments to other regions will fall below expectation. Such provincial (*mestnicheskie*) tendencies cannot be tolerated because they hamper the development of the socialist economy.

Also included in the plan of wholesale trade is an indicator of inventory accumulation. Because of the effect of direct transit sales, the size of inventory stocks is not related to the general wholesale volume of sales but only to the sales of the warehouse. A typical plan of wholesale trade might look like this:

Warehouse inventory and en route at beginning of year.........	20
Planned wholesale trade including	250
Sales from warehouse	110
Direct-transit sales	140
Norm of warehouse inventory and stocks en route..............	30
Planned shipments to the warehouse........................	120

$$(110 + 30 - 20)$$

FIGURE 1

THE WHOLESALING PROCEDURE IN THE SOVIET UNION

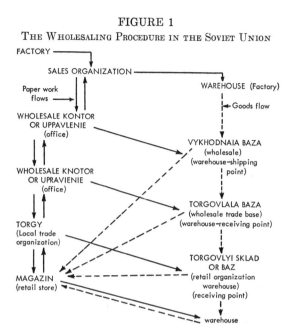

——————— paper work flow

— — — — — goods flow

Source: Marshall I. Goldman, *Marketing in the Soviet Union* (Glencoe, Ill.: Free Press, 1962).

Inventory norms are set so that there will be a continuous flow of goods to the retail network and other consumers. This means that the assortment must be complete and that interregional deliveries will also be provided. The special problems created by seasonal inventory demands and early shipments must also be anticipated.

Finally, in judging the success of the wholesale plan, it is also necessary to consider the success of the retail plan. The work of the wholesale base can be called successful only if the goods which it supplies to the retailer permit the latter to meet his retail sales plan. The pace of retail sales must be smooth without any disruptions because of inadequate stocks.

TABLE 1*

ORGANIZATION OF THE SOVIET MINISTRY OF TRADE, January, 1959

A. Administration and control

    1. Administration (*Upravlenie*) of: Food sales, Bakery product sales, Manufactured goods, Restaurants, Planning economic commission, Organization of trade, Technology and capital constructions, Cadres.

    2. Department (*Otdel*) of: Pricing, Labor and Wages, Productive Enterprises, Transportation, Finance, Legal Matters, Accounting, Complaint Bureau.

    3. Main Administration (*Glavnoe Upravlenie*) of: Inspection, Resort Areas, Far North, Material Technical Supply (*Glavsnab*).

B. Operational and wholesaling (offices and warehouses)

1. Office (*Kontor*) of: *Rosmiasorybtorg* (meats, fats, fish), *Rosbakaleia* (groceries), *Rostekstiltorg* (textiles), *Rostorgodezhda* (clothes), *Rosobuvtorg* (shoes), *Roskhoztorg* (household goods), *Roskultorg* (cultural and sporting goods), *Rosgalantereia* (haberdashery, toiletries, cosmetics, perfumes), *Roslesstroitorg* (lumber and construction material), *Rosiuvelirtorg* (jewelry).

C. Functional services

1. *Posyltorg* (mail order).
2. *Torgposredkontora* (commission agent office—trade fairs).
3. *Rostorgmontazh* (refrigeration operation and service).
4. *Rostorgstroi* (construction and repair).
5. *Torgreklama* (advertising offices).

* Source: *Sovetskaia Torgovlia*, January 8, 1959, p. 4.

FIGURE 2

CHAIN OF COMMAND IN TRADE AS OF THE FALL OF 1960

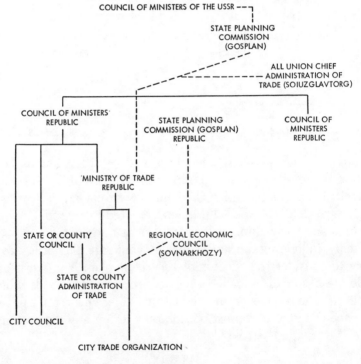

Source: Marshall I. Goldman, *Marketing in the Soviet Union* (Glencoe, Ill.: Free Press, 1962).

COMMUNIST CHINA

The reader of this chapter may be led to doubt some of the advantages claimed for planned wholesaling in contrast to capitalistic wholesaling, as set forth in the exposition of wholesaling in the Soviet Union. The writer indicates that economic efficiency is not the inevitable outcome of state planning. The excess of middlemen attributed to capitalism is found to be a real and even more besetting problem where the state attempts to determine through whose hands products should pass.

Of particular interest in this chapter is an explanation of how the distributive system may be made the instrument through which state control is gained over the entire economy. The commercial or distributive portion of the economy was subserved through progressive stages of control over the sources of supply to retailers. The industrial or manufacturing segment of the economy, on the other hand, was socialized through progressive control over the outlets for finished goods. Distribution became dominated through organization of small establishments into co-operatives, through joint state ownership of business organizations, through complete nationalization, and, finally, through the establishment of rural communes. Production became dominated through strategic order placing, through purchasing of entire output, through joint state-private operation, and, finally, through the "buying-up" of the enterprise by the state.

The complexity of the wholesaling system in China may be more apparent than real, in some respects. It is the author's conclusion that the nationalization experience has proved the inherence of need for wholesaling in given market situations. The simplicity of this fact, however, is obscured by ideological substitution of public for private institutions and by the peculiar restrictions placed upon economic

251

institutions for the achievement of political ends. One who is familiar with the free-market operations of wholesaling will see, in its more restricted setting, counterpart activities and organizations.

Wholesaling in Communist China

YU-MIN CHOU [*]

Distribution in the Chinese market has undergone considerable transformation since the Communists took power in 1949. At that time, the public sector of the economy began to exert a controlling influence in the distribution of goods, and marketing became a weapon for the eventual introduction of over-all economic planning by the state.

The government enforced restrictions on the free exchange of goods by introducing state control over the sources of supply for major commodities. This was known as "planned purchase and planned supply." At the same time, small commercial units were converted into co-operatives. Then, gradually, larger private enterprises were merged into the public sector through joint state-private operation, and eventually these were completely nationalized. With the introduction of the rural communes in 1958, the socialization of the domestic marketing channels was virtually complete. All these changes occurred in less than a decade.

An examination of wholesaling in Communist China shows the effect direct control of an economy has on market intermediaries. It also demonstrates that in a given social or market situation certain wholesaling functions are inherent and can not be eliminated merely by elimination of private middlemen. It also demonstrates the vital relation of the distribution system to the entire economy, evidenced by the vulnerability of the economy when control is gained over the distributive mechanism.

DOMESTIC MARKETING IN TRANSITION

The effect on wholesaling of the process of socialization since 1949 is indicated in Table 1. Three evolutionary steps were undertaken in

[*] Dr. Yu-min Chou is Assistant Professor of Economics, Hanakamer School of Business, Baylor University, Waco, Texas. He was educated in China through junior college. Having come to the United States in 1951, he received from the University of Illinois his B.A. in 1954, M.A. in 1955, and Ph.D. in economics in 1960.

253

socializing private commerce—the socialization of small enterprises, the socialization of large enterprises, and the establishment of state trading companies.

TABLE 1

WHOLESALE SALES BY OWNERSHIP OF ESTABLISHMENTS
COMMUNIST CHINA, 1950–55
(Percentages)

	1950	1951	1952	1953	1954	1955
Total wholesale volume	100	100	100	100	100	100
State trading companies	23.2	33.4	60.5 ⎫			
Co-operative commerce	0.6	1.0	2.7 ⎭	69.2	89.3	94.8
Joint state-private commerce	0.1	0.2	0.5	0.5	0.5	0.8
Private commerce	76.1	65.4	36.3	30.3	10.2	4.4

Source: H. Chin et al., Changes in Our Country's Industry and Commerce over the Past Seven Years, 1949–1956 (Peking: Finance and Economics Press, 1957), pp. 54, 121.

Socialization of Small, Individualistic Commercial Units

The processes of socialization were applied alike in due course to traders, handicraft producers, and farm commercial organizations.

Peddlers and Small Traders. The transformation of peddlers and small traders into a more socialistic organization took two forms: co-operative groups and co-operative stores.[1] Vendors comprising the co-operative groups retained their individual operation; the co-operative stores exchanged individual for collective operation—in the co-operative stores peddlers and small traders operated stores together and shared profits jointly. Both co-operative groups and co-operative stores acted as distributors, commission agents, or purchasing agents for the state enterprises. Their operations resembled those of co-operative chains in the United States, except that they also acted as purchasing agents for the state enterprises in acquiring local products.

Eventually, co-operative groups and co-operative stores were closely integrated into the public sector through state control over sources of supply. This process was completed in 1958, when the rural communes were created. Most of the co-operative groups and stores were then taken over as the supply and marketing departments of the communes.

---

[1] For detail about co-operatives, see M. C. Hsueh et al., The Socialist Transformation of the National Economy in Communist China (Peking: Foreign Language Press, 1960), pp. 159–165.

Individual Handicraft Producers. Although actually producers, handicrafters were also important distributors of goods; hence they were regarded as an instrument for socialization. Until during the 1950's, handicraft products accounted for about 60–70 per cent of the total industrial products supplied to farmers.[2] According to the state plan, the transformation of individual handicraft producers into co-operatives was to take three forms: the supply and marketing groups, the supply and marketing co-operatives, and the producers' co-operatives.[3]

The supply and marketing groups were organized for the purpose of purchasing raw materials from, or selling products to, state commercial establishments and handicraft supply and marketing co-operatives. They also accepted orders from handicraft supply and marketing co-operatives for processing.[4]

The supply and marketing co-operatives were organized on a larger scale, consisting of a number of handicraft producers and supply and marketing groups.[5] Their objective was to solve the common problem of raw-material supply and marketing for the members. They differed from supply and marketing groups not only in the scale of operation but also in the nature of their organization. In the supply and marketing co-operatives, the members owned shares of the co-operatives and some common property, and there was more division of work.[6]

As the experience in the collective work of marketing increased and common property accumulated, producers' co-operatives were formed. In this manner, production and marketing of handicrafts were unified. Today, most handicraft co-operatives are merged into state industries, communal industries, and communal supply and marketing departments.

Farmers' Commercial Organizations. By the time the rural communes were created, farmers had also been organized into co-operatives for marketing, finance, and production. In marketing, the agricultural supply and marketing co-operatives became commercial

---

[2] T. H. Hsu, *The Economic Analysis of Our Country during the Transitional Period* (Peking: Science Publication Press, 1957), p. 94.

[3] *Jen-min Jih-pao* (*People's Daily*), July 13, 1954.

[4] Hsueh *et al., op. cit.,* p. 149.

[5] A Japanese source reported that a supply and marketing group consisted of at least three handicraft producers in the rural areas and five handicraft producers in the urban areas, while a supply and marketing co-operative consisted of at least eleven households in the rural areas and twenty households in the urban areas. See Asahi Shinbunsha Research Department, *The True Picture of the Chinese Socialist Economy,* Vol. I (Tokyo: Asahi Shinbunsha, 1958), p. 321.

[6] Hsueh *et al., op. cit.,* p. 149.

organizations which served as an important link between the state trading companies and the farmers in the distribution of goods.

The objectives of the agricultural supply and marketing co-operatives were twofold. They were, first, to increase the flow of goods between the cities and the rural areas, through co-operative organiza-tion in supply and marketing. Second, they were to draw the farmers closer to state planning by increasing trade between the state trading companies and the co-operatives and by eliminating private whole-salers.[7] The state trading companies acted as both suppliers and marketing agents for the co-operatives. However, the latter appears to have been more important.[8] It was by this means that the state gained control over the products produced by the farmers.

Socialization of Industry and Commerce

Like the smaller private enterprises, larger enterprises of industry and commerce also became socialized.

Industry. Socialization of industries also affected the structure of the marketing channels. Through the state trading companies, the state expanded its activities to include schemes such as "processing," "placing orders," "purchasing the entire output of private enter-prises," and "marketing all finished products of private enterprises." Eventually these schemes were replaced by joint state-private opera-tion and, finally, by full-state operation of private enterprises.[9]

In "processing," the state sector supplied the capitalist industry with raw materials or semifinished products for processing in the re-quired quality and quantity within a stated time. The finished prod-ucts were then procured by the state trading companies for distribu-tion in the market. In some instances, orders by the state trading companies were placed directly with the capitalist industry. This scheme was known as "placing orders." When necessary, the state trading companies might pay part of the price or supply part of the raw materials in advance. Free disposal of any excess above the quota was permitted the private enterprises under "processing" and "plac-ing orders" arrangement.

---

[7] *Jen-min Jih-pao,* November 30, 1954.

[8] Of the trade (in value) between the agricultural supply and marketing co-operatives and the state trading companies, the supply portion accounted for 47.3 per cent and the marketing portion accounted for 52.7 per cent in 1951. They were 43.7 and 56.3 per cent in 1952, 37.5 and 62.5 per cent in 1953, 28.9 and 71.1 per cent in 1954, respectively (Asahi Shinbunsha Research Department, *op. cit.,* Vol. II).

[9] For details about the socialization of industries, see T. T. Kuan, *The Socialist Trans-formation of Capitalist Industry and Commerce in China* (Peking: Foreign Languages Press, 1960), pp. 59–72, 75–88.

Under the "purchasing the entire output of private enterprises" arrangement, the state trading companies possessed the exclusive right to purchase, on a long-term basis, certain important industrial products from private enterprises at appropriate prices.

In contrast with the socialization of small, individualistic commercial units, where an attempt was made to control the sources of supply for those units, the socialization of the capitalist industries seemed to seek control over the outlets of the finished products. Eventually, by investing in these industries with a scheme known as joint state-private operation, the state acquired fuller control over the production and marketing activities of the capitalist industries. Since 1956, the capitalist industries have been fully integrated into the state sector. This full state operation was achieved through the policy of "buying up," which meant that the state would acquire full ownership of the capitalist industries in return for a payment of 5 per cent interest per annum until 1962 to the previous owners of the property.[10]

Commerce. The process of socialization of commerce took the following steps: private stores acted as retail distributors of the state; private stores acted as commission agents for the state; the state invested in private stores in joint state-private operation; the state acquired full control of private stores through the "buying-up" policy.[11]

Where private stores acted as retail distributors of the state, retail stores were made retail distributors of the state trading companies. The state trading companies supplied the private stores with goods and set their retail prices. The difference between the wholesale price (the price charged by the state trading companies) and the retail price then became the profit of the retail stores. This arrangement was also applied to the private wholesalers when they were made wholesale distributors for the state. The private wholesalers purchased goods in cash from the state trading companies and sold them at wholesale. This was done according to the state plan and other specific conditions.

When private stores served as commission agents, they had to deposit a certain sum with the state trading companies as guarantee that the goods would be sold on a commission basis according to the state plan and at the prices set by the state trading companies. Private import and export concerns were also made commission agents for the state trading companies in foreign trade.

[10] *Ibid.*, pp. 86–87.
[11] For detail, see *ibid.*, pp. 59–62, 75–88.

In contrast with the socialization of the capitalist industries, the socialization of commerce was achieved through control over the source of supply to the retailers. As with industries, the state absorbed commerce, first by joint state-private operation and then by full state operation through the "buying-up" policy in 1956. In this manner, former private commercial enterprises became a part of the state commercial establishments.

State Trading Companies

As indicated in the previous sections, the state trading companies performed a leading role in the socialization of Communist China's domestic market. The state trading companies were able to link the private sector with the public sector either through control over the source of supply to the private enterprises or through control over the outlet of the finished products. Their mounting influence is indicated in the increasing share of their trade in the total wholesale volume shown in Table 1.

Trading companies for different commodities were established under the jurisdiction of the Ministry of Commerce. They maintained extensive chains down to the local levels (i.e., provincial and prefectural state trading companies) in the procurement and distribution of goods.[12] They are listed below in the chronological order of their establishment: [13]

1. Petroleum Company, 1949
2. Grain Company, 1950
3. Cotton Cloth Company, 1950
4. Mining and Construction Machineries Company, 1950
5. Native Products Company, 1950
6. The National Department Stores, 1950
7. Oil and Paints Company, 1950
8. Salt Company, 1950
9. Small Equipments and Machineries Company, 1952
10. Chemical Raw Materials Company, 1952
11. Land Transportation Company, 1952
12. Transportation and Electrical Equipments Company, 1952
13. Foodstuffs Company, 1953
14. Tobacco and Liquors Company, date of establishment not known

---

[12] A province is equivalent to a state, and a prefecture to a county, in the United States.

[13] Ajia Seikei Gakkai, *A Survey on Chinese Politics and Economy* (Tokyo: Hitotsubashi Book Co., 1960), p. 535.

15. Cultural Materials Company, 1955
16. Chinese Medical Materials Company, date of establishment not known
17. Movie Distribution Company, date of establishment not known
18. Western Medicine Company, date of establishment not known
19. Fabric Company, 1955
20. Marine Products Supply Company, 1955
21. Vegetables Company, 1955

When the movement to decentralize national economic control started in 1958, these state trading companies, with chains of command in centralized head offices, were abolished. Subsequently, their local establishments were placed under the control of the provincial and prefectural governments.[14]

WHOLESALING TODAY IN THE DOMESTIC MARKET

Little published information on wholesaling in Communist China exists, probably because of the traditional lack of emphasis by Marxists on marketing and the complex and transitory nature of the marketing channels in Communist China. In fact, wholesaling as a private activity carried on through independent channels hardly exists today. It has been knit into the state-operated commercial network, in which wholesaling channels are only a part of the whole network.

In Communist China, goods are distributed through a variety of channels. The channels used depend partly upon the nature of the goods handled—whether they are capital goods or consumer goods, agricultural or industrial products. Not all the goods are distributed through channels involving middlemen. Generally, capital goods are distributed directly between state enterprises under direct allocation administered by the State Council. Hence these goods do not enter the channels which are normally under the jurisdiction of the Ministry of Commerce and the commercial departments of the local authorities. Consumer goods are the main items distributed through such indirect marketing channels.

Distribution of Goods under the State Council's Direct Allocation Method

Ordinarily, important raw materials, metals, large machinery, and

---

[14] State Council, *Collection of Laws, Regulations, and Statements of the People's Republic of China* (Peking: Law Press, 1957), Vol. VI, p. 355. In some localities where circumstances did not permit an immediate abolition, the original form of the state trading companies was retained.

equipment—capital goods produced primarily by the state enterprises
—are directly allocated. The State Planning Commission, established
under the State Council, plans the allocation of such goods in co-
ordination with the producers and the users.[15] The actual allocation,
however, is administered by the State Economic Commission (also
an organ of the State Council) in co-ordination with the related
ministries.[16]

In order to facilitate the direct distribution of goods, special
material-supply bureaus have been established in various parts of the
country. These supply bureaus, which provide storing facilities, are
controlled directly by the State Council rather than by the Ministry
of Commerce.[17]

Goods Distributed through Marketing Channels

Goods which are distributed through the existing marketing channels consist mostly of consumer goods, products of both agriculture
and industry. The supply of some of these goods may be placed under
the jurisdiction of various ministries, such as the Ministries of Grain,
Foreign Trade, Light Industries, and Marine Products. However, the
supply of most such goods is placed under the jurisdiction of the Ministry of Commerce. Regardless of under whose jurisdiction they fall,
all goods are distributed to the ultimate consumer through the marketing channels provided by the Ministry of Commerce or by the commercial departments of the local governments.[18]

The selection of the marketing channels is determined by the nature of the goods handled and the areas to which they are distributed.
Some simple illustrations are presented on the following pages to indicate the prevailing distribution system.[19]

Distribution of Manufactured Products. As indicated in Charts I
and II, most manufactured products are produced either by centrally
controlled or by locally controlled state industries. In order to facili-

[15] *Ibid.,* Vol. VIII, pp. 96, 100.

[16] C. M. Li, *Economic Development of Communist China* (Berkeley: University of
California Press, 1959), p. 19.

[17] H. Yonezawa, "Pricing Policies in Communist China," *Chugoku Kenkyu Geppo,*
No. 156 (February, 1960), pp. 13–14.

[18] For further detail about this distribution, see State Council, *op. cit.,* Vol. VIII,
pp. 100–101; Vol. IX, pp. 158–63, 167–68.

[19] K. Asakawa and M. Suganuma, "The Structure of Market Distribution in Communist China," *Chugoku Shiryo Geppo,* No. 82 (December, 1954), pp. 25–31. The
information given in this article is rather out of date. Illustrations are based also on
information obtained from other sources. See also *Ta Kung Pao,* issues in 1958, 1959,
and 1960 (this paper specializes in economic and business affairs); Chugoku Kenkyusho,
China Annual (Tokyo: Iwazaki Book Co., 1961), pp. 221–23; Chugoku Kenkyusho,
Research on Chinese Socialism (Tokyo: Godo Press, 1959), pp. 74–80; State Council,
op. cit., Vol. VIII, pp. 45–49, 100–101; Vol. IX, pp. 158–63, 167–68.

CHART I

DISTRIBUTION OF MANUFACTURED PRODUCTS FROM CENTRALLY CONTROLLED SOURCES

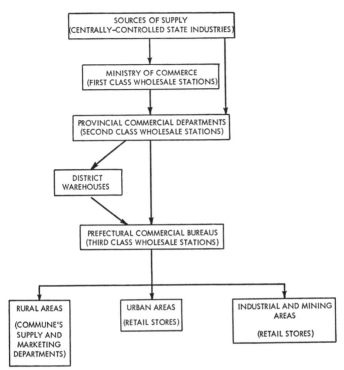

tate their distribution to the retail stores, various types of wholesale stations have been established.

The Ministry of Commerce maintains "first-class" wholesale stations in large cities and ports where the production of finished products is concentrated. Presumably, these wholesale stations handle mainly goods which are produced by centrally controlled state industries; hence they are likely to be goods which are vital to the welfare of the people.[20] Along with the first-class wholesale stations are warehouses and large-scale refrigeration facilities also maintained by the Ministry of Commerce.

On the provincial level, there are "second-class" wholesale stations maintained by the provincial commercial departments. These wholesale stations are located in the cities and major areas of production in the province. They purchase, supply, store, and transport locally produced products. Each second-class wholesale station specializes

---

[20] This inference is drawn from a speech made by the then Deputy Minister of Commerce. See I. L. Yao, "Three Directions to Which Commercial Advancement Ought to Pay Attention," *Hsing Hua Pan Yueh Kan*, No. 131 (May, 1958), p. 107.

CHART II

DISTRIBUTION OF MANUFACTURED PRODUCTS FROM LOCALLY CONTROLLED SOURCES*

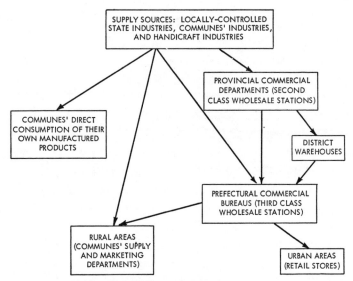

* By May, 1959, 64.7 per cent of the handicraft industries (in terms of membership) had been integrated into locally controlled state industries and communes' industries (see *Jen-min Jih-pao*, September 17, 1959). Since this integration has increased further, it may be concluded that the amount of finished products supplied by the handicraft industries is negligible today.

in certain commodities as indicated by the following names: the Chiansu Provincial Lumber Supply Station, the Shanghai Educational and Cultural Supplies Station, and the Shanghai Clothing, Shoe, and Hat Company.[21]

The second-class wholesale stations may extend their operation further by creating their own wholesale outlets. In such case, the negotiation for transaction with the retailers is handled by the whole-sale stores, leaving the second-class wholesale stations to engage primarily in purchasing the supplies and storing the stock of merchandise. For example, in Shanghai the Shanghai Textile Company (a second-class wholesale station) set up five wholesale stores, in order to meet the demand of the retail stores scattered in the different parts of the city.[22]

On the prefectural level, there are "third-class" wholesale stations, which supply commodities primarily to the local department stores. There is not much information about the operation of these stations. However, it seems that they engage primarily in the negotiation of

---

[21] In some cases, the name "company" is retained instead of the name "station." Whether it is named "station" or "company," the function performed is the same.

[22] Chugoku Kenkyusho, *China Annual*, p. 222.

transactions, serving as a link between the second-class wholesale stations and the retailer.[23]

Distribution of Agricultural Products. Since the drive to establish rural communes started in 1958, the commune system of agricultural production appears to have been completed. It seems, therefore, that the supply of agricultural products today originates primarily from the communes. A simplified illustration of this is shown in Chart III.[24]

In the state regulation promulgated in 1958, agricultural products were divided into three categories. In 1959, these were expanded to include also finished industrial goods for consumers. Generally, the first and second categories include products that are vital to the welfare of the people or products for which there is an extensive market demand. Consequently, their procurement and distribution are centrally controlled. The third category, which comprises a wide variety of agricultural products and small-itemed finished products, is placed under local control; hence free local distribution is permitted.[25]

It appears that products in the first and second categories are distributed direct from province to province, with the responsible ministry retaining administrative control. Possibly, they may also be sent to the respective national ministries for redistribution to other provinces.

Variation of Distribution Channels. The channels of distribution presented in the preceding sections are by no means uniform throughout the country. In some localities there are more intermediary channels, and in others there are less. On the whole, the commercial network tends to be concentrated in the urban areas. In some cases there are an excessive number of intermediary channels, which have resulted in wasted manpower, high cost of distribution, and even excessive damage to the commodity handled. It is reported, for instance, that eggs produced in An Juei (a province less than 500 miles from Shanghai) took more than twenty days to reach Shanghai market, after having gone through five distribution agencies. Consequently, by the time the eggs were offered for sale in the market, they had spoiled.[26]

When feasible, attempts have been made to simplify the distribution system by eliminating some of the intermediary channels. One

---

[23] *Ibid.*

[24] The reference used here is the same as those listed under footnote 19.

[25] State Council, *op. cit.*, Vol. VIII, pp. 174–77; Vol. IX, pp. 158–63.

[26] *Ta Kung Pao*, April 30, 1958. For further criticism about the existing marketing channels, see a special article written by T. K. Chou in *Ta Kung Pao*, of the same date as above; also see H. Kao, "Cutting Excessive Channels of Distribution Is a Managerial Revolution," *Ching-chi Yen-chiu* (October, 1958), pp. 58–67.

CHART III

DISTRIBUTION OF AGRICULTURAL PRODUCTS

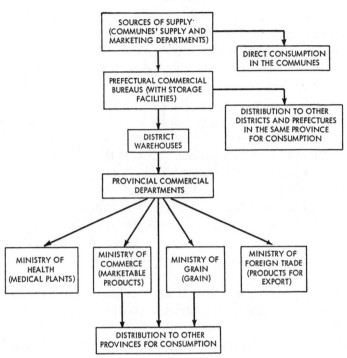

example is the adoption of a more direct route of distribution for industrial products between the wholesale stations and the retail stores in some cities. The method adopted requires direct shipment of goods, whenever feasible, from the factory or from the railroad station direct to the retail stores (as happened in Shihchianchuang, a city in northern China) or from the main wholesale station direct to the retail stores, bypassing auxiliary wholesale stations (as in Peking department stores).[27] Similar attempts have also been made to simplify the channels of distribution for agricultural products. For example, the district warehouse, which was a superfluous channel, was bypassed in the distribution of hogs. As a result, delivery was speeded up and the cost of distribution lowered.[28]

In order to improve the effectiveness of the marketing channels, a "contract" system in transactions between the suppliers and the users has been introduced. In wholesaling, such contracts are drawn up between the wholesale stations or stores and the retail stores. By deter-

[27] *Ta Kung Pao,* April 26, 1958, and April 4, 1959.
[28] *Ta Kung Pao,* June 3, 1958.

mining in advance the supply and demand for goods, it is hoped that no serious shortage or surplus will develop. In agriculture, the contract is made between the communes and the state commercial establishments. However, in this case the contract involves both the communes' supply of goods to the state and the state's supply of goods to the communes.[29]

The contract system and the shortening of the route of distribution in Communist China's market is an attempt to balance demand and supply and draw retail stores closer to the source of supply. As a result, it may appear that the importance of intermediaries has been reduced. However, even if it were possible for some factories to ship goods directly to the retail stores, wholesale stores cannot be eliminated, given the diversity of industries, dispersion of their location, and the bottleneck in transportation. Moreover, the supply of and the demand for many small-item consumer goods cannot be controlled fully unless all goods are rationed—and they are not. It is in this respect that the wholesale stations still constitute an important link between production and consumption in Communist China's market. As an official planner points out, the level of wholesale stations' inventory is the barometer for measuring changes in demand and supply; inventory fluctuations serve as a guide for production policy.[30]

Thus the contract system of transactions and the attempt to shorten the route of distribution do not eliminate the wholesale function. While some auxiliary wholesale establishments may be eliminated in the process of rationalizing the channels of distribution, the over-all effect is to strengthen those wholesale activities that remain. Simplification means the elimination of the unnecessary channels of distribution, leaving fewer wholesale stations to provide wholesale services. Hence the role of the remaining wholesale stations will be enhanced. As sales volume expands in the future, wholesaling should become even more important.

Some Effects of the Rural Communes on the Structure of the Domestic Market. The communes are an experiment hitherto unattempted. Because of their radical nature, their establishment is expected to have a significant effect on the structure of the domestic market.

From a theoretical point of view, the communal system of organization raises a basic question about the distribution of goods—whether

---

[29] For the nature about the contract system, see State Council, *op. cit.*, Vol. VIII, pp. 48–49.
[30] Yao, *op. cit.*, p. 108.

to produce goods for self-consumption in a self-contained communal economy or to produce goods for exchange. If the former case prevailed, it would decrease the volume of goods circulated in the market and would seriously curtail marketing activities. It seems that there was such a tendency earlier in 1958.[31] As a result, wholesaling activities diminished.

The disregard for market exchange inevitably led to the neglect of specialization in the communes' production and lowered the communes' productivity. Apparently, the state recognized this problem. A directive was issued calling for increased effort to step up communes' production for marketable products for outside exchange.[32]

The attempt to increase marketing activities eventually led to the formation of "commodity exchange fairs," which aimed at increasing the circulation of goods between the cities and the rural areas. These commodity exchange fairs are held several times a year in different localities and are attended by representatives of industries, government, and communes. Contracts are signed, and production is then planned accordingly. In this way, it is expected that production and marketing will be drawn closer to each other.[33]

In some respects, the commodity exchange fairs may be likened to a Western trade fair or the operation of the grain market. However, unlike the grain market, at the commodity exchange fairs prices are regulated by the state; therefore, they are not likely to fluctuate with changes in demand and supply.

Since a wide latitude of power is given to the local authorities in commodity exchange fairs, it appears that negotiations are confined primarily to local distribution. Mainly, commodities under local control are traded. However, of commodities under central control—products vital to the public welfare—the excess of supply over the allotted quota may also be traded in the commodity exchange fairs.[34]

If the distribution of commodities under local control is not properly organized and co-ordinated, it may retard marketing activities and thereby disrupt production. Closer contact between the producers and the buyers via "contract" or "commodity exchange fairs" will alleviate this problem. But, considering the wide diversity of transactions and the small scale of the activity, marketing efficiency may be better achieved through the use of middlemen.

---

[31] See a report by the Minister of Finance, H. N. Li, "An Observation on People's Communes," *Hung Chi*, May, 1958, p. 6.

[32] State Council, *op. cit.*, Vol. VIII, pp. 33–34.

[33] *Ibid.*, Vol. IX, pp. 166–68.

[34] *Ibid.*, pp. 158–63, 166–68. Also, see Ajia Seikei Gakkai, *op. cit.*, p. 548.

Another consequence of the organization of communes is the virtual disappearance of the local free market. The establishment of the communes has brought about fuller socialization of local commercial channels.[35] However, it may be too early to conclude that free market is gone forever. There seems to be an indication that the open market is being revived for the transaction of less important agricultural byproducts produced by the sideline activities of commune members.[36] Prices in the open market are regulated by the state, however.

There is some question concerning the relationship of the communes' commercial establishments to former agricultural supply and marketing co-operatives. There is evidence to suggest that the latter have been integrated into the former.[37] Nevertheless, how complete this integration has been, is not clear, for agricultural supply and marketing co-operatives have continued to be listed as one of the marketing channels in the rural areas. It is possible that these co-operatives are actually the communes' supply and marketing departments except that the name "co-operative" is retained. It is also possible that, in the course of the experiment over the last two years, there has been a disintegration of the communal organization.

All considered, it seems that wholesaling process will not be eliminated, despite the establishment of the communes.

FINANCING AND PRICING IN WHOLESALING

The financing and pricing of wholesaling activities have certain distinctive characteristics.

Financing

Financing market transactions in Communist China seems to be rigidly controlled by the People's Bank (the state bank). Unlike wholesalers in the United States, who may grant credit to retailers in their transactions, credit (short-term credit) in Communist China is granted by the People's Bank alone. The following regulations indicate how rigidly credit is controlled:

1. Capital for purchasing by all commercial enterprises must be integrated into the credit plan of the People's Bank. Credit for transactions can be obtained only from the local office of the People's Bank.

[35] See a report by the Minister of Finance, H. N. Li, "How to Recognize the Improvement in Rural Finance and Trade Control System," *Hung Chi*, January, 1959, p. 3.
[36] Chugoku Kenkyusho, *China Annual*, p. 225.
[37] See Hsueh *et al.*, *op. cit.*, p. 138; Chugoku Kenkyusho, *Research on Chinese Socialism*, pp. 76–77.

2. For transactions which extend beyond a local area, payment must be cleared through the local office of the People's Bank where the buyer's credit is deposited. Buyers are permitted to carry only a small amount of cash.

3. Buyer's credit transferred to another area for purchasing must be deposited in the local office of the People's Bank in that area immediately. Credit is designated for a particular transaction only and cannot be used for any other purposes.[38]

Even though financing is strictly controlled by the state, there seems to be some latitude within the power of the wholesale establishments to facilitate market transactions financially. This can be done, for instance, by making payments at more frequent intervals to the suppliers (producers) or lengthening the interval of collection from the retailers. In this manner, the problem of capital shortage of the producers and retailers may be lessened.[39]

Pricing [40]

The methods of pricing differ between industrial and agricultural products. In general, as in the United States, wholesale establishments in Communist China are expected to earn enough margin to cover the cost of merchandise and to sustain their operation.

Pricing Industrial Products. In pricing industrial products, the difference between the price at which sale is made at the factory and that at which sale is made by the wholesale establishment constitutes the wholesale margin. This wholesale margin is used to cover "circulation costs," which include interest on borrowed capital, storage cost, insurance, operating costs, merchandise loss and depreciation, and profits.

The following factors also are taken into account in determining the wholesale price: the importance of the commodity for the welfare of the people, the market demand and supply conditions, and the availability of the raw materials needed in producing the commodity. In general, the wholesale prices for commodities that are important for the welfare of the people are maintained at low levels, even when there is a shortage. For other commodities, some consideration is given to the market demand and the availability of supply in determining their wholesale prices. Since the "circulation costs"

---

[38] State Council, *op. cit.*, Vol. IX, pp. 129–31.

[39] *Ta Kung Pao*, April 26, 1958.

[40] The major sources of reference for "pricing" are H. Yonezawa, "Pricing Policies in Communist China," *op. cit.*, pp. 1–30; H. Yonezawa, "Commodity Pricing in Communist China," *Ajia Keizai Junpo*, July 1, 1960, pp. 5, 6–14.

of the wholesale establishments in Communist China are relatively fixed, the level of wholesale price is determined mainly by varying the level of profits. Hence profits are used not only as a measurement for operational efficiency but also as a means to adjust production by varying the price.

Despite this practice, wholesale prices over the past decade appear to have been quite stable. The difference between factory price and retail price appears to be usually about 40 per cent.[41] Although few data are available, Tables 2 and 3, based upon information from an independent source, both indicate a relatively stable wholesale price level. They show, however, only the average of the wholesale prices of the various products and do not preclude fluctuations in the wholesale price of an individual product.

TABLE 2		TABLE 3	
WHOLESALE PRICE INDICES OF URBAN AREAS, 1950–57 (1952 = 100)		WHOLESALE PRICE INDICES (Nation-wide Average Prices of Preceding Year = 100)	
1950	84.7	1952	100.1
1951	99.8	1953	98.7
1952	100.0	1954	100.4
1953	98.7	1955	100.6
1954	99.1	1956	99.5
1955	99.7	1957	100.9
1956	99.2	1958	100.0
1957, Jan.–June	99.9		

Source: C. M. Li, *Economic Development of Communist China* (Berkeley: University of California Press, 1959), p. 25.

Source: State Statistical Bureau, *Ten Great Years* (Peking: Foreign Languages Press, 1960), p. 172.

Pricing Agricultural Products. There are only two prices for agricultural products: state purchase price from the producers and state selling price to the consumers.

In determining the state purchase price, the historical price of the individual product and its cost of production are taken into consideration. For those products that are vital to the development of the economy and important for the welfare of the people, selling prices are maintained at low levels. It is reported that in some instances the selling price is only 8 per cent above the purchase price.[42] This may be a result of an attempt to encourage production by raising the procurement price paid to the farmers.

In general, low selling prices have been maintained for agricultural products. In order to sustain the narrow margin between the purchase

[41] C. M. Li, *op. cit.*, p. 28.
[42] Chugoku Kenkyusho, *China Annual*, p. 226.

price and the selling price, marketing efficiency must be improved. This explains, in part, why there has been so much emphasis made on the simplification of the channels of distribution.

CONCLUSION

The simple conclusion to which this analysis leads relates to the question: Can a controlled, socialist economy dispense with wholesaling? The answer is, No. In Communist China, wholesaling as a function not only has played an effective role in improving the efficiency of the distribution system but has also served as an important means of obtaining control by the state over the economy.

YUGOSLAVIA

Yugoslavia lies economically between other Communist countries and the capitalistic countries. Thus her marketing system partakes of the characteristics of both. On the one hand, since the administrative management of industry was eliminated in 1950, initiative for planning production and distribution have been returned to individual entrepreneurs. On the other hand, those individuals are still under the control of the council of consumers and the communes, who, through marketing inspections, observe the performance of the "private" business activities.

It is interesting to note that, notwithstanding contrary claims of some Communists, the decentralization of administration seems to have increased efficiency in the performance of marketing. When responsible for making his own market plans, each manufacturer is said to feel more keenly the importance of planning, research, and sales activities.

In many respects, the wholesalers in Yugoslavia are described as performing the functions that are commonly ascribed to them in other more developed economies.

Wholesaling in Yugoslavia

JERKO RAZUM *

INTRODUCTION

As of 1961, the economy of Yugoslavia was still undergoing a considerable transition. Since 1962 it has become a goods-monetary type of economy, and, consequently, there are certain functions which marketing is now called on to perform to aid in the over-all economic development of the nation. Trade plays an important role in this development, not only from the point of view of the social community, but also from that of the producer and consumer. The services of trade are both useful and necessary, because these services speed up the process of production and exchange with less usage of the country's economic resources. If the services of marketing were not indispensable, it would inevitably be excluded from the economic process.

Today, trade in Yugoslavia is an independent economic activity. There are some unsatisfactory traits and characteristics to be found in distribution at present. However, there are conditions and forces at work to make distribution completely a service activity. The goal of marketing is not to help itself but to bring together the producer and the consumer as quickly, efficiently, and rationally as possible. In other words, trade becomes the means through which the exchange and distribution of the social end product is achieved. As a service activity, trade works to serve the interests of consumers as well as those of producers and tries constantly to improve the efficiency of its services. In a sense, marketing is losing some of its independence, but trade organizations will remain legally independent. "They remain legally independent, with certain rights and responsibilities, but they are no longer the equals of producers. They lose the right to take working surplus that is made only in production."[1] There are many

* Jerko Razum is a graduate of the University of Zagreb. He is at present employed in the Federal Center in that city, is a member of the Management Board of the Association of Advertisers of Croatia, and is the author of several books and articles dealing with marketing and management subjects.

[1] Dr. S. Novakovic, "Goods Exchange and Trade," *Booklet for Economy of Yugoslavia* (Beograd: published by "RAD"), p. 291.

possible ways of curtailing the independence of the marketing network; however, the nature and development of the Yugoslav economy does not as yet permit this.

POSTWAR DEVELOPMENT OF THE YUGOSLAV ECONOMY

The development of the present Yugoslav economy can be divided into two basic periods. A study of the distribution of goods must be similarly divided.

The first period (1941–50) was characterized by administrative management by the state. During this period the state dominated the economic life of the country; planned and centrally administered economic activities; and regulated the marketing of goods through competent organs. These organs of the state carried on the planning of production; administered the distribution of stocks of goods; prescribed fixed prices; and so on.

As a result, the distribution process had no independent commercial function. Marketing personnel were not stimulated to increase efficiency and reduce costs, because the refunding of trade costs was prescribed in the form of the rebate and margin. Salaries of tradespeople were not affected by their efforts or by the success of their enterprises. A complete review of the early period would take too much space, but we should note that there were also some benefits in the regulation of the distribution of goods.

In the second period (since 1950), the administrative management of industry by the state was eliminated, and regulation of the distribution of goods by administrative decree virtually disappeared. Intervention by organs of the state in the exchange process and state determination of the mix of products to be manufactured have been reduced. Relations in the market are regulated almost completely by the free influence of economic laws. Self-government of industrial organizations requires greater rights in establishing proper market relationships. Producers manufacture the goods for which there is a demand without formal control over quality, the volume of production, or the product line. Relations between sellers and buyers are freely established, and prices are determined freely, although certain limitations set by the community must be taken into consideration. The sources for meeting the costs of distribution are no longer prescribed, but costs are covered through the difference between the purchasing and selling prices of the goods. From this margin, it is possible to reward the staff according to the success of the business.

We need not point out the many positive and important results made possible by the adoption of this system. Enterprises are interested in the quality of the product and in widening the product line. They strive to lower costs, which, in turn, produce greater consumer satisfactions. Of course, this "new" system of distributing goods has brought with it certain new problems that did not appear in the earlier period. Many efforts have been made to reduce these problems.

ROLE OF THE MARKET IN THE YUGOSLAV ECONOMY

The existence of the market is necessary because the Yugoslav economy has a money-commodity character. However, it has far less importance and less influence on the direction of development of the economy than in a capitalistic economy. In Yugoslavia the determination of "direction" is undertaken by the social community. The social community consciously plans the direction of economic development of the country as a whole and the role of particular industrial fields. The instrument for carrying out this function is the social plan, through which the basic distribution of national income is achieved. However, this does not mean that the market has no important economic functions.

We shall mention only a few of these functions. The market influences prices of particular goods. The success of the individual industrial organization, which affects the salary and the income of workers and employees, and the real value of the income received are adjusted by the market. These functions are basic to the regular and harmonious development of the Yugoslav economy.

In every market, including the Yugoslav, various problems of imbalance appear. The causes for different market disturbances and fluctuations are to be found in the interpretation of factors which define the volume and product mix. There are also some causes which have tended to sharpen the imbalance of the market. The basic task of present policy in Yugoslavia is the stabilization of the market, and the efforts made to reach this objective have been quite successful.

THE FUNCTION OF PRICES IN THE YUGOSLAV ECONOMY

The function of prices in the Yugoslav economy can be listed briefly as follows:

a) The exchange of goods in the market is carried out by means of prices. Therefore, pricing is a basic function of the economy.
b) Through prices, the real income of the working people is established.

c) Prices serve as a means of establishing regular relations in the exchange between city and village.

d) Prices are a handy instrument by means of which the quantity and mix of consumption can be influenced.

e) Prices serve as an instrument for determining the size and distribution of inventory accumulations.

The basic instrument for regulating the level of prices is the turnover tax. This tax is paid as a certain percentage of the selling price. Trade organizations independently determine their selling prices to cover their expenses, their transportation costs, and certain constant contributions to the community. They also pay a tax according to sales income. The purpose of the tax on sales income (and profits) is in accordance with the concept that there should be no work surplus in trade. Therefore, the trade organizations have little incentive to raise prices above the necessary level. Rather, they are stimulated to adopt more effective and efficient methods of operation.

ORGANIZATION OF THE GOODS EXCHANGE IN YUGOSLAVIA

The physical size of Yugoslavia and the dispersion of markets make it necessary for producers to use trade organizations to sell their products. With the yearly increase in production and in population changes, there are greater and more complicated problems facing trade organizations. There are two kinds of trade organizations in Yugoslavia:

1. Trade organizations for buying and selling of goods, or trade organizations in the narrow sense (merchant middlemen)
2. Economic organizations which offer services in the wider sense (agents and facilitating agencies)

The first group covers (1) trade enterprises, (2) trade shops, (3) purchasing-consuming associations, and (4) handicraft purchasing-consuming co-operatives. The second group covers (1) trading agencies, (2) mediating enterprises, (3) commission enterprises, (4) storage facilities, (5) expediting enterprises, (6) quality and quantity control enterprises, and (7) enterprises for representation in international firms.

A certain enterprise is a "trading enterprise" if it deals continuously with buying and selling as a basic activity. Its activities are based on the elementary business principles of socialistic industrial enterprises, such as the principle of economic accounts, the principle of workers' self-government, and the principle of economic unit and profitability.

Trade enterprises may be classified in the following ways:

1. According to *volume of business:* retail stores (specialty shops) which buy goods from producers or wholesalers and sell to consumers in small quantities; department stores, where almost all that is necessary for consumers is sold; wholesalers, who buy goods from manufacturers and sell to retail stores and large consumers (institutions). The large volume of the wholesalers allows them to specialize in a certain line of goods.
2. According to *basic type of product:* commercial enterprises distributing industrial goods and those distributing agricultural products.
3. According to *type of products sold:* enterprises for the distribution of textiles, shoes, hardware, etc. Fields of specialization are defined according to certain rules. Each commercial enterprise receives permission to trade certain types of goods from the registrar of industrial organization.
4. According to *type of market:* domestic enterprises; enterprises for foreign trade divided into import, export, and import-export; agencies that represent domestic or foreign companies in import or export of goods; and transitive companies, which buy goods from foreign suppliers and resell these goods abroad.

In planning for the development of trade in Yugoslavia, a substantial increase in the volume of trade has been anticipated. In the near future it will be necessary to modernize the operations of present organizations and to increase the numbers of various types of commercial enterprise to handle the expected volume.

Basic control of the activities of commercial organizations is exercised by "communes" (people's committees of the community or district), usually through marketing inspections. Higher organs of the state administration also have the right to follow up on the performance of commercial activities. In addition to marketing inspections, some measure of control is given to the council of consumers (in some ways similar to Better Business Bureaus), which may also suggest measures for business promotion and which may participate in decisions affecting the proposed or continuing existence of companies in its area.

With the development of its workers' self-government type of economic system and the elimination of many functions of the state in the direction of the economy, Yugoslavian businesses have found it necessary to organize into various "chambers." Today there are municipal, district, and republic commercial chambers, in which various commercial and other marketing-service organizations may enroll. The aims of each chamber are to help in solving the problems common to its members, to act on their behalf in various matters, and, at the same time, to project the interests of its social community. The work of the chambers is carried out by means of boards and commissions of either temporary or permanent nature.

MARKETING ACTIVITIES OF MANUFACTURERS

In the first period of centralistic management of the economy, the role and tasks of the commercial department in a company were quite restricted. Now, however, the new system of free exchange has made the activities of the commercial department much more important to the success of each company. Each company must make and sustain its own business relations with suppliers and customers.

With this change, the services of the commercial department in each company has assumed great importance. In general, the present-day commercial department is charged with establishing and maintaining strong relationships with both suppliers and customers and is responsible for obtaining the best price possible for the products of the company. Conversely, the commercial department is also held responsible for any mistakes in the procurement of goods and for any failure to sell the company products. Consequently, much effort has been made to improve the organization and methods of work in the commercial department. In particular, a great deal of attention has been given recently to the selection of personnel and to the training of personnel by sending staff members to various schools and seminars.

Specifically, the tasks of the commercial department are: to determine the optional procedures (marketing strategy) for marketing the products of the company; to define the market for the company's products; to determine what customers need; to sign sales contracts and see that these contracts are fulfilled; to help determine the quality, quantity, and product mix to be manufactured; to build an efficient procurement and sales organization; to administer warehousing services and facilities; to co-operate with production in meeting delivery dates; to help collect payments promptly; to work harmoniously with other departments in the company; to follow all regulations concerning the commercial business of the enterprise; to report regularly to the management and to the administration; and to control all other commercial activities of the company.

In Yugoslav practice we find the typical commercial department organized in one of two different ways. In some enterprises the commercial department is responsible for both the purchasing and the selling functions. At the head of this department is the commercial director. In this case, the commercial department is broken down into departments, and each department has its head. Typically, the commercial department consists of the following departments: sales, purchasing, statistics, accounting, storage, transportation, and import-export.

In other companies the commercial department is divided into two separate divisions—selling and procurement. The selling division may consist of sales, marketing research, advertising, legal, export, inventory, expediting, and other departments.

Separate accounting records are kept for each division. Each has its own plans and costs and is responsible for controlling and reducing its costs. The head of each division is on the same level as the heads of the other functional divisions of the company: production, personnel, and economic accounting (controller). The first form of organization, having only one division, is being abandoned in favor of the second form, as the size of the companies grow and as the operations of the market become free.

There are two basic channels of distribution used by companies to sell their products: direct selling and selling through middlemen. In the case of direct selling, the task of reaching customers is carried out in several different ways. Typically, merchant-travellers (company salesmen) are used by companies that produce consumer goods. On the other hand, companies that do not produce goods for mass consumption use representatives (agents), who are not employees of the company.

Some companies have their own stores, particularly in the larger industrial centers. Participation in fairs is one of the customary ways of making direct-selling contacts with buyers. There are many fairs (specialized and general) held in Yugoslavia throughout the year. Advertising is being used also as a means of promotion and selling. The use of advertising is a recent development in Yugoslavia.

A study of Yugoslav practice shows that any of these ways (or a combination) can be used to reach customers efficiently. However, many companies are not successful in using these methods because they fail to emphasize the sales function and they do not research adequately the specific conditions of their business and of the Yugoslav market.

Up to this point we have been describing, in a general way, the economic system, the marketing system, and the marketing activities of manufacturers. Such explanation is needed as background if we are to understand the role and the functions of a wholesaler in Yugoslavia.

WHOLESALE ENTERPRISES

Wholesalers have appeared in Yugoslavia because they are needed if quantities of goods are to be marketed efficiently. Wholesalers are needed especially to carry out the functions of assembly, selection, handling, and storing. Because retailers could not successfully perform these functions, the problem was solved by establishing wholesaling enterprises. However, there was a great deal of debate about the economic wisdom of such a solution. Many people felt that the costs of distribution would be increased by the addition of one more middleman between producer and consumer.

Wholesale enterprises have taken over many important marketing functions. They strongly influence the selection of the types and qualities of goods to be produced and insist on greater standardization of products. By storing finished goods in their warehouses, they provide industry with the opportunity for steady production throughout the year. They help retailers save work and time and reduce investment in inventory. They give retailers a great deal of advice about the market. In some economically less developed districts, where retailers have little business experience, poorly trained personnel, and low sales volume, wholesalers play an important, and sometimes decisive, role in supplying this district. Generally, wholesalers specialize in handling a particular line of goods and concentrate on supplying a particular area of Yugoslavia.

Functions Performed for Manufacturers

Determining and defining consumer demand is one of the most important functions performed by the wholesaler for the manufacturer. Many manufacturers are very much occupied with problems of production and productivity and take no time to deal with marketing research. Most companies have no marketing research department, which means that they receive little information about their customers. Usually, wholesalers are specialized, and through their knowledge of a market and their research work they can throw light on the present and future market for products in which they deal. Additionally, they provide industry with valuable data and advice about product quality and other characteristics of a product, such as packaging.

Wholesalers make extensive use of salesmen, which means that manufacturers need employ only as many salesmen as are needed to maintain contact with wholesalers and thereby can greatly reduce selling costs. Through salesmen, wholesalers keep in continuous touch with the retailers they serve. This means that retailers often become permanent customers of the manufacturers.

As mentioned above, the wholesaler contributes to the stability of production. This stable utilization of basic resources enables the manufacturer to lower the price at which he sells goods to the wholesaler. Practice has shown that in most cases the wholesaler can store goods more efficiently than the producer or the retailer. We should also mention the extent to which the producer and retailer benefit because they do not have to manage and administer this function.

In addition, the wholesaler helps industry in another way. By using the services of wholesalers, a manufacturer can substantially cut down his accounting, storage, transportation, packaging, insurance and consignment costs, and the amount of time and administration he must give to these functions also is considerably reduced.

Wholesaler Services to Retailers

From the point of view of the retailer, the wholesaler is more than a supplier. The wholesaler stores goods in different places, so that these goods may be shipped quickly and at low cost. In some cases, the wholesaler grants credit to the retailer, enabling retailers to buy in quantities which insure a rapid turnover. The retailer may keep only a minimum stock of goods, which reduces risks from deterioration or spoilage and lowers his investment in inventory. As a result of his market studies, the wholesaler gives the retailer data about the demand for his goods.

The wholesaler does not brand the merchandise he sells, but, in a way, he guarantees the quality of the goods he sells. Thus the retailer is not required to analyze the quality of the goods if he has had continuous relations with a particular wholesaler. In case of claims, the wholesaler serves as the mediator between manufacturer and retailer.

The wholesaler provides other services. His salesmen give advice about demand and fashion, and they assist in making effective counter and window displays in the stores.

THE ORGANIZATION OF A WHOLESALE COMPANY

The organizational structure of individual wholesalers will vary, depending on many factors within the company. Generally, the typical wholesale organization is as shown below:

Worker's Council
Management Board
Director

General Affairs	*Commercial*	*Accounting*
Personnel	Purchasing	Financial accounting
Legal	Pricing	Inventory accounting
Office services	Sales	Personnel accounting
Auxiliary personnel	Invoicing	Treasurer
	Advertising	Statistics and economic
	Transportation	analysis
	Storage	

CONCLUSIONS

ROBERT BARTELS

Several types of conclusions may be dawn from the foregoing material. If the studies are considered separately, they represent simply a number of distinct situations whose differences are more apparent than their similarities. Superficial observation always produces this impression and leaves one with a feeling that dissimilarities are not related. Businessmen and casual tourists have returned from foreign forages contrasting how "they" engage in marketing with how "we" do it. Studying and writing of our own domestic marketing activity for years has deepened a tendency to make ethnocentric analyses and to resist assimilation of divergencies into established patterns of thought and action. Upon this type of thinking is based an attitude that where there are differences, one behavior is "right" and the other "wrong," one "efficient" and the other "inefficient," one "modern" and the other "out-of-date." To regard differences in marketing practices among nations in this manner is to miss completely the meaning of comparative marketing.

A second conclusion reached from such studies minimizes the differences and emphasizes the similarities in the practice of marketing in different countries. Abstracting practice to a set of generalizations, one may go even so far as to say that the "principles" of marketing are universal, that differences of fact merely represent the obverse of a general truth, a fundamental law. Traditional marketing study until recent years has encouraged this type of conclusion, for, lacking awareness of the social orientation of our own marketing system and practice, one was inclined to underestimate the significance of cultural differences in the other environments in which marketing occurs. This has led exporters to treat foreign markets as they do their domestic markets, to apply the same policies to different international regions. Business consultants and government administrators have displayed this same delusion in disseminating American marketing technology in other lands.

A third conclusion reconciles these differences and similarities. Differences in marketing systems and practice are recognized, but they are harmonized through a consistency of marketing thought. Differences in marketing are recognized as differences in social behavior, as indigenous to different societies. Differences in marketing are seen to be not a divergence in scientific marketing practice but the agreement of marketing with its social orientation. To the extent that principles of social action and organization can be postulated, the existing body of marketing thought finds a broader setting and new meaning. Thus differences in marketing lose the character of being typical or atypical, centric or eccentric. Neither are they explained away by the established framework of marketing thought. Rather they are interpreted in a new dimension and integrated into a broader logic, which is identified as comparative marketing.

Inferences can be drawn from these studies of wholesaling to enrich our concepts of marketing, wholesaling, and comparative marketing, as follows:

Marketing—a means conceived, organized, and sanctioned by society for meeting its needs for consumption goods and services; an elaborate and technical system, with practices characteristic of the market economy, employed in the distribution of products; systems or sets of interactions among individuals, enterprises, and groups acting in positions or roles which they hold in organized society.

Wholesaling—that part of marketing mainly through which society acts to achieve order, harmony, integration between production and consumption; a focal point of entrepreneurial, as well as of sovereign, power essential to the fulfillment of private or social objectives of marketing; an area of marketing strongly characterized by the interaction of countervailing power structures in the accomplishment of marketing objectives; the predominant concentration of functions related to assembly, bulk handling, and movement of products.

Comparative marketing—the interpretation of marketing as social activity and as a component part of the economic institution of our society; the explanation of marketing structure and practice in terms of market task, work flows, interaction, and social attitudes; interpretation of marketing in terms of not only the economic institution but also other major social institutions; the conceptual approximation of a socio-economic process viewed from the standpoint of what that process means to the people involved in it.

The "Problem" of Wholesaling. In appraising these studies of wholesaling, one cannot avoid comparing them with early study of wholesaling in this country. In 1920, wholesaling problems plagued the country; yet no one thought that wholesaling was a suitable subject for scientific study. The problem of the period was the plague of ignorance concerning the essential nature of those distribution functions which were being performed between the point of production and the level of retail distribution. Meaningful statistics were nonexistent, for no census of distribution had yet been taken and a rational appraisal of wholesaling had not yet been developed. Gradually, however, classical concepts of production as the creation of different types of utility were applied particularly to wholesaling, and, through a combination of inductive and deductive reasoning, a rationale for this activity was constructed.

These comparative studies of wholesaling in several countries reflect similar circumstances. The awareness of "problems" is the starting point for each analysis, and in each article may be seen the principal wholesaling problem with which the respective country has been confronted in recent years. In Germany, for example, the big problem has been that of the demise and renaissance of the regular wholesaler. In this decline and revival of an important marketing agency are epitomized much of the competitive interplay that has characterized German distribution for the last forty years. In Finland, the dominant feature of wholesaling in recent years has been the development of marketing blocks, the countervails of small-scale inefficiency, large-scale tyranny, and political ineffectuality; in Africa, the marketing boards, serving somewhat the same purpose as the Finnish blocks but reflecting the waning influence of colonial overseeing; in Australia, the transition from national to local wholesalers; in Russia, the use of wholesalers for planning and adjusting market distribution; in Yugoslavia, the decentralization of administrative control over wholesaling. The "problems" identified by the writers' choice of subject matter, however, are not basically wholesaling problems. They are, instead, *social* problems, giving rise to wholesaling problems. Specifically, they are problems of national industrialization, of shifting social classes, of the infusion of new political philosophies, etc.

Whatever may be the stage of wholesaling practice in a country, the verbalization of that practice is itself a problem, and a writer's conceptual approach to this task also reveals interesting comparative phenomena. In general, two rationales for wholesaling are explicit in the articles: that of the emergence of enterprises to perform the functions of a free market and that of the interactions of agencies in the planned economies of Communist countries. Writers in countries whose economies are modeled according to classical concepts justify wholesaling in similar fashion. It may further be noted that they seem to show a strong compulsion to *have* to justify it, as though there still lingered suspicions of what the Russian writer points to so confidently as the faults of capitalistic enterprise: excessive duplication, profiteering, and lack of co-ordination. Productivity is imputed to wholesaling in the creation of utility, as explained in both economics and marketing writings since the beginning of this century. Thus there appears to be a stage in the intellectualizing of free marketing where economic justification is essential to the resolution of social and marketing problems. In general, these explanations follow a pattern.

Not so in Communist logic, however, where rationalization of the presence and problems of wholesaling rehearses a prescribed doctrine and appraises the technical performance of a system charged with designated responsibilities. The reasoning of the Yugoslavian writer to the effect that a "working surplus" resulted only from physical production is sharply in contrast to that of the Netherlander, who regarded the economic transformation wrought by marketing as productive as the technical transformations wrought by manufacturing. It is obvious from this that what appears to the writers to be the "problems" of wholesaling are not only the external conflicts of the business world but also the internal conflicts of their intellectual worlds.

However viewing wholesaling, authors have dealt with it more from the standpoint of macro- than of micro-analysis. Very little attention has been given to technical or mechanistic aspects of wholesaling; little concern has been shown for the management processes per se in wholesaling. On the contrary, the preoccupying subjects have been those of wholesaling structure, channels, institutional interrelations, functions to be performed, and utilities being created. Interest has been focused, moreover, more on wholesalers, or wholesale establishments, than with wholesaling, upon the interactions of functionaries rather than upon divisibility of functions. Inductive generalizations were fitted to deductive reasoning, but few reliable statistics were available in any country for support of the prevailing beliefs about wholesaling.

Instrumental Uses of Wholesaling. In addition to the fact that many social circumstances and problems are reflected in wholesaling, these articles further demonstrate that the area of economic activity identified as wholesaling serves instrumentally for the conscious achievement of certain social ends. Perhaps most evident is that wholesaling is a locus of power for those who can gain control of its strategic positions. Various groups aspire to this authority, and the success of one or another strongly influences both economic and social circumstances. Where the government has seized the key posts in wholesaling, as it has in most of the Communist countries by imposing restrictions upon buying and selling, it has been able to use the wholesaling system for carrying out the designs of its political philosophies. Formulation and administration of state plans, stimulation or depression of certain types of economic activity, equalization and adjustment of production, distribution, and consumption, and control over prices—these are some of the ends to which control over wholesaling activity and agencies is put by governments.

Almost as complete control over the power resident in wholesaling has been gained also by private interests. Where trading activity has been depreciated in social esteem, as in Japan, Africa, and India, there has arisen a social class of merchant traders to whom the power obtained through control of the wholesaling processes was compensation for occupational status abasement. Organizers of the Zaibatsu enterprises in Japan, Levantine merchants in Africa, and colonial enterpreneurs in many places typify a socio-economic class who have used the power obtained through wholesaling for their own economic and political ends. Prominence in manufacturing has always provided both power and status, but in some countries these ends are also obtainable through wholesaling activity.

Where neither sovereign nor private interests have amassed the power inherent in control over the wholesaling processes, this power has been organized by semiprivate or quasi-public groups. Producers' co-operatives represent such a seat of this power; so also do the "blocks" of Finland, the cartels of Western Europe, and the marketing boards in Africa. Rather than creating a power dominance, these institutions have sought in different ways the power inherent in this segment of economic activity.

In still other ways, this power has been shifted among manufacturers and tradesmen as their capacities permitted. Under some circumstances, manufacturers have grasped this power, eliminating wholesalers from the distributive channel and holding control over both the processes of production and those of distribution. This type of power play has often been regarded merely as the working of individual initiative in a free market or as the manifestation of monopoly, integration, etc. More than this, it is a type of the social power which inheres in wholesaling. The fact that in our society wholesaling may be used somewhat less instrumentally for achieving public or social ends than in others does not make it less so.

The role of the wholesaler may rise or fall with social change, but wholesaling itself represents a basic type of behavior, or work flows and interactions, which are pervasive and take different forms under the pressures prevailing in different localities. It is a type of social power which opposing interests seek to control. It is a medium through which society is exposed to both the evil and the good designs of those who wield this power.

Social Influences upon Wholesaling. The manner in which wholesaling evolves in any country is a function of the social organization and institutions of that country. To delineate all the social influences upon the development of any part of marketing would require giving consideration to all the major institutions of the society. For example, it would consider the impact upon marketing or wholesaling of the family organization, economic incentives and agencies, educational facilities, and the like. While a list of such topics was proposed in the guide for comparative study recommended to the writers, it has not been uniformly followed in the preparation of these articles. Nevertheless, many of the influences which shape the course of wholesaling are evident in these studies. A few might profitably be pointed out.

One is the general attitude of a society toward trade, particularly toward wholesale trade. Lying apart from the daily experiences of most people, wholesaling is subject to much ignorant criticism, which reaches the extent of social taboos and even restrictive legislation. Wholesaling has thus been hampered, as in Africa, by suspicion or, as in India, by total indifference of manufacturers to distributive responsibilities and activities. Likewise, the failure of a society to distinguish between commercial property and personal property, even though owned by the same individual, impedes the entrepreneurship necessary for wholesaling. Where the extended family structure is prevalent, common claims to property may deplete commercial assets for personal use. This is a real impediment to the accumulation of capital and management of enterprises. Exclusion of employees other than a proprietor's family, as in Italy, is another factor which has prevented the development of marketing establishments. Similarly, preference for the independence of self-employment, as against employment by others, has also kept enterprises small and has produced a wholesaling structure that differs from that found where commercial enterprise is more impersonally conducted.

The means and rate of capital formation are another influence on the conduct of wholesaling in a country. In underdeveloped countries the absence of widely held liquid savings places a premium upon available funds. Frequently, too, an economy has not a banking system or banking attitudes which produce funds. Consequently, wealth constitutes a leverage for gaining power, and this is sometimes used to gain control over the power inherent in wholesaling. The use of wealth in this manner in Japan has produced a merchant caste whose economic and social influence extends forward and backward from the controlling wholesale merchant and even into international business. In similar manner but in lesser degree, financial strength determines in our own economy who performs the wholesaling functions. The financing of distribution is usually a principal part of wholesaling, and the residence of financial control determines the shifting of wholesaling activity among producers, wholesalers, and retailers.

Little need be added to what has already been said concerning the role of the state, the philosophies of individualism, and the automatism of the market in determining the configuration of wholesaling in a society. To these influences may be added the state of technology—mechanical and conceptual—in the distributive arts; the economic status of women—their presence in retailing but their absence from wholesaling; and the customs of a people relating to work specialization, working hours, occupational class mobility, and the uses of leisure. The effects of all such factors on wholesaling are apparent in the studies here presented.

Social Expectations of Wholesaling. The character of wholesaling or of marketing in general, in a society, reflects not only the general aspects of the society but also the particular expectations concerning the wholesaling system. Cross-cultural studies indicate widely differing expectations of the economy. In some societies the economy performs a subordinate and passive supplying of society's consumption needs. Some expect the economy, and particularly the market mechanism, to play a more prominent role in attaining social objectives. The rise and decline of central administrative control over distribution in Yugoslavia illustrates a changing social expectation. Originally expected to perform with maximum economy and efficiency under state control, the wholesaling system was relieved in some measure from this objective as the expectations of state planning diminished. In Communist societies the expectations of the economy and its components are more explicit than in free-market countries, but in the latter they are no less present, no less apparent, when marketing is analyzed in its social setting.

More specific expectations of wholesaling are apparent in these studies. For example, it is evident from the shift of power centers in wholesaling from wholesalers to manufacturers, because of alleged inefficiencies of wholesalers, that society expects of the wholesaling system a certain amount of innovation and initiation. Where this expectation has not been fulfilled by traditional wholesalers, where vested positions have been held by perpetuation of the status quo, the pressure of social expectations has shifted authority to innovative producers and sometimes to innovative retailers. Taking the initiative which wholesalers did not, manufacturers have circumvented wholesale middlemen. Where this has not occurred in the development of industrializing economies, as the writer suggests it has not yet in Italy, change in the future is certain, if not imminent. This lack of initiative on the part of wholesalers, the subsequent action of manufacturers, and the ultimate reaction of wholesalers describe the renaissance of wholesalers in Germany.

A second expectation of wholesaling is that in the performance of the wholesaling task the interests of subordinate, but participating, parties be not abused. In a free competitive market, buyers and sellers are not always equal in bargaining strength. Wholesale buyers, with a power dominance, in agricultural countries have often withheld from producer-sellers the services needed and the prices of the market. Such default in fulfillment of normal expectations has resulted in the organization of producer co-operatives or of government agencies to provide needed service and protection. Failure to meet expectations, in other words, has invited the rise of countervailing institutions and the shift of distributive power to new institutions.

A third expectation which society has of wholesaling is that the physical volume of goods will be moved to the market. Fulfillment of this is achieved through the organization of physical facilities for handling goods—shipping companies, distributors and assemblers, and various facilitating agencies. The degree to which this has been fulfilled in a society determines also the allocation or reallocation of power.

These expectations of wholesaling are independent of the social structure in which they may be involved. The studies show that the measure of their success is the cause of the interplay among the components of the distributive channel. Assuming fluidity of factors of production, one may anticipate the gravitation of wholesaling power to the enterprise which best fulfills these expectations. It has also been shown that a free competitive market is more likely to be conducive to this sort of social interaction than the planned economy.

Patterns of Wholesaling Structure. A prominent and visible subject of interest in comparative analysis is that of trade structure or system. Considering that translation of technical terms for different types of middlemen may not preserve the implications of names used for institutions in other tongues, one perhaps should not be surprised to find a high degree of uniformity in the wholesaling structure in different countries when the types of establishments are expressed in English. Even then, however, some different names are used. Thus it becomes a question of whether the differently named establishments perform similarly, or whether terminological differences are indicative of functional differences. This question is not fully answered in these studies, but some conclusions seem warranted.

1. There appear to be more similarities and fewer dissimilarities in the channel components among Western, democratic, free-market countries than between those countries and the Eastern, Communist, planned-economy countries. This is due in part to the superimposition in the latter countries of arbitrarily determined institutions upon the remnants of their former free-market types. Thus various types of state-owned and co-operative units appear in the marketing structure, sometimes complementing, sometimes supplementing, sometimes replacing, voluntary establishments. There is no way of predicting the degree or form which social-political objectives will take in the formation of such a distributive structure. The functions of governmental ministries, of remote assembly stations, or of agencies for the adjustment of market supplies to demand are mainly arbitrary.

2. There is a pervasiveness of certain basic types of functionaries, whether their market environment is planned or unplanned. Local assembly and urban concentration of agricultural products are indispensable, for the simplest kind of economic reasoning concerning scale advantages demonstrates the merits of these functions. Consequently, in all countries there are agencies in the agricultural producing areas which consolidate the goods for shipment. These may be private, co-operative, or state-owned organizations, but their func-

tions are essentially the same. There is universally less need, on the other hand, for the assembly of manufactured goods, and they flow either directly to the market or through similar dispersion agencies.

3. The prominence of the wholesaler in the distribution structure has been proportional to the indifference of producers to marketing responsibility. Such indifference, producing a structure strongly influenced by wholesaler dominance, is found in lesser developed economies, where manufacturing is regarded as a greater social contribution than trade or where local inertia has attracted foreign wholesale tradesmen. The obverse condition prevails where economic progress and management initiative produce quickened competition in wholesaling and where, as a result, the regular wholesaler is complemented by various types of establishments and by other circumventing channels. When their indifference to distribution is overcome, producers often become initiators of new structural patterns.

4. Wholesaling structures differ quantitatively, as well as qualitatively, among countries. The ratio of retail to wholesale establishments, as well as the ratio of regular wholesalers to other types, and of establishments handling farm products to those handling manufactured goods reflect both economic and social circumstances— economic, by showing the relative volume of different types of productive activity; social, by expressing predilections for one level of trade over another, kinship limitations upon enlargement of enterprise, shopping habits, retailing regulations, etc.

5. The wholesaling system is the design of a social power structure. Aspects of this have already been discussed from the standpoint of the power inherent in the wholesaling function. It need only be mentioned, therefore, that the interactions by which power is shifted become crystallized in types of wholesale establishments.

6. The patterns of the wholesaling structure and practice are determined not only by internal management strategy producing differential competitive advantage but also by a variety of external circumstances: geographic dispersion of wholesale trade, historical origins of business enterprise, extent of social planning for business, and the nature of the economic task in a society.

Social Dynamics and Wholesaling. Another conclusion that may be drawn from these studies is that wholesaling is a dynamic institution. It initiates change; it is responsive to change. Its recent history in almost every country analyzed is one of initiative or responsive change. Even where its character has been most unchanging, analysts of its socio-economic environment predict change. In general, it appears that wholesaler dominance of channels yields to manufacturer dominance, that change is followed by counteraction, and that wholesaler defensiveness evolves into wholesaler offensive tactics. As depicted herein, the situation in Italy illustrates these points, where ensconced interests have maintained wholesaler dominance but where changing economic conditions portend a rise of other innovators, a counteraction of the shift of power away from wholesalers, and a renaissance of the wholesaler, such as has been experienced in Germany, where it is said that the wholesaler has become less a merchant adventurer and more a provider of goods and services.

Dynamics in marketing has been termed "adaptivity" in recent years, but it is implied by comparative analysis that change in patterns of wholesaling practice and structure is the result of no mere passive, conforming adaptivity on the part of marketing institutions. Neither is it merely the interaction of competing wholesaling institutions, but the interaction of the entire marketing mechanism to all other social changes. Economic development, particularly, is the impelling change which imposes new expectations on the existing wholesaling structure. Wholesalers' insensitivity to economic change does not reduce the dynamics involved but rather accentuates it, for the dynamism is a socially inspired and not merely a technically contrived phenomenon.

Numerous influences combine in this social impulsion and marketing adaptivity. Among those noted in the studies are the following: transition from sellers' to buyers' market, local politics at variance with federal policy, and tax structures discouraging risk venture.

Summary. Marketing is a social process; it is more than a business technique or even an economic activity. Marketing is an arm of the social body, a pattern of behavior, an institution. As a process, it is comprised of innumerable work flows involving individuals in diverse interrelationships in the positions they take in the social organization. These are relationships both within marketing enterprises and outside them among the parties who participate in marketing as a social process. The behavior of individuals in their respective roles is one of interaction: initiative and response, innovation and emulation, leadership and loyalties, power and countervails, and individuals and groups. The patterns of interaction in marketing are determined by the socio-economic circumstances prevailing in the environment in which it occurs. These consist of the attitudes, customs, mores, and institutions of the people. They are adaptive to social change.

Wholesaling, as a principal part of the marketing process, is a power center for the accomplishment of social and economic, private and public objectives. To the extent that existing participants in wholesaling fulfill the social expectations of the system, stability characterizes wholesaling. To the extent that these expectations are not fulfilled or to the extent that social change introduces now expectations, dynamism is introduced, which reallocates wholesaling power. The rate or time at which this occurs in different societies is not uniform nor coincident, and the commonality which can be found in wholesaling or in marketing through comparative study derives from the similarity of the societies to which marketing is adapted.

A pioneering effort in comparative marketing study is no place for a "final" word. It is expected that this book will constitute a beginning, rather than a terminal, appraisal either of the content or of the method of comparative marketing. If the present studies have demonstrated anything, however, it is that marketing has a dimension never plumbed and scarcely imagined in our traditional expositions of the subject. It is a dimension of social scope. Advances must be made along lines of this dimension if marketing is to fulfill the responsibility which all who engage in it have to society, *whether this fact is recognized or not.*

APPENDIX

Outline For
Comparative Marketing Analysis

ROBERT BARTELS

Introduction

A comparative marketing analysis may well begin with a brief statement about marketing in the country. As this is followed by several
sections devoted primarily to social and economic factors, such an
introduction will avoid the appearance that one is engaged solely
in a social analysis. It will also serve to point up some of the key
marketing issues for which solution must be found in an interpretation of the social circumstances.

This introduction might consist of a broad characterization of marketing in that environment, of the role which it plays, of the stage
of its development, of the principal marketing problems, and the
like. It is merely introductory.

The Nation

A brief description of the nation should be given. This is to orient it
in place, in time, and in the framework of the world's nations.

It might include something concerning its size, location, physical features, natural resources, racial stock, sovereign identity, age, and
distinctive features as a world community. Whatever is selected for
inclusion should be chosen as bearing directly upon the marketing
analysis which is to follow.

The Society

A somewhat detailed analysis of the society furnishes a basis for interpreting marketing as a social phenomenon—as a type of social
behavior within the framework of the economic institution.

Characterize the society, for example, as religiously oriented, busi-
ness-oriented, militarily oriented, or whatever it may be. This will
indicate the nature of the principal wants and needs of the people
and of the dominant determinism in their philosophy.

Distinctive features of each of the major social institutions should be
indicated:

Family. The family unit, solidarity, interdependence, role dominance, size, formation, rate of growth, fertility, age composition, bonds, coherence in economic pursuits.

Church. Basic religious commitments; prevailing concepts of God and man's relation to Him; devotional practices; the religious calendar; consumption prescriptions and restrictions; influence upon mental outlook, ambition, ethics.

School. Literacy; educational programs and facilities; level of educational achievement; technology in education; education for business; vocational training in marketing.

Government. Form of government; relation of government to business; means and extent of governmental economic planning; governmental engagement in business; marketing laws; official attitudes concerning justice, fairness, competition, etc.

Military. Claim upon economic resources; commitments affecting international relations and influencing balances of payments and trade; means of distribution of products through channels of the military organization.

Leisure. Predilections for leisure rather than work; leisure versus unemployment; time periods spent in leisure; recreational practices; facilities employed in leisure; expenditures for leisure activities; individual and group leisure behavior patterns; effects of leisure activities.

The purpose of this portion of the analysis is to depict the means by which the basic needs and wants of the society are supplied. Such wants are mainly nonmaterial wants, for the latter are supplied largely by the economy. It might be pointed out that depending upon the dominant institutions of the society and the extent to which any given institution may or may not be fulfilling its basic purpose, the functions generally performed by one institution may be taken over by another. This ultimately may have strong implications concerning marketing.

The Economy

Because the economy is the social institution, or set of relationships, with which the analyst is principally concerned, it is set aside for especially detailed consideration. The economy, in whatever form it is organized, is the means by which society provides for its material needs. It embraces the production and distribution of goods. It is an important instrument in a nation's raising its standard of living, establishing security, and gaining status in the world.

As practically all but the most primitive economies today are market economies, this condition may almost be taken for granted. An analyst should keep in mind, however, that the market economy is but one form of economy, and that there are many variations of market economies. It should be observed, also, to what extent the market economy is an exchange economy, a credit economy. Other aspects of the economy which must be considered as relevant to marketing are the degree of self-sufficiency of the economy, in contrast to the dependence the nation may have upon other nations for essential materials and markets; the principal forms of production, whether agricultural, handicraft, or manufacturing, and the extent to which services, including marketing services, constitute part of the nations production; the stage of technology, in science and in art, in theory and in practice; employment; distribution of wealth and income; scale of business operations; balances of trade and of payments; national industrialization programs in effect.

The Market

Although the market is in one sense comprised of both buyers and sellers, it may also be regarded as society in the role of customers, buyers, or users of the products which the economy has evolved to supply. Satisfaction of the market—the supplying of consumers' material wants—is the objective of the social activity of which marketing is a part. Knowledge of the circumstances of the market, therefore, is essential to an understanding of the marketing mechanism—extant and potential.

The market has both physical and conceptual aspects. Physically, the market may be described by the number of consumers, their purchasing power, location, purchasing and patronage habits, etc. Conceptually, the essence of a market is the occurrence of a transaction. Traditional theory of market behavior has presumed certain conditions of demand and supply which effect transactions in a market economy. Actually, these assumptions do not always correspond to conditions. As it is the task for marketing to bring about the occurrence of transaction in the existing circumstances of the market, description of the market must include all of the aspects by which demand is separated from supply, customers are separated from producers, the unfulfilled material wants of society constitute an expectation that the social mechanism (relationships) will satisfy those wants.

The following types of separation in the market determine the task for the marketing mechanism and the functions which must be performed:

Functional separation. The fact that some individuals are consumers and others are producers makes it necessary to provide places where transactions may occur. A largely or partially self-sufficient people, as a rural or agricultural people, have fewer expectations of stores. On the other hand, a more highly specialized consumer market has many expectations of merchandising establishments, including expectations of assortment, service, shopping atmosphere, etc. Producers and consumers are also functionally separated by intermediate customers, or distributive middlemen.

Informational separation. Lack of knowledge among buyers and sellers concerning products and conditions of the market —knowledge assumed in classical concepts of the market— constitutes a need for selling and advertising, for buying activity, for product identification, and for market research.

Spatial separation. Physical distance between producers and consumers necessitates the transporting of goods.

Temporal separation. Time differences between when goods are produced and when the market wants to purchase or consume them necessitates the storing of products. Seasonality of production and consumption, as well as the existing facilities for holding goods for the market, must be included in a description of the market.

Financial separation. Needs of the market to be financed, whether it be the ultimate, industrial, or distributive market. Financial needs of buyers have important effects upon marketing and differ markedly among countries.

Marketing

The heart of a comparative marketing study is the understanding of the manner in which marketing takes place, or should take place, in the existing circumstances. It is not enough, however, merely to describe the way in which institutions perform functions in the distribution of products. This is to view marketing not as a social process but as a mechanistic business or economic process. The purpose of the social analysis made thus far is to give marketing a social orientation, to indicate the social wants that a social process is called forth to supply. Marketing, therefore, must be viewed as the action and interaction of people in the process of a certain type of want fulfillment. Marketing is nothing more or less than what the people do. Therefore their behavior in solving the various types of market "separation" must be analyzed in terms of concepts of social behavior—the behavior of people as individuals in groups, or in role positions, seeking the fulfillment of their expectations and fulfilling their obligations to individuals in other positions.

Analysis of marketing may begin with observation of the manner in which the work of distribution is divided among several parties:

1. State agencies versus private agencies.
2. Profit agencies versus nonprofit (co-operative) private agencies.
3. Producers versus distributors.
4. Wholesale institutions versus retail institutions.
5. Business establishments versus consumers.

This will indicate the relative dominance of the government and the economy in distribution. It will indicate also the degree of economic specialization which characterizes marketing.

The functions of marketing are implicit in the market situation, they differ in different circumstances, and they are derived from the extent and type of "separation" found in the market. Thus:

1. Functional separation gives rise to merchandising and store keeping.
2. Informational separation gives rise to buying, selling, advertising, grading, standardizing, branding, and market research.
3. Spatial separation gives rise to transportation.
4. Temporal separation gives rise to storage.
5. Financial separation gives rise to credit and marketing finance.

Marketing Structure. Social action directed toward supplying economic needs occurs generally in the organized form of marketing establishments. Abstractly considered, they represent various combinations of economic units, such as labor, capital, facilities, etc., and various combinations of factors in marketing management, sometimes called the "marketing mix." Specifically, these establishments constitute diversified groups of organizations which together comprise the "marketing structure." The term "institutions," is often used as synonymous with "organization" or "establishment," but as such it must be recognized as having a distinctly different and narrower connotation than when used to describe marketing itself as a social institution.

The establishments of the marketing structure embody manage-

ment concepts of means by which part of all of the marketing task
may be accomplished relative to meeting certain economic needs.
They are institutions particularly of an economic nature, but no less
of a social nature inasmuch as social factors determine economic (nar-
rowly conceived) and marketing behavior alike.

The organic components of the marketing structure as expressions of
  management concepts of how best to accomplish the marketing
  task in the light of prevailing circumstances, may be interpreted as
  follows:
Direct marketing
  Prevalence of the practice
  Circumstances in which most used—consumer products, industrial
    products
Retailing system
  Quantitative aspects
    Number of stores and volume of sales
    Classification and numbers, classification and volume of sales
    Locations
    Size—number of employees
  Scale of operation
    Types and prevalence of small-scale operation
    Types and prevalence of large-scale operation
    Means by which scale of operation is increased
    Obstacles to large-scale retailing
  Role of the single-line independent
    Lines or portions of lines handled
    Typical gross and net margin of profit
    Sources of merchandise
  Service policies—credit delivery, adjustment
    Voluntary association—horizontal and vertical
    Sources of permanent and temporary financing
    Modernity
    Nature of competition—differential advantage
  Multi-line stores
    Department stores—role and status, operating statistics, integra-
      tion, branches, research and innovation, differential ad-
      vantage
    Others
  Multi-store organizations
    Corporate chains—lines in which common; competitive merits;
      buying; selling; operations; differential advantages

Co-operative chains
Voluntary chains
Nonstore retailing
Mail selling
Itinerant vending
Automatic and mechanical vending
Miscellaneous forms of retailing
Markets
Auctions
Exchanges
Shopping centers
Fairs
Bazaars
Government-owned outlets
Wholesaling System
Agricultural products assemblers
Concentration of products—rural assembly areas, functions, independent middlemen, co-operatives, disposal of products
Terminal markets—middlemen, locations, functions performed, price-making forces, price behavior
Circumstances affecting channels and policies
Co-operation
Handicrafts—location and scale of operation; control or integration of production from standpoint of quality, design, marketability; manner and scale of payment; training
Manufacturers' sales organizations
Methods of selling—salesmen, branches, middlemen
Integration—horizontal, vertical, factors influencing, effects upon trade and competition
Competition—price competition, nonprice competition, scale of operation and competition, competition based upon research activities, competition based upon emulation, constructive and destructive competition
Product diversification
Distributors
Wholesaling structure—concepts of institutional types; number of establishments; typical functions; relationships; trends relating to circumvention, integration, specialization
Channels used for typical product groups
Agency relationships
Principal functions performed by distributors

Physical facilities—character, adequacy, labor-saving devices
Integration
Monopoly
Facilitating Marketing Institutions
Warehouse facilities—adequacy, location, distributive services
rendered
Credit information services—credit bureaus, collection services,
etc.
Advertising agencies—nature of operation, relations with adver-
tisers and with media, services rendered, manner of com-
pensation, ethical standards
Standards associations—private and public, procedure for de-
veloping and enforcing standards
Financing agencies
Business financing—factors, banks, finance companies, other
lenders, mercantile credit terms and practices
Sales financing—character of operations, relations with sellers
and buyers, regulation, rates charged
Consumer lending—agencies, public and private regulation,
sources of funds, rates charged, nature of competition
Consumer open account facilities—institutions offering, attitudes toward, credit practices, collection problems
Trade protective groups—associations, co-operative agencies,
public agencies
Marketing Interaction. While the structural or institutional approach will provide an interpretation of marketing comparable to
that which is widely given domestic marketing, a useful alternative
is that which can be made of the role positions engaged in the work
flows of marketing.
The following are the roles in which people participate in the work
of marketing:

Managers	Customers
Employees	Intermediate customers
Owners	Resources
Other investors	Competitors

Government
Community

Marketing consists of the sets of actions and interactions between
the related roles. It is the action of expressing and fulfilling the expectations of the respective roles.
The likelihood of differences between interactional behavior pat-

terns resulting from contrasting social values and expectations in different countries is greater, and more apparent, than the likelihood of marketing practices differing internationally when interpreted only in terms of entrepreneurial objectives and entrepreneurial cost-profit considerations. This implies that an understanding of the interaction patterns *between* buyers and sellers may be more meaningful for interpreting marketing than is an understanding of buyer behavior or seller behavior as though they were separate and unrelated. To understand buyer-seller interaction is to understand how two parties act under the influence of their total culture, and it is possible to make meaningful comparisons between the interaction patterns of people in similar roles but in different cultures or societies. This is, in other words, the essence of comparative analysis—*the study of behavior in a framework of fixed variables but of cultural differences.*

Sociological research has contributed not only the concept of roles but also that of personal involvement, which is explained in terms of such other concepts as initiative, dominance, competition, conflict, loyalties, reward, leadership, etc. Thus such concepts are employed in explanation of the relationships among role positions both internal and external to the firm—both among the positions within its own organization structure and among those external to it which involve the essential functions of marketing.

Thus, for example, in a market situation where information is lacking, the interactions of buyers and sellers may depend upon initiative being taken by buyers; sellers are passive. In many countries producers not only take no initiative in distribution but will not participate in it because of certain attitudes. Behavior in such circumstances obviously is quite different from that in the United States, where both sellers and producers take marketing initiative.

In this manner, the analytical methods of social analysis may be applied to behavior and interaction involved in each of the work tasks or flows (functions) needed for resolving the problems (market separations) which prevent consumers from immediately satisfying their economic wants. One must ask such questions as these: Who is the dominant party (role position) in the performance of storage, financing, etc? Is loyalty prominant in the relations of sellers and business buyers, of sellers and distributors?

Control of Marketing

As a social activity, no major institution is autonomous; rather each is subject to the checks and balances of the society as a whole. Society exercises a control over its institutions, and this is accomplished in different ways in different societies. The final section of the comparative marketing study should indicate the nature and performance of the control mechanisms. The following are means by which this is accomplished:

1. Pre-planning—government planning, market research, budgeting, etc.
2. Automaticity of the market mechanism—long- and short-run adjustments in demand and supply.
3. Countervailing powers—inter-institutional and intergroup actions and reactions.
4. Cost data—the imperative of meeting costs, making profit, etc.
5. Voluntary restraint—co-operation, collusion.
6. Government regulation—laws, administrative control.
7. Social ethics—restraints imposed by awareness of the expectations of various social groups, self-control.
8. Consumer resistance—organized and unorganized expressions of consumer attitudes toward economic want satisfaction.

BIBLIOGRAPHY

Bibliography*

TROPICAL AFRICA

BOOKS

BALDWIN, K. D. S. *The Marketing of Cocoa in Western Nigeria.* London: Geoffrey Cumberlege, Oxford University Press, 1954.

BAUER, P. T. *West African Trade.* Cambridge: Cambridge University Press, 1954.

BENEVISTE, GUY, and MORAN, WILLIAM E., JR. *African Development—A Test for International Cooperation.* Menlo Park, Calif.: Stanford Research Institute, 1960.

BOWER, P. A., *et al. Mining, Commerce, and Finance in Nigeria.* London: Faber and Faber Ltd., 1947.

CARNEY, DAVID E. *Government and Economy in British West Africa.* New York: Bookman Associates, 1961.

CARTER, GWENDOLYN M., and BROWN, WILLIAM O. (eds.). *Transition in Africa: Studies in Political Adaptation.* Boston: Boston University Press, 1958.

COXE-GEORGE, N. A. *Finance and Development in West Africa.* London: Dennis Dobson, 1961.

FEARN, HUGH. *An African Economy—A Study of the Economic Development of the Nyanza Province of Kenya, 1903–1953.* New York: Oxford University Press, Inc., 1961.

FORDE, DARYLL, and SCOTT, RICHENDA. *The Native Economies of Nigeria.* London: Faber and Faber Ltd., 1954.

DEGRAFT-JOHNSON, J. C. *An Introduction to the African Economy.* Bombay: Asia Publishing House, 1959.

HANCE, WILLIAM A. *African Economic Development.* New York: Harper & Bros., 1958.

HILL, J. F. R., and MOFFETT, J. P. *Tanganyika—A Review of Its Resources and Their Developments.* The Government of Tanganyika, 1955.

---

* Submitted by authors for the respective countries.

311

INTERNATIONAL BANK FOR RECONSTRUCTION AND DEVELOPMENT. *The Economic Development of Nigeria.* Baltimore: The Johns Hopkins Press, 1955.

INTERNATIONAL BANK FOR RECONSTRUCTION AND DEVELOPMENT. *The Economic Development of Tanganyika.* Baltimore: The Johns Hopkins Press, 1961.

INTERNATIONAL LABOUR OFFICE. *African Labour Survey.* Studies and Reports, New Series, No. 48. Geneva: I.L.O., 1958.

DU JONCHAY, IVAN. *L'Industrialisation de L'Afrique.* Paris: Payot, 1953.

KARP, MARK. *The Economics of Trusteeship in Somalia.* Boston: Boston University Press, 1960.

KIMBLE, GEORGE H. T. *Tropical Africa,* vols. I and II. New York: The Twentieth Century Fund, 1960.

KRUEGER, KARL. *Afrika.* Berlin: Safari Verlag, 1952.

MARCUS, EDWARD and MILDRED. *Investment and Development Possibilities in Tropical Africa.* New York: Bookman Associates, 1960.

MARZORATI, DEM. AFRED. *Aspects de l'Industrialisation en Afrique Centrale.* Brussels: Institut des Relations Internationales, 1953.

MENIRU, G. UDEGBUNEM. *African-American Cooperation.* Glen Gardner, N.J.: Libertarian Press, 1954.

MUDDATHIR, AHMED. *Die Industrialisierung der wirtschaftlich unterentwickelten Afrikanischen Laender und ihre Auswirkungen auf die Weltwirtschaft.* Berlin: Duncker & Humblot, 1957.

PEDLER, F. J. *West Africa.* London: Methuen & Co., Ltd., 1959.

SIMOONS, FREDERICK J. *Northwest Ethiopia—Peoples and Economy.* Madison, Wis.: The University of Wisconsin Press, 1960.

THOMPSON, VIRGINIA, and ADLOFF, RICHARD. *The Emerging States of French Equatorial Africa.* Stanford, Calif.: Stanford University Press, 1960.

UNITED NATIONS. *Structure and Growth of Selected African Economies.* New York: United Nations, 1958.

U.S. DEPARTMENT OF COMMERCE. *Investment in the Federation of Rhodesia and Nyasaland.* Washington, D.C.: U.S. Government Printing Office, 1956.

WILSON, CHARLES. *The History of Unilever,* Vol. II. London: Cassell & Co., Ltd., 1954.

WOYTINSKY, W. S., and E. S. *World Commerce and Governments.* New York: The Twentieth Century Fund, 1955.

————. *World Population and Production—Trends and Outlook.* New York: The Twentieth Century Fund, 1953.

WRIGHT, FERGUS CHALMERS. *African Consumers in Nyasaland and Tanganyika.* London: H. M. Stationery Office, 1955.

PERIODICALS

AMERICAN UNIVERSITIES FIELD STAFF. Selected letters and reports from foreign countries.

MARCUS, EDWARD. "Selling the Tropical African Market," *Journal of Marketing*, July, 1961, pp. 25 ff.

MARCUS, MILDRED RENDL. "Merchandise Distribution in Tropical Africa," *Journal of Retailing*, Winter, 1959–60, pp. 197 ff.

The New York Times. Selected issues.

CENTRAL AMERICA *

MARTZ, JOHN D. *Central America: The Crisis and the Challenge.* Chapel Hill, N.C.: University of North Carolina Press, 1959. 356 pp.

Individual chapters on the political affairs of each of the six Central American countries covering chiefly the years since World War II.

WILSON, CHARLES M. *Challenge and Opportunity: Central America.* New York: Henry Holt, 1941, 303 pp.

A survey not only of the Central American republics and Panama, but also touching upon Colombia and Cuba. Contains information on the history, climate, politics, people and commerce, with particular attention to agriculture.

Costa Rica

BIESANZ, JOHN B., and BIESANZ, MAVIS. *Costa Rican Life.* New York: Columbia University Press, 1944, 282 pp.

Chapter 6 contains specific references to markets and throughout the book are references to economic and commercial development.

El Salvador

"El Salvador: A Market Study," *International Trade Review*, February, 1959, pp. 14–15.

Many statistics and facts on geography, trade regulations, and market economy.

Guatemala

BUNZEL, RUTH L. *Chichicastenango, a Guatemalan Village.* Publications of the American Ethnological Society, Vol. XXII. Locust Valley, N.Y.: J. J. Augustin, 1952, 464 pp.

The section on trade, pp. 67–76, describes the village market, including a sketch of the market place, and a discussion of trading by the villagers.

HUXLEY, ALDOUS. *Beyond the Maxique Bay.* New York: Harper, 1934, 295 pp.

Although dealing with other countries somewhat, Huxley writes mainly about Guatemala, and his descriptions of small local markets are in Guatemalan villages.

INTERNATIONAL BANK FOR RECONSTRUCTION AND DEVELOPMENT. *The Economic Development of Guatemala.* Baltimore: The Johns Hopkins Press, 1951, 323 pp.

As in other books in this series, background material important in understanding this country's marketing problems is found throughout, with some specific references.

KELSEY, VERA, and OSBORNE, LILLY D. *Four Keys to Guatemala.* Rev. ed. New York: Funk & Wagnalls Co., Inc., 1961, xiv. 332 pp.

Chapter 4 presents a description of markets and fairs; Chapter 18, the economic outlook for domestic trade; and Chapter 21, the markets of Guatemala City.

LISTER, JOHN H. *Agricultural Markets in Guatemala and Improvement Possibilities,* 2 vols. Guatemala: Ministerio de Agricultura, SCIDA, 1956.

Vol. 1. Discusses briefly the principal agricultural products of Guatemala and the present methods of marketing. Suggests improvement especially through the development of co-operative marketing associations. Vol. 2. Organization forms for Farmer's Corn Storage Association.

WAGLEY, CHARLES. *Economics of the Guatemalan Village.* Memoirs of the American Anthropological Association, No. 58. Menasha, Wis.: American Anthropological Assn., 1941, 85 pp.

Both the chapters on "Economic Cycle" and "Consumption" deal with marketing in a primitive village.

Honduras

KASSEBAUM, J. C. *Review of Grain Storage and Grain Marketing Program of the National Development Bank of Honduras.* Teguci-

galpa: Banco Nacional de Fomento, 1957, 17 pp.
Reviews grain storage and marketing conditions in Honduras
and outlines the accomplishments of the Bank's storage construction and minimum price purchasing program.

WELLS, WILLIAM V. *Explorations and Adventures in Honduras.*
New York: Harper & Bros., 1957, 612 pp.
Descriptions of stores in larger towns are found on pp. 224–26.
Chapter 24, pp. 558–67, is entitled "Commerce."

COMMUNIST CHINA

I. Chinese Language Sources:

A. BOOKS

CHING, H., *et al. Changes in Our Country's Private Industry
and Commerce over the Past Seven Years, 1949–1956.*
Peking: Finance and Economics Press, 1957.

HSU, T. G. *The Analysis of Our Country's Economy during
the Transitional Period.* Peking: Science Press, 1957.

KUAN, T. T. *Market under Socialist System.* Peking: People's
Press, 1959. This book is not available.

STATE COUNCIL. *Collection of Laws, Regulations, and Statements of the People's Republic of China,* Vol. VI, VIII, and
Vol. IX. Peking: Law Press, 1957, 1958, 1959.

B. JOURNALS

CHAO, C. C. "A Preliminary Study of the Opening of the
Free Market under State Direction," *Ching-chi Yen-chiu,*
No. 3 (June, 1957), pp. 78–99.

CHING, L. F. "People's Communes Must Greatly Expand
Commodity Production," *Ching-chi Yen-chiu,* No. 30 (January, 1959), pp. 42–47.

CHU, C. N. "Discussion of Commodity Exchange and Commodity Direct Distribution," *Chai-ching Yen-chiu,* No. 17
(February, 1959), pp. 14–17.

HSU, T. H. "Discussion on Commodity Production and Value
Theory after the Communes," *Ching-chi Yen-chiu,* No. 30
(January, 1959), pp. 14–17.

HSUEH, M. C. "A Few Opinions on the Question of Commodity Production and Value Theory," *Ching-chi Yen-chiu,*
No. 30 (January, 1959), pp. 14–17.

KAO, H. "Cutting Excessive Channels of Distribution is a Managerial Revolution," *Ching-chi Yen-chiu*, No. 27 (October, 1958), pp. 58–67.

LI, H. N. "An Observation on People's Communes," *Hung Chi* (May, 1958).

————. "How to Recognize the Improvement in Rural Finance and Trade Control System," *Hung Chi*, No. 16 (January, 1959), pp. 1–8.

WAN, LI. "The Current Form of Our Country's State Capitalism," *Hsin Hua Pan Yueh Kan*, No. 77 (February, 1956), pp. 53–54.

YAO, I. L. "Three Directions to Which Commercial Advancement Ought to Pay Attention," *Hsin Hua Pan Yueh Kan*. No. 131 (May, 1958), pp. 106–8.

————. "Commerce over the Past Ten Years," *Hsin Hua Pan Yueh Kan*, No. 165 (October, 1959), pp. 70–75.

YU, K. Y. "Discussion on the Problem of Commodity Production under Socialist System," *Ching-chi Yen-chiu*, No. 37 (July, 1959), pp. 19–51.

C. NEWSPAPERS

Jen-min Jih-pao.

Ta King Pao.

II. English Language Sources:

A. BOOKS

ADLER, S. *The Chinese Economy*. London: Routledge and Kegan Paul, 1957.

CHAO, K. C. *Economic Planning and Organization in Communist China*, 2 vols. Cambridge, Mass.: Harvard University Center for East Asian Studies, 1959.

HSUEH, M. C., *et al.* *The Socialist Transformation of the National Economy in China*. Peking: Foreign Languages Press, 1960.

KUAN, T. T. *The Socialist Transformation of Capitalist Industry and Commerce in China*. Peking: Foreign Language Press, 1960.

LI, C. M. *Economic Development of Communist China*. Berkeley, Calif.: University of California Press, 1959.

STATE STATISTICAL BUREAU. *Ten Great Years.* Peking: Foreign Languages Press, 1960.

WU, Y. L. *An Economic Survey of Communist China.* New York: Bookman Associates, 1956.

YIN, H., and YIN, Y. C. *Economic Statistics of Mainland China, 1949–1957.* Cambridge, Mass.: Harvard University Center for East Asian Studies, 1960.

III. Japanese Language Sources:

A. BOOKS

AJIA SEIKEI GAKKAI. *A Survey on Chinese Politics and Economy.* Tokyo: Hitotsubashi Book Co., 1960.

ASAHI SHINBUNSHA. *The True Picture of the Chinese Socialist Economy.* Tokyo: Assahi Shinbunsha, 1958.

CHUGOKU KENKYUSHO. *Research on Chinese Socialism.* Tokyo: Godo Press, 1959.

———. *Dictionary of Modern Chinese Affairs.* Tokyo: Iwazaki Book Co., 1959.

———. *China Annual.* Tokyo: Iwazaki Book Co., 1961.

KUSANO, F. *Research on Communist China's Economy.* Tokyo: Government Security Office, 1958.

B. JOURNALS

ASAKAWA, K., and SUGANUMA, M. "The Structure of Market Distribution in Communist China," *Chugoku Shiryo Geppo,* No. 83 (December, 1954), pp. 1–37.

FUJIMOTO, A. "The Question of Free Market in China," *Ajia Kenkyu,* IV, No. 3 (March, 1958), pp. 17–40.

YONEZAWA, H. "Pricing of Commodities in Communist China," *Ajia Keizai Junpo,* No. 436 (July 1, 1960), pp. 5–14.

———. "Pricing Policies in Communist China," *Chugoku Kenkyu Geppo,* No. 156 (February, 1960), the whole issue.